D1609874

*Gladstone: Ireland and Beyond*

# Gladstone
## Ireland and Beyond

Mary E. Daly & K. Theodore Hoppen

EDITORS

FOUR COURTS PRESS

Set in 10.5 on 12.5 point Ehrhardt for
FOUR COURTS PRESS LTD
7 Malpas Street, Dublin 8, Ireland
e-mail: info@fourcourtspress.ie
www.fourcourtspress.ie
*and in North America for*
FOUR COURTS PRESS
c/o ISBS, 920 N.E. 58th Street, Suite 300, Portland, OR 97213.

A catalogue record for this title
is available from the British Library.

ISBN 978-1-84682-298-8

ACKNOWLEDGMENT
The editors and publishers would like to acknowledge the generous support
of the Commemorative Initiatives Fund of the Department of the Taoiseach
for providing a grant towards the publication of this volume.

Printed in England
by Antony Rowe, Chippenham, Wilts.

# Foreword

MARTIN MANSERGH

The bicentenary of Gladstone's birth in 1809 provided an opportunity to re-appraise, using the latest research, the legacy of the pre-eminent British statesman of the second half of the nineteenth century, whose Irish mission became central to his premiership. His memory is still honoured in Ireland. There is a main thoroughfare called Gladstone Street in Clonmel, and, when I was younger, I remember a portrait of him in a solicitor's office in Tipperary.

Many British prime ministers, such as Pitt, Peel, Asquith, Lloyd George, Churchill, Heath, Thatcher and Major, had an important influence on Irish affairs (in some cases not always positive), but it was not until Tony Blair that Gladstone's contribution was surpassed. An Indian obituary of Gladstone in 1898, cited by David Omissi in this volume, said that to Indians his name was 'a synonym for justice, wisdom and high resolve'.[1] Contemporaries, especially opponents, were conscious of the underlying political skills, and viewed the professed high ideals in a much more cynical way.

Gladstone was driven by a strong sense of responsibility, even guilt, at the mismanagement of Ireland, and the nemesis that this might bring, which he publicly acknowledged. His contribution to Ireland was threefold; disestablishment, land reform, and the commitment to Home Rule, which formed a new baseline, despite Conservative and Unionist resistance, for solving what was often called at that time the Irish Question. The debate about whether Home Rule was an historic compromise that turned into a huge missed opportunity, or an exercise in naïveté that excluded his party from power for most of twenty years and in the long run helped to destroy it, will continue.

Gladstone also left a quite different legacy to independent Ireland, worthy of greater exploration – the Gladstonian tradition of public finance, which, along with Sinn Féin economics, strongly featured for at least a generation post-independence. Eamon de Valera, with his frugal approach to public expenditure and to the trappings of power, embodied the spirit, without, however, having to apply Gladstone's intellectual rigour to a policy area, in which he never exercised direct responsibility. Successive finance ministers up until the 1950s operated in much the same vein, though soon after the war T.K. Whitaker, who saw the

---

1 See below, p. 198.

5

budget as a means of demand management, argued that 'the Gladstonian ideal of a budget, which was both balanced and as small as possible, has long since gone by the board, in practice at any rate, and to a greater extent, nowadays in theory'.[2]

The procedure by which the budget is subsequently incorporated into the finance bill was inaugurated by Gladstone as chancellor of the exchequer in 1861. He also made the budget statement a major news event. Rigorous paring of public expenditure and an opposition to extravagance, as the enemy of thrift and industry, were his declared guiding principles.

It was a great pleasure to be once again at St Deiniol's Library in Hawarden, looking out at the imposing statue of Gladstone in the garden that had been earmarked for Dublin, when Home Rule came. It never did, but the battles over it were a stage on the journey to the fullest form of self-government, a sovereign independent Ireland. Home Rule for other countries of the United Kingdom, with the exception of the Government of Northern Ireland at Stormont between 1921 and 1972, had to wait for 'New' Labour at the end of the twentieth century.

---

2 Cited in Ronan Fanning, *The Irish department of finance, 1922–58* (Dublin, 1978), p. 385.

# Contents

SECTION C: MATTERS OF THE MIND

SECTION D: THE WORLD BEYOND

# Contributors

EUGENIO BIAGINI is a Fellow of Sidney Sussex College and Reader in Modern British and European History at the University of Cambridge. He has written on the history of democracy, liberalism and republicanism in the nineteenth and twentieth centuries. His publications include *British democracy and Irish Nationalism, 1876–1906* (2007).

QUENTIN BROUGHALL is an IRCHSS Scholar at the National University of Ireland, Maynooth. He is currently completing a PhD thesis entitled 'The rehabilitation of ancient Rome in English culture, *c.*1870–1918'. His academic interests are centred upon the historical reception of antiquity, Victorian and Edwardian culture, and the British Empire.

MARY E. DALY is a member of the UCD School of History and Archives and Principal of the UCD College of Arts and Celtic Studies at University College Dublin.

K. THEODORE HOPPEN is Emeritus Professor of History in the University of Hull. He has published extensively in seventeenth- and nineteenth-century Irish and British history. In 2001 he was elected a Fellow of the British Academy and in 2010 an Honorary Member of the Royal Irish Academy.

ALVIN JACKSON is Sir Richard Lodge Professor of History and Head of the School of History, Classics and Archaeology at the University of Edinburgh. He is the author of numerous books, including *The Ulster Party* (1989), *Home Rule: an Irish history* (2003) and *Ireland, 1798–1998* (2nd ed. 2010). His comparative history of the British-Irish and Anglo-Scots unions is being published by Oxford University Press in 2011.

JOHN-PAUL MCCARTHY recently completed a DPhil dissertation at Exeter College Oxford entitled 'Gladstone's Irish questions, 1830–86: an historical approach'. This explores Gladstones intellectual life and the way in which his religious and historical sensibilities shaped his Irish analysis.

DEVON MCHUGH is a doctoral candidate at the University of Edinburgh, specializing in the cultural history of Ulster. Her research interests include British and Irish art, architecture and design in the nineteenth and twentieth centuries, elite family life, and the sporting and leisure practices of the landed classes.

KEVIN MC KENNA graduated from NUI Maynooth in 2005 with an honours degree in History and Anthropology. He is presently researching a PhD thesis entitled 'Power, resistance and ritual: landlord-tenant relations on the Clonbrock estates, 1828–1917' at the Department of History, NUI Maynooth. Kevin was awarded a John and Pat Hume Scholarship in 2006 and an IRCHSS Postgraduate Scholarship in 2007.

PATRICK MAUME is a graduate of University College Cork and Queen's University Belfast. He has published extensively on nineteenth- and twentieth-century Irish cultural and political history with particular reference to the politics of literature and newspaper history. He has published biographies of Daniel Corkery and D.P. Moran and a study of nationalist political culture in early twentieth-century Ireland. He is currently a researcher with the Royal Irish Academy's *Dictionary of Irish Biography*.

PAULA MURPHY lectures in Art History in University College Dublin, where she specializes in the teaching of nineteenth- and twentieth-century art, with particular emphasis on sculpture. She is widely published on Irish art. Her most recent publication is *Nineteenth-century Irish sculpture, native genius reaffirmed* (2010). She has served on the board of the Irish Museum of Modern Art and the Sculptors' Society of Ireland (now Visual Artists Ireland).

DAVID OMISSI is Senior Lecturer in History at the University of Hull. He graduated with a First in History from the University of Lancaster, and gained his MA and PhD in the Department of War Studies at King's College, London. He was previously a Prize Research Fellow at Nuffield College, Oxford. His publications include 'Europe through Indian eyes: Indian soldiers encounter England and France, 1914–1918', *English Historical Review*, 122:496 (2007); 'India: some perceptions of race and empire' in D.E. Omissi and A.S. Thompson (eds), *The impact of the South African War* (2002); and (as editor) *Indian voices of the Great War: soldiers' letters, 1914–1918* (1999).

BERNARD PORTER is Emeritus Professor of History in the University of Newcastle. He took his degrees at Cambridge University, becoming a Fellow of Corpus Christi College, before moving on to a Lectureship at Hull, a Chair at Newcastle and Visiting Professorships at the Universities of Yale and Sydney. His books include *Empire and superempire* (a comparison between British and American 'imperialisms'; 2006), *The absent-minded imperialists* (2004) and *The lion's share* (4th ed. 2004). He lives mainly in Sweden.

MELANIE SAYERS has recently completed her doctoral thesis entitled 'Philip Kerr and the Irish Question' at the University of Edinburgh.

# Illustrations

# Abbreviations

| | |
|---|---|
| *DIB* | *Dictionary of Irish Biography* |
| HC | House of Commons |
| IHTA | Irish Historic Towns Atlas |
| IRCHSS | Irish Research Council for the Humanities and Social Sciences |
| *IT* | The *Irish Times* |
| *JRSAI* | *Journal of the Royal Society of Antiquaries of Ireland* |
| *KJV* | *King James Version* [of the bible] |
| NLI | National Library of Ireland |
| NUI | National University of Ireland |
| *ODNB* | *Oxford dictionary of national biography* |
| *PRIA* | *Proceedings of the Royal Irish Academy* |
| ser. | series |
| UCD | University College Dublin |

# Acknowledgments

This book presents the proceedings of a conference at St Deiniol's Library, Hawarden, in September 2009, to mark the bicentenary of the birth of W.E. Gladstone. The conference was funded by the Northern Ireland section of the Department of the Taoiseach; the department has also provided a generous grant to assist the publication of this volume. Dr Martin Mansergh, minister of state at the Department of Finance and the Department of Arts, Sports and Tourism, who attended the conference and participated fully in the discussions, spoke eloquently about Gladstone and Ireland at the conference dinner, and has also furnished a foreword to the present volume. Barbara Jones, counsellor at the Irish embassy in London, also participated fully in the conference proceedings. The warden of St Deiniol's Library, the Revd Peter Francis, made us very welcome, with a tour of the library and its history. We would like to thank St Deiniol's Library and the National Library of Ireland for permission to reproduce the images in this volume. We owe an enormous debt of gratitude to Elaine Cregg, who handled all the administrative arrangements for the conference, and has played a critical role in bringing this volume to publication. Martin Fanning, Michael Potterton and the team at Four Courts Press have been patient and efficient with the editors. Our final thanks go to the contributors for a stimulating conference, and the subsequent papers.

Mary E. Daly & K. Theodore Hoppen
February 2011

# Introduction

## K. THEODORE HOPPEN

Anniversaries, especially when expressed in large and round numbers, lie close to the human heart, in part at least because – whether for individuals, nations, religions or organizations – they help to connect the present with the past. The year 2009 marked the two-hundredth anniversary of the birth of two distinguished Englishmen: Charles Darwin and William Ewart Gladstone (the latter a keen, if not very well informed, appreciator of the former).[1] The international nature of science ensured that Darwin's anniversary was marked by celebrations and conferences throughout the world. But Gladstone too, given the wide geographical reach of his interests and agitations, received commemoration, not only in the form of a grand international conference at the University of Chester, but also (perhaps more modestly but no less significantly) by means of conferences sponsored by the New University of Bulgaria in Sofia and by the government of Ireland.[2] Indeed, the Bulgarian ambassador in London declared in February 2009 that, while 'some of my countrymen might be admirers of Margaret Thatcher or Tony Blair ... William Gladstone will always be the number one as far as we're concerned'.[3] And, in a matching act of honour and recognition, the Irish government sponsored a conference on Gladstone held at St Deiniol's Library in Hawarden (the only such institution ever erected in honour of a British prime minister) in September 2009, from which the essays in the present volume originate.

More generally, Gladstone's gift for striking language still has the power to illuminate and sharpen our perception of the conflicts that characterized these two nations during his own lifetime. His best-selling pamphlet *Bulgarian horrors and the question of the East* of 1876 memorably demanded that the Turks take themselves off 'bag and baggage' with 'their Zaptiehs and their Mudirs, their Bimbashis and their Yuzbachis, their Kaimakams and their Pashas ... from the province they have debased and profaned'.[4] In Ireland's case, he had less fierce but no less eloquent words when he identified his 'mission to pacify' that country

---

1 M.R.D. Foot & H.C.G. Matthew (eds), *The Gladstone diaries*, 14 vols (Oxford, 1968–94), xiv, 352–3, 661; D.W. Bebbington, *The mind of Gladstone: religion, Homer and politics* (Oxford, 2004), p. 236. For his part, Darwin was a staunch Gladstonian Liberal, dying four years before the party split over Home Rule when so many intellectuals took the Unionist side.   2 On Gladstone's involvement with the two countries, see R.T. Shannon, *Gladstone and the Bulgarian agitation, 1876* (London, 1963) and the out-dated but still valuable J.L. Hammond, *Gladstone and the Irish nation* (London, 1938).   3 *New Statesman*, 19 Feb. 2009.   4 J. Morley, *The life of William Ewart Gladstone*, 3 vols (London, 1903), ii, 554.

and when (at the end of the debates on the first Home Rule Bill in 1886) he
identified

> one of the golden moments of our history – one of those opportuni-
> ties [for good] which may come and may go but which rarely return,
> or, if they return, return at long intervals, and under circumstances
> which no man can forecast ... We believe and we know we have the
> promises of the harvest of the future.[5]

And had Afghanistan today a more settled polity it too might have celebrated
Gladstone's denunciation of Britain's shambolic invasions of the late 1870s as 'a
war as frivolous as ever was waged in the history of man'.[6]

Not only, however, is Gladstone a suitable candidate for anniversary celebration on account of the lasting power of his political words (which of course often
disguised hard-headed imperatives), but because he was himself a dedicated
memorialist, and especially so in the case of his own life and career. Amidst his
vast *Nachlass* – 15,000 columns in *Hansard*, over 200 books and articles,
thousands of memoranda, a diary of forty-one volumes, and several hundred
thousand surviving letters[7] – are to be found annual reflections written on his
birthday (29 December) and at the end of each calendar year as well as occasional
papers characterizing personal strengths and (at least as often) personal failings.
It is notable, for example, how already on his fifty-ninth birthday he felt himself
to be descending 'the hill of life', though this notable failure in perception was
more than matched by an insight few politicians attain: 'swimming for his life, a
man does not see much of the country through which the river winds, and I
probably know little of these years through which I busily work and live'.[8] What
these reflections most typically reveal is the close juxtaposition of grand claims
and eager self-abasement. Thus in 1872, while 'truth, justice, order, peace,
honour, duty, liberty, piety' are confidently claimed as the blazons of his political
shield, 'all the rest is summed up in "miserere"'.[9]

---

5 Ibid., 252; *Hansard* 3: 306, 1237–9 (7 June 1886). 'The extent to which he would have been
aware, however, that one of the commonest initial thrusts of Irish nationalist response to the
[Bulgarian] atrocities was to equate the Turks and English as alien oppressors ... is not clear'
(R.T. Shannon, *Gladstone: heroic minister, 1865–1898* (London, 1999), p. 208). 6 W.E.
Gladstone, *Political speeches in Scotland: November and December 1879* (London, 1879), p. 92.
7 D. Beales, 'History and biography' in T.C.W. Blanning & D. Cannadine (eds), *History and
biography: essays in honour of Derek Beales* (Cambridge, 1996), p. 277; R.J. Olney, 'The Gladstone
papers, 1822–1977' in J. Brooke & M. Sorensen (eds), *The prime ministers' papers: W.E. Gladstone*,
4 vols (London, 1971–81), iv, 118–30. John Morley, who wrote the authorized biography, is said
to have remarked that only two things in life had ever frightened him: his first sight (as chief
secretary) of Dublin Castle, and his first sight of the Gladstone papers (ibid., i, 1). 8 Foot &
Matthew (eds), *Gladstone diaries*, vi, 654–5 (29 & 31 Dec. 1868). 9 Ibid., viii, 264 (29 Dec.
1872); also ix, 471 (28 (*sic*) Dec. 1879): 'Last among the last/Least among the least/Can there be
a place for me/At the wedding feast?'

Not much could drive him away from the task of recording these annual reflections, one of the very few exceptions being the problems of Ireland, which prevented the usual outpourings in both 1880 and 1885.[10] Yet it was Ireland that furnished what Gladstone believed to be two of the only four occasions during the whole of his life upon which he might be said to have shown something akin to 'anything which may be called a striking gift ... what may be termed appreciation of the general situation and its result', namely, the 'proposal for religious equality ... in 1868' and that for 'Home Rule ... in 1886'.[11]

One memorial task which proved less congenial, though unavoidable, was the Commons speech required of Gladstone as prime minister on the death of Disraeli in April 1881. Gladstone thought Disraeli a charlatan, but, ever the keen annalist, he was determined to combine honesty with the requirements of the moment. And it was brilliantly done. Hitting upon two of his opponent's characteristics which none could dispute – his 'great parliamentary courage' and his 'profound, devoted, tender and grateful affection for his wife' – Gladstone produced a Rolls Royce performance complete with the mandatory Virgil quotation (in Latin, no translation or indeed reference being required by Victorian parliamentarians) and a generous, if not entirely accurate, reference to the deceased's strong and consistent 'sympathy with his race'.[12] What, however, in the wider context is perhaps the most interesting aspect of this episode is that Gladstone was immediately followed by the radical Henry Labouchere, who saw no reason why Disraeli should be given a public memorial in Westminster Abbey, and by Arthur O'Connor, who denied that any 'Irishman' would want to honour him at all.[13] Seventeen years later, when Gladstone's own death was being recorded in the Commons, John Dillon spoke of 'the love which he bore to our nation', Arthur Balfour turned graceful phrases, and no one had the bad taste to undermine the solemnity of the occasion.[14]

The core of Gladstone's engagement with Ireland (and indeed with the world 'overseas' generally) came more and more to revolve around ideas of nation and nationality, both in the sense that these were growing realities of contemporary life and because they could also stand as public manifestations of the differing but equally significant worth of individual human societies. A growing

10 Ibid., ix, 655 (29 Dec. 1880) & xi, 465 (29 Dec. 1885).   11 'General retrospect' (Gladstone papers, B[ritish] L[ibrary] Add. MS 44791) in J. Brooke & M. Sorensen (eds), *Prime ministers' papers: W.E. Gladstone*, i, 136. The other occasions were 'the revival of the income tax in 1853' and (somewhat bizarrely) 'the decision for a dissolution of parliament in the beginning of 1894'.   12 *Hansard* 3: 256, 38–45 (9 May 1881): 'Aspice, ut insignis spoliis Marcellus opimis/Ingreditur, victorque viros supereminet omnes' ('Look, how Marcellus goes forth distinguished with the spoils of honour/And as victor above all men').   13 Ibid., 48–54.   14 *Hansard* 4: 58, 118–32 (20 May 1898). While Disraeli's family chose a private funeral (which Gladstone declined to attend), Gladstone's agreed to mighty public obsequies (recorded on film) and burial in Westminster Abbey, where the unbelieving Darwin had been interred in 1882. See also Foot & Matthew (eds), *Gladstone diaries*, x, 52, 56, 63.

recognition of the value of 'organic', even primitive, ideas of human behaviour as seen in a historical context led Gladstone, as it did many others, to move away from a generalized, universal and not infrequently utilitarian view of society and economics towards a recognition of particular local and national differences that were themselves the products of what became increasingly known as 'natural' and 'authentic' developments over long periods.[15]

Nationalism in all its complex forms constituted, therefore, not only a reaction to concrete situations, but also a product of a certain kind of thinking about human society in general. If for Gladstone the notion of community was central to his social understanding, his application of this to the Irish situation was a comparatively late development. It can, however, be seen clearly in the memorandum he produced for the cabinet while preparing the first Home Rule Bill in which he firmly denies that the idea of 'Irish nationality' was 'of necessity a thing unreasonable and intolerable' and insists that the Irish possessed in every sense those 'strong permanent instincts of a people and the distinctive marks of character, situation and history' which require that their 'laws should proceed from a congenial and native source'.[16] Again, during the parliamentary debates that followed, his use of the words 'nation' and 'nationality' became, in the Irish context, frequent, grinding and passionate. 'Irish nationality vents itself in the demand for ... separate and complete self-government, in Irish, not in imperial, affairs' (the rider was important). Ireland was a distinct 'nation'. 'Can anything', he asked in almost Parnellian language, 'stop a nation's demand?' And though Scottish virtues were ever admired by Gladstone the arch-Caledonian, the admission that notions of 'local patriotism' were 'stronger in Ireland even than in Scotland' was a mighty admission indeed.[17] After the Liberal defeat at the subsequent general election he insisted that the mere fact of an election having 'been contested on grounds of nationality, of itself gives a new place to nationality as an element of our political thought'.[18] In 1889 he argued that it was 'of no avail to say ... that the people of Ireland are not a community, but only a portion of the [United Kingdom] community' because, if one could but imagine oneself, not an 'Englishman or Scotchman' but an 'Irishman', the direct opposite would immediately and quite naturally become apparent.[19]

It was precisely these notions which Unionists denied and mocked. The Irish were no 'true ... race'; the people of Ireland included no small proportion of

---

15 C. Dewey, 'Celtic agrarian legislation and the Celtic revival: historicist implications of Gladstone's Irish and Scottish land acts, 1870–86', *Past & Present*, 64 (1974), 30–70; H.C.G. Matthew, *Gladstone, 1809–1874* (Oxford, 1986), p. 74; also K.T. Hoppen, 'Gladstone, Salisbury and the end of Irish assimilationism', below.   16 'Irish Nationality', Mar. 1886, BL Gladstone papers Add. MS 44772.   17 *Hansard* 3: 304, 1081 (8 Apr. 1886); ibid., 1542 (13 Apr. 1886); *Hansard* 3: 306, 1237 (7 Apr. 1886); *Hansard* 3: 304, 1082 (8 Apr. 1886).   18 W.E. Gladstone, *The Irish question: I, history of an idea; II, lessons of the election, with an addendum on the legislative union* (London, 1886), p. 18.   19 W.E. Gladstone, 'Plain speaking on the Irish Union', *Nineteenth Century*, 149 (July 1889), 5.

Teutons, who constituted 'the most energetic, prosperous and leading portion of the community'. The Irish had never been a 'separate nation'. 'There were two Irelands; there were two races'.[20] And Unionist leaders were no less strong of view than their followers. Salisbury, having once grandly denounced the Irish in general as 'Hottentots', later insisted upon their complex differentiations of 'race, traditions, long history and mutual ill-will', all of which rendered them at best a mongrel people.[21] Arthur Balfour thought 'Ireland' merely an 'arbitrarily-selected area', while the Liberal Unionist duke of Argyll (Gladstone's one-time cabinet colleague) can be seen taking himself off to some distant political planet, not indeed because of his denial that Ireland possessed 'a separate nationality', but because of the high-pressure rage in which he informed the House of Lords that Gladstone must now be regarded 'as I look upon the Mahdi, or any of the dervishes in the Valley of the Nile, as a pure fanatic'.[22]

Not the least remarkable aspect of the late-Victorian political elite's involvement with the Irish question is how little *direct* knowledge the prime ministers of the time possessed about the island that so moved their passions. Earlier in the century, men like Wellington, Melbourne, Peel and Derby had all served as chief secretaries for Ireland. Russell often visited Ireland and Palmerston (and Derby) owned substantial properties there. Disraeli, however, never came to Ireland at all; Gladstone's three-week tour of 1877[23] and his day-trip in 1880 hardly amounted to much in the way of physical engagement; Salisbury eventually got round to dropping by in 1893. Many years later, when talking of the parliamentary debates on Home Rule, Sir Wilfrid Lawson recalled how

> one of the speakers said he had two very good reasons for knowing a great deal about Ireland. The first was that he had never been there, and the second was that he once met a commercial traveller who told him a great deal about it.[24]

Indeed, it is tempting to suggest that certain aspects of Britain's late-Victorian Irish 'policy' are best understood if decoded with the help of precisely this kind of 'commercial traveller' mode of analysis.

---

**20** *Hansard* 3: 304, 1236 (8 Apr. 1886) Sir John Lubbock; *Hansard* 3: 322, 608 (16 Feb. 1888) Edwin de Lisle; *Hansard* 4: 11, 143 (12 Apr. 1893) Gerald Loder.　**21** K.T. Hoppen, *The mid-Victorian generation, 1846–1886* (Oxford, 1998), p. 686; *Hansard* 4: 8, 23 (31 Jan. 1893), also 17, 631 (8 Sept. 1893).　**22** *Hansard* 4: 8, 1404 (13 Feb. 1893) Balfour; ibid., 17, 204, 217 (6 Sept. 1893) Argyll. See also the latter's *Irish nationalism* (London, 1893).　**23** See Kevin McKenna, 'From private visit to public opportunity: Gladstone's 1877 trip to Ireland', below.　**24** *Hansard* 5 [Commons]: 53, 1528 (10 June 1913). See the marquess of Londonderry's localist version of this: 'I honestly say that I do not myself frequently visit the south and west of Ireland ... but I have met a large number of people who have travelled through the south and west ... and have found that there is no desire amongst the people there for Home Rule', *Hansard* 5 [Lords]: 14, 978 (15 July 1913).

If, therefore, Gladstone's attitude to Ireland was not informed by personal knowledge of the country and if some contemporaries could only see him as a politician of almost deranged fanaticism, the man himself was capable of taking up points of view which suggest a surprising degree of mental flexibility. Striking in this context was his reaction to Parnell, particularly the 'reflection' he sent to his Liberal colleagues after the Irish leader's visit to Hawarden in December 1889.

> He appeared well and cheerful and prepared to accompany (without a gun) my younger sons who went out shooting. Nothing could be more satisfactory than his conversation, full as I thought of good sense from beginning to end in so far as I could judge; nothing like a crotchet, or an irrational demand, from his side, was likely to interfere with the proper freedom of our deliberations when the proper time comes for practical steps.[25]

But, then, cases are altered by the perspective of the beholder, and what might have struck some as open-mindedness, would, to others, have resembled nothing so much as unprincipled opportunism.

The present volume of essays seeks to shed light upon some aspects at least of Gladstone's multifaceted character, interests and influences. The magnificent index volume in the late Colin Matthew's edition of the diaries pins down with lepidopterist precision the enormous range of Gladstone's activities and preoccupations. The section devoted to 'Dramatis personae' covers pp 1 to 283; that on 'Gladstone's reading' an astonishing 326 pages (285–610);[26] the subject index a mere 252 pages (611–862). The diary was, as he told one of his sons in 1872, 'an account-book of the all-precious gift of time',[27] and for Gladstone time well-spent meant time crammed with ceaseless work and endless activity. It was, indeed, this extreme commitment to constant busyness and to busyness in every field that struck contemporaries as forcibly as all the other characteristics of Gladstone's complex personality. In September 1881 his secretary noted how

> The other day while he was writing to Forster on Ireland, to Lord Granville on public affairs generally, to Blennerhassett on Dr Döllinger and religion, he was also writing to some American

25 Memorandum in Gladstone's hand, 23 Dec. 1889, BL Gladstone papers Add. MS 44773 circulated to, among others, Spencer, Rosebery, Harcourt, Granville, Hershell, Kimberley & Morley. 26 This was by no means always 'serious'. Gladstone was once spotted in his club deep 'in the perusal of a book' and 'when eventually he put the book down and left the room, the engrossing volume proved to be ... [Rhoda Broughton's] *Red as a rose is she*' of 1870. See R.C. Terry, *Victorian popular fiction, 1860–1880* (London, 1983), p. 4. 27 Morley, *Life of William Ewart Gladstone*, i, 205.

professor on the cosmology of Homer and expressing the hope that the time would soon come when he would be able to test thoroughly the theories propounded.[28]

Few individuals can, in their diaries or in other productions, have offered to (in this case a probably astonished) Almighty so bulging a record of their time spent in this valley of tears.

While, therefore, no book or even collection of books can address the full gallimaufry of Gladstone's interests, the Hawarden conference from which these essays emanate (and which was marked by a deliberate commitment to featuring the work of younger as well as of established scholars) sought to examine four of the chief areas of Gladstonian concern, but to do so within the broad (though not exclusive) context of the Irish preoccupations which took up so much of his time and energy. In Section A ('British dimensions'), Alvin Jackson looks at long-term relationships within what was then, but is no longer, the United Kingdom of Great Britain and Ireland. Theo Hoppen argues that deeper similarities in the direction of travel underlay the often bitter surface differences over Ireland between Unionists and Liberals in late-Victorian politics. And Melanie Sayers identifies Gladstone's ghost hovering over the men involved in the making of the Government of Ireland Bill of 1920. In Section B ('Irish settings'), Gladstone's strangely distanced visit to Ireland in the autumn of 1877 is discussed by Kevin Mc Kenna, while Devon McHugh uses the family relationship between Gladstone and the Irish aristocracy (a niece was married to the fourth earl of Belmore) to unravel unexpected connections and to examine the manner in which these illuminate the position of Irish peers more generally. Both Patrick Maume and Eugenio Biagini undertake close studies of the ways in which the Irish newspaper press – in particular the *Dublin Evening Mail* and the *Irish Times* – viewed Gladstone while alive and after his death. Section C ('Matters of the mind) looks at how religion, the very core of Gladstone's being, affected aspects of his Home Rule analysis (in John-Paul McCarthy's essay) and at how the ancient classics provided yet another theatre for the playing-out of the conflict between Gladstone and Disraeli (in Quentin Broughall's piece). Section D ('The world beyond') considers the importance for both Gladstone and his supporters and opponents of seeing contemporary politics (and not least the matter of Ireland) through the prism of imperial preoccupations. Bernard Porter analyzes Gladstone's relationship with imperialism in general, while David Omissi looks in more detail at the special case of India. Finally, Paula Murphy discusses the troubled history of the bronze statue of Gladstone by John Hughes (illustrated in this volume) which was intended for – but never

---

28 D.W.R. Bahlman (ed.), *The diary of Sir Edward Walter Hamilton, 1880–1885*, 2 vols (Oxford, 1972), i, 170. See also D.W. Bebbington, *The mind of Gladstone*, passim.

erected in – Dublin and which now stands in front of St Deiniol's Library at Hawarden.

With Gladstone, as with many other politicians, the intention and the thought were by no means always fathers of the deed. In the case of Ireland, his opponents certainly exulted in his failure after the defeats of the first and second Home Rule Bills. Even so, a species of cross-party agreement on the question of Irish land meant that not all went down in the wreckage, though it did mean that this part of the Gladstonian legacy was given a distinct (and to Gladstone an unwelcome) Tory/Unionist twist. When it came to Empire more generally, it remains one of the ironies of the age that Disraeli, the supposedly great 'imperialist', annexed almost no new territory, while Gladstone, especially in the 1880s, found himself engaged in hoovering up large tracts in South Africa, Egypt, the Sudan and elsewhere. Small wonder that the colonial governor, Sir Hercules Robinson, thought it 'strange ... that the [Liberal] government which came in on the platform of curtailing imperial responsibilities should be likely to add more to them than any previous ministry'.[29] However that may have been, Gladstone was never one to feel permanently disheartened or put off his stride. The 'Old Sinner' (his own words) could always rely upon the resource that would (indeed could) never disappoint: 'The Almighty seems to sustain me for some purpose of His own deeply unworthy as I know myself to be. Glory to His Name'.[30]

29 Robinson to J.X. Merriman, 3 Jan. 1884, P. Lewsen (ed.), *Selections from the correspondence of J.X. Merriman, 1870–1890* (Cape Town, 1960), p. 155 (Van Riebeck Society Publications No. 41). See B. Porter, 'Gladstone and imperialism', below, pp 169–78.   30 Foot & Matthew (eds), *Gladstone diaries*, vi, 654 (29 Dec. 1868).

# Gladstone, Ireland, Scotland and the 'Union of heart and spirit'

ALVIN JACKSON

Gladstone's engagement with Ireland and Home Rule are comparatively well-researched historical themes; but they still have subsidiary aspects that have received slighter attention. This essay addresses three of these secondary motifs, beginning with the ways in which Gladstone's achievement has been communicated to later political leaders active in the field of British-Irish and Anglo-Scots relations. It also looks (aside from any question of legislative or policy influence) at those aspects of Gladstone's life and political style that appear to have had a continuing relevance for the British-Irish relationship. And lastly, the essay suggests that Gladstone's Big Idea – a comprehensively reformed United Kingdom, which was capable of accommodating Irish national sentiment – simultaneously looks back to the experience of Scotland under the Union, and forward to those seeking more equitable constitutional relationships in the twenty-first century. Not the least of the curiosities of the literature on Gladstone is that so little should have been written about the Grand Old Man and his effective homeland, Scotland.

Gladstone is associated of course with the effort to achieve Home Rule for Ireland; but his importance extends much further than this. Gladstone in fact embodies or symbolizes the British-Irish relationship in its complexity, and exercised a form of influence on this relationship beyond the grave. One of the central themes of the essay, therefore, is that Gladstone is important not just as a British sympathizer with the national cause, or as a promoter of a new union, but as an ongoing point of reference within Irish politics and as a source both of practical ideas and stimulus for future action.

## THE TRANSMISSION OF THE LEGACY

Gladstonian Home Rule and the personalities associated with it still exercise 'an inherent fascination' and an influence.[1] For the Liberals Gladstone and

* The reference in the title is taken from Gladstone's Southport speech of December 1867. This essay was written during my tenure of a British Academy-Leverhulme Senior Research Fellowship. I am grateful to both the Academy and the Leverhulme Trust for the scholarly opportunities created through this award. 1 Paul (Lord) Bew, *Ireland: the politics of enmity,*

Gladstonian Home Rule bestowed a complex legacy of moral vindication, combined with short-term division and defeat. The parameters of this question have been well-explored: the Liberal Party may have been morally and strategically correct in supporting the demand of the Irish people for Home Rule, and Home Rule may indeed – as Eugenio Biagini has suggested – have provided a 'humanitarian' focus around which the Party was subsequently reconstructed.[2] But Ireland also, clearly, divided Liberals and represented a damaging electoral distraction. Gladstone himself for long remained a point of reference for Liberals and others: his very name 'was a potent force in Liberal politics' in the inter-war era, while Gladstonian ideas on humanitarianism and internationalism exercised an influence far beyond the confines of the Liberal party.[3] For the Conservative Party, however, the challenges posed by Gladstone and Home Rule were no less clear and lasting: the outrageous loyalist oratory of Lord Salisbury in 1885–6 and the political brinkmanship of Andrew Bonar Law in 1912–14 continue to unsettle and divide even convinced Conservative partisans. The sanction bestowed by the Tory leaders upon the most extreme forms of Ulster Unionism (and I have suggested elsewhere that it is likely that Bonar Law was informed of the gunrunning at an early stage) during the third Home Rule crisis has burdened the party with an extremely awkward political legacy.[4] For both Tories and Liberals, Gladstone and Gladstonian Home Rule live on.

In addition, Gladstone remains an occasional point of reference within contemporary Irish politics and political commentary. Indeed, one of the minor themes of Roy Foster's recent commentary on contemporary Irish history, *Luck and the Irish: a brief history of change, 1970–2000* (2007), has been the continuing relevance of the debates of the late nineteenth century to Irish politics of the late twentieth century. Foster has gently poked fun at the Progressive Democrat minister, Tom Parlon, who 'called up the shades of Charles Stewart Parnell and Michael Davitt, who, he [Parlon] said, "gave their lifetimes" to the creation of a nation of property-owning farmers – an achievement he proceeded to use as a rationale for allowing land developers to run riot unimpeded by legislation'.[5] But significantly, for Foster, Garret FitzGerald was 'in so many ways Gladstone to [Charles] Haughey's Disraeli'.[6]

There have in fact been several generic ways in which Gladstone has served

*1789–2006* (Oxford, 2007), p. 348. For a radical reinterpretation emphasizing Gladstone's empathy with Catholic Ireland, see J.-P. McCarthy, 'Gladstone's Irish questions, 1830–86: an historical approach' (DPhil, Oxford, 2010). **2** Eugenio Biagini, *British democracy and Irish nationalism, 1876–1906* (Cambridge, 2007). **3** Christopher Wrigley, '"Carving the last few columns out of the Gladstonian quarry": the Liberal leaders and the mantle of Gladstone, 1898–1929' in David Bebbington & Roger Swift (eds), *Gladstone centenary essays* (Liverpool, 2000), p. 256; Eugenio Biagini, 'Gladstone's legacy' in Roger Swift (ed.), *Gladstone: bicentenary essays* (London, 2011). **4** Alvin Jackson, *Home Rule: an Irish history, 1800–2000* (London, 2004), pp 154–5. **5** R.F. Foster, *Luck and the Irish: a brief history of change, 1970–2000* (London, 2007), p. 68. **6** Ibid., p. 85.

as a point of reference for subsequent Irish and other politicians. Firstly, Gladstone has supplied an exemplar to those either seeking to emulate his strategies (or, more often) wanting to be seen so to do: Chris Wrigley's work on the deployment of the Gladstone mystique within Liberalism between 1898 and 1929 illustrates the kind of uses and abuses to which the great man's name has been applied, while others have traced the influence of Gladstonianism over British domestic and foreign affairs as far as the late twentieth century.[7] Second, Gladstone has been a source of guilty regret for some later leaders, who (regarding the evident mess of British-Irish relations at particular junctures) came to see his efforts as a pivotal missed opportunity: George V evidently came to lament the wasted opportunity created by Gladstonian statesmanship in the mid-1880s, and destroyed by Unionism.[8] Gladstone is conspicuously absent from the memoirs of most Conservatives, but even some Tories and Unionists by the 1930s were beginning to feel that, given the course of the British-Irish relationship, Gladstone had somehow been 'right'. Biagini's work on the ex-Unionist Dublin press of the inter-war years suggests that this kind of critical reappraisal was in full-flow in the decades after Gladstone's death.[9] Thatcherism has been occasionally seen as the Conservatives' 'Gladstonian moment'; and while the analogies have generally been applied within the realms of political economy, there is also a sense in which Thatcher, like Gladstone (if somewhat more reluctantly), signed up to the notion of a reformed union.[10]

The memory of Gladstone's efforts and achievements in Ireland and beyond has been communicated through a variety of media to later generations of politicians and civil servants and within a wider, popular, culture. Only the barest outline of these interactions can be offered here, but (given the paucity of this theme within the current literature) even this sketch is worth offering. First, there is a material legacy of prints, portraits and commemorative ware which was generated at the highpoints of Gladstone's political career – Midlothian, 1886 – and, in great profusion, at the time of his death in 1898. The range and ubiquity of this material is astonishing. When Gladstone visited Ireland in 1877 he was immediately recognized by a news vendor.[11] At the time of the first Home Rule Bill, *United Ireland* sold 125,000 copies instead of the usual 90,000, when it gave away a printed portrait of the GOM.[12] Cartoons featuring a flattering rendering of Gladstone were in fact a regular feature of the paper at this time. Gladstone continued to attract veneration even after the Parnell Split;

7 Wrigley, 'Last few columns', pp 243–59; Biagini, 'Gladstone's legacy'. 8 George V's relationship with Ireland and the Irish is usefully discussed in James Loughlin, *The British monarchy and Ireland: 1800 to the present* (Cambridge, 2008), pp 271–343. 9 See Eugenio Biagini, 'The *Irish Times*, southern Protestants and the memory of Gladstone, 1898–1938', below, pp 122–41. 10 Biagini, *British democracy and Irish nationalism*. 11 Kevin McKenna, 'From private visit to public opportunity', below, pp 77–89. 12 David Bebbington, *William Ewart Gladstone: faith and politics in Victorian Britain* (Grand Rapids, MI, 1993), p. 216. See also David Bebbington, *The mind of Gladstone: religion, Homer and politics* (Oxford, 2004).

and Gladstone prints were used during election contests (as at Longford in 1892), while his name was invoked in the dedication of nationalist works of literature.[13] 'By 1895', in a recent argument, 'Gladstone had been elevated to the status of a lay saint in Nationalist hearts – "he is a miracle, not a man"'.[14] Gladstone of course received somewhat less respectful treatment at the hands of Unionist cartoonists like the professional Tom Merry in the *St Stephen's Review*, or the amateur, Colonel Edward Saunderson, one of whose renditions of the GOM, in the feral or deranged mode favoured by Unionists, was reproduced in the Reginald Lucas biography of 1908.[15]

What has been described by Mark Nixon (in a contribution to an earlier bicentenary conference) as 'the material Gladstone' has an undervalued significance.[16] The range of Gladstonian pottery, china and glass commemorative ware is bewildering, though some indication may be provided by the varieties of ware produced by the Doulton factory alone. In 1898, in commemoration of the GOM's death, the factory produced at least three different types of commemorative jug. The most common of these products was inscribed with the legend 'England's Greatest Commoner' and the less than pithy Gladstonian sentiment 'effort – honest, manful, humble effort – by its reflective action upon character, better than success'. A pair of plates, bearing the images of William and Catherine Gladstone, was mass produced and adorned more modest households than the Doulton wares. Staffordshire fairings of William and Catherine were produced in abundance. Pressed glass sugar bowls and cream jugs spelt out the great man's name in capital letters. Ceramically, there was also a counter-attack by the Belleek company (who, famously, produced a chamber pot adorned with the image of the GOM in its bowl), and (again) Doulton, who (ever willing to play the field of national sentiment) manufactured a range of wares commemorating the betrayal of General Gordon in 1885 ('Hero of Heroes: Betrayed Jan. 26 1885'). No other nineteenth-century Briton, with the exception of Queen Victoria, was commodified so thoroughly and so energetically as Gladstone.

Gladstone was relayed, not only through material representation, but also intellectually: his ideas had an archival life, and a life in print. Historians are increasingly interested in the ways in which British official policy has been shaped by historical readings and precedents: the work of Peter Beck on the post-war treasury and foreign office is a recent case in point.[17] The use of historical precedent as a means of sculpting policy has been a given within much writing on the British-Irish relationship, and the historicist Gladstone, converted to an historical antipathy towards the Union, has been given pretty full

13 Biagini, *British democracy and Irish nationalism*, pp 158–9. 14 Ibid., p. 160. 15 Reginald Lucas, *Colonel Edward Saunderson MP: a memoir* (London, 1908), p. 150. 16 Mark Nixon, 'Material Gladstones', paper delivered at the 'Gladstone Bicentenary International Conference', Chester, 8 July 2009. 17 See Peter Beck, *Using history, making British policy: the treasury and the foreign office, 1950–76* (London, 2006).

examination by (in particular) James Loughlin.[18] Less attention has been devoted by scholars to the ways in which the fertility of Gladstonian legislative invention was communicated to subsequent generations of politician and statesman through the official archives. Patricia Jalland and Nicholas Mansergh's exposition of some of the Gladstonian origins of the acts of 1914 and 1920 are honourable exceptions to the rule that the kinds of question and solution that Gladstone applied to the challenges of the British-Irish relationship have had an ongoing, if neglected, relevance through civil service procedures and files.[19]

Related to this, the wide range of biographical literature on Gladstone has been an independent influence, though it is admittedly not always easy to gauge the extent of this impact within an Irish context. The evidence, short of a dedicated research project on this issue, remains for the moment fragmented and impressionistic. Irish leaders like Justin McCarthy, J.G. Swift MacNeill and T.P. O'Connor contributed to a celebratory biographical genre with productions such as O'Connor's (co-authored) *Gladstone, Parnell and the great Irish struggle: a graphic story of the injustice committed upon the Irish tenantry and a graphic history of the gigantic movement throughout Ireland, America and Great Britain for Home Rule* (originally published in 1886, but reprinted in 1891). The precise readership in Ireland of works such as this, and the avalanche of commemorative literature produced in 1898, is unclear, though Biagini's essay later in this volume makes an important contribution to understanding the reception of the literary Gladstone among southern Irish Protestants. We know that a range of earlier activists within the British-Irish relationship read and were seemingly influenced by biographical portrayals of Gladstone. We know, from its sales and multifarious editions and reprints, that the Morley 'Life' of 1903 was an important medium for the GOM's reputation. We know (in terms of Unionists), for example, that Philip Kerr, whose significance in the making of the Government of Ireland Act is revisited by Melanie Sayers later in the volume, read admiringly at least one Gladstone biography (by Erich Eyck).[20] We know that one of the leading Fianna Fáil ministers of the mid-twentieth century, Sean MacEntee, bought and read Philip Magnus' 1954 biography of Gladstone (since MacEntee's library was sold after his death in 1984, and included a marked copy of this volume).[21]

Indeed, turning to the impact of these literary and material legacies, Tony Blair was by no means the first within the Labour tradition with a critical role to play in Ireland and Northern Ireland to be influenced by either Gladstone or his biographical legacy. Not all were impressed, however. Clement Attlee, whose

---

18 James Loughlin, *Gladstone, Home Rule and the Ulster Question, 1882–1893* (Dublin, 1986): see McCarthy, 'Gladstone's Irish questions'. 19 Patricia Jalland, *The Liberals and Ireland: the Ulster Question in British politics to 1914* (Brighton, 1980); Nicholas Mansergh, *The unresolved question: the Anglo-Irish settlement and its undoing, 1912–72* (London, 1991). 20 See below, pp 64–76. 21 Private information.

father was a Gladstonian, encountered the Magnus biography shortly after its publication, and was emphatically not persuaded by its subject: 'he really was a frightful old prig', Attlee wrote to his brother,

> Fancy writing a letter proposing marriage including a sentence of 140 words all about the Almighty … he was a dreadful person. His guidance by the Almighty was worse than Cromwell's. He seems to have had as little idea of managing a cabinet as he had of dealing with Queen Victoria. Curious his complete blindness to all social problems except prostitution.[22]

The lawyer and Irish historian, Austen Morgan, in his 1992 biography of Harold Wilson, emphasizes the somewhat more elevated Gladstonian hinterland to his subject: as a young civil servant during the War, Wilson 'seemed to know a great deal of history and was always quoting Gladstone'.[23] Philip Ziegler's authorized biography emphasizes Wilson's family origins in Lib-Labism, and briefly discusses the ubiquity of Gladstoniana in the Wilson household in Huddersfield: the family dinner table was adorned with a black-edged cloth commemorating Gladstone's death, and Harold's bedroom was dominated by a print of the Millais portrait of the GOM.[24] Wilson's view of Britain's external relations was, by the early 1960s, in Morgan's formulation, 'Gladstonian'.[25] Certainly, in terms of Ireland there is evidence of a specifically Gladstonian inheritance: Wilson's experience of working with a very small parliamentary majority in 1964–6 had convinced him that action was necessary to disenfranchise the dozen or so Ulster Unionist MPs who acted, in effect, as an adjunct to the Conservative Party. Despite the existence of a 'Home Rule' devolved parliament, Stormont, these Ulster Unionists had the right to vote on all British and foreign matters before the Commons, and this provided a recurrent grouse for Wilson in his contact with Stormont: he continually and unavailingly flagged the issue as one wherein a deal might be struck. The precedent that he long had in mind was Gladstone's 'in and out' arrangement with the Home Rule Bill of 1893, whereby Irish parliamentarians would be excluded from specifically British debates and divisions, but admitted to all others (in fact Gladstone subsequently abandoned the idea).[26]

Gladstone continued to preoccupy Wilson in his strange and haunted final years in office: he 'saw himself as a *melange* of Gladstone, Lloyd George and Churchill'. Several contemporaries (including Bernard Donoghue) recorded

---

22 Quoted in Kenneth Harris, *Attlee* (London, 1982), pp 3, 525.   23 Austen Morgan, *Harold Wilson* (London, 1992), p. 68.   24 Philip Ziegler, *Wilson: the authorised life* (London, 1993), p. 8.   25 Morgan, *Wilson*, p. 245.   26 Jackson, *Home Rule*, pp 275–6. See also Alvin Jackson, '"Tame Tory hacks"? The Ulster Party at Westminster, 1922–72', *Historical Journal*, forthcoming.

Wilson's suspicion that, if Gladstone had been a presiding image in Huddersfield, then – almost literally – he was watching over Wilson's final years in office: Wilson came to believe that the secret services were bugging his study, using a portrait of Gladstone as cover for their electronic surveillance (in fact the 'bug' appears to have been either an old light or a picture fitting).[27]

We are (as it happens) even better informed than this about Tony Blair's reading of Gladstone. We not only know that Blair possessed at least one biography of the GOM (by Roy Jenkins); we also know that Blair read this work against the background of the Good Friday Agreement, saw meaning in it for himself, and actively used Gladstone as a point of reference. In his memoir of the peace process, Blair's aide, Jonathan Powell, recorded that 'Tony had been an enthusiastic reader of Jenkins' life of Gladstone, and saw parallels with his own career, not least with the Irish question. He was constantly ordering me to make impossible things happen'.[28] Northern Ireland, Powell recorded, was also a key priority for the incoming Labour government in 1997, 'probably for the first time for a newly elected prime minister since Gladstone'.[29] Later in the memoir, Powell observed that Gladstone 'was just about the only British prime minister to enjoy a degree of popularity in Ireland until Tony Blair … driven by his Christianity, … developed a crusading enthusiasm for Home Rule'.[30]

It should be conceded that an alternative reading is possible, and indeed has been supplied by exasperated Conservative commentators. It is, for example, possible that Powell's memoir says more about the ways in which Blair wanted (and wants) to be presented than about substantive historical connections; but of course even this illustrates the continuing importance of Gladstone, if only as a point of current political reference. Dean Godson, Trimble's biographer, and formerly a leader writer on the *Daily Telegraph*, has observed the same connection being adumbrated, but is somewhat more dismissive: 'like Gladstone, Blair was essentially in thrall to a nationalist interpretation of recent Irish history (subsequently, on the floor of the House of Commons, John Reid explicitly likened Blair's efforts to settle Northern Ireland to those of the GOM, although more cynical observers believed that this lay more in the realm of flattery of the "boss" than of serious historical analysis)'.[31]

Brief allusion has been made to Gladstone's standing within Irish nationalism, and Alan O'Day and others have devoted more attention to this theme than is possible here: in general, Gladstone received an (in some ways, given the circumstances of the Parnell Split) unexpectedly kindly handling from the historian-politicians whom O'Day reviews (and including Justin McCarthy, R. Barry O'Brien, J.G. Swift MacNeill and P.S. O'Hegarty).[32] George Boyce has

**27** For example, Morgan, *Wilson*, p. 514.   **28** Jonathan Powell, *Great hatred, little room: making peace in Northern Ireland* (London, 2008), p. 3.   **29** Ibid., p. 8.   **30** Ibid., pp 39–40.   **31** Dean Godson, *Himself alone: David Trimble and the ordeal of Unionism* (London, 2004), p. 690.   **32** Alan O'Day, 'Gladstone and Irish nationalism: achievement and reputation' in Bebbington &

investigated Gladstone's standing among Irish Unionists.[33] This was initially, and unsurprisingly, poor: the (for Unionists) fatally damning notion of 'surrender' – the accusation that Gladstone had given in to Nationalist violence – is a theme in some of their renderings of the GOM (as in Ronald McNeill's *Ulster's stand for Union*).[34] The image of the solipsistic, fevered and essentially deranged Gladstone generated and favoured by British Tories and Unionists in the 1880s was a long time dying within those party circles. But even here, among Ulster Unionists, there was by the late twentieth century some evidence of reconsideration: Terence O'Neill, writing in 1972, was evidently interested in Gladstone's achievement. In associating himself with the Gladstonian legacy, O'Neill emphasized a letter from Gladstone to O'Neill's maternal grandfather, and concluded his autobiography with what seems like an act of identification with the GOM (he wondered whether 'Gladstone's Irish policies [would] have succeeded, had he been allowed to carry them out?' and lamented that 'the only tangible result of his courage was to sow the seeds of the break-up of the Liberal Party').[35]

## THE NATURE OF THE LEGACY

If Gladstone has been a personal and political preoccupation for successive generations of British and Irish politicians, what were the practical implications of this? How has his biography – his personal and intellectual concerns and approaches – been relevant to later politicians, active within the British-Irish relationship?

Blair was (so far as we can at present tell) a very much less cerebral or ascetic figure than his perceived historical model, but like Gladstone and other British Liberals, he accepted that the British record in Ireland had been inglorious, and he evidently had some sense of the broader historical resonances of his actions. One of Blair's earliest actions as prime minister was to offer the Irish an expression of regret over the Irish Famine of 1845. In his personal interventions to salvage the peace process, he has famously (eschewing sound bites) referred to the 'hand of history'. There is some evidence to suggest that Blair, beyond Jenkins on Gladstone, has read into contemporary Irish history. But Blair, like Gladstone, was also a highly religious individual. And, just as Home Rule for Gladstone was partly a personal spiritual enterprise, so the Good Friday Agreement and the restoration of a devolved government in Belfast were, it might be argued, an expression of Blair's religiosity.

Swift (eds), *Gladstone centenary essays*, pp 164–81.  **33** D. George Boyce, 'In the front rank of the nation: Gladstone and the Unionists of Ireland, 1868–93' in Bebbington & Swift (eds), *Gladstone centenary essays*, pp 184–201.  **34** Ronald McNeill, *Ulster's stand for Union* (London, 1922), p. 30.  **35** Terence O'Neill, *The autobiography* (London, 1972), p. 138.

Gladstone believed until 1892–3 that Home Rule was a providentially ordained political opening and opportunity, and he acted accordingly. As the work of David Bebbington and others has underlined, it seems clear that religious faith played its part in the motivation of Gladstone in approaching the issue of Home Rule, which he defined as a great providentially ordained opportunity to affect a reconciliation in the British-Irish relationship. Gladstone's introduction of the Home Rule Bill in April 1886 was, famously, a spiritually charged occasion, the success of which he attributed to providential intervention, and the role of prayer: 'voice and strength and freedom were granted me in a degree beyond which I could have hoped. But many a prayer had gone up for me, and not I believe in vain'.[36] Bebbington has memorably suggested that Gladstone treated 'Irish policy as a branch of Christian ethics'.[37]

If religious faith, or a sense of Providence, helped with the birth of Home Rule, then it has had a continuing importance for those seeking political consensus in Ireland. Gladstone moved from an evangelical family background towards High Church Anglicanism; Blair has moved towards Catholicism from some family roots in an Orange evangelicalism. There can be little doubt, on the basis of the available evidence, that Ian Paisley's otherwise surprising evolution after 2005 towards the St Andrews' Agreement in 2007 has been rooted, in part, in issues of religious faith and spirituality. His relationship with Tony Blair is of course, the classic expression of this shared religiosity: a critical aspect of the prelude to the St Andrews' Agreement was the increasingly frequent personal meetings between Blair and Paisley, some of which have been recorded by Jonathan Powell: 'there would be lots of laughter from behind the closed door to the [prime ministerial] den, and when I went in I would often find little religious tracts left behind for Leo'.[38] In December 2006, at a strained time of relations, Blair 'called Paisley from the King David Hotel in Jerusalem, looking out at the Mount of Olives, and after a discussion of the biblical scene, ... suggested some language Paisley could use to indicate that he was sympathetic to the Sinn Fein wish for a conditional timetable for the devolution of justice'.[39] Gladstone, with his interest in classical and biblical geography and landscape, and within his real sense of the imminent presence of God, would have fully understood.

Through the history of Home Rule the British have regularly oscillated between policies of criminalization and accommodation – between outlawing Home Rulers and later nationalists, and then seeking to win their allegiance. Here, Gladstone, notorious – even among his most devoted lieutenants – for his casuistry, was of course a particular pioneer and a precedent.[40] As is well known, Gladstone moved from the prosecution of the IRB to disestablishment, from the proclamation of the Land League, the motor force of the Home Rule movement,

---

36 Quoted in Bebbington, *Gladstone*, p. 214.  37 Ibid., p. 223.  38 Powell, *Great hatred*, p. 275.
39 Ibid., p. 296.  40 Wrigley, 'Last few columns', p. 246.

to the creation of a 'union of hearts' between the Liberals and the Irish Parliamentary Party in 1886 and afterwards. Between 1882 and 1886, he had moved from seeking to criminalize Parnell and Parnellism to reaching a political accommodation that would bring a limited devolution of state power to the latter. Arthur Balfour and the Tories shifted from a vigorous pursuit of the national movement in the shape of the Plan of Campaign towards the more emollient strategies associated with 'constructive Unionism'. Lloyd George pursued his bloody war against the IRA in 1919–21, only to seek an accommo-dation with the representatives of the Dáil government through the Truce and the negotiations for the Anglo-Irish Treaty. After detonating Unionist 'Home Rule' in 1972, the British moved uncertainly between criminalizing the leader-ship of the IRA and private negotiation. Ultimately, in the latest instalment of Home Rule, the British have helped to devolve the vestiges of state power upon those who recently were leading a counter-state insurgency. This process of military and legal resistance, accompanied by historical education, and resulting in political accommodation, essentially began with Gladstone.

Linked with this, of course, are the ways in which political and personal histories may be manipulated for contemporary effect. As has been suggested, Gladstone's historicism has had an ongoing relevance: guilt and a sense of 'the hand of history' have been influences upon those politicians who since Gladstone have sought to devolve power to an Irish or Northern Irish assembly. The historicist nature of Gladstone's commitment to Home Rule is familiar enough. But it is not just the case that (for example) Gladstone read, shaped and applied a particular version of Irish history; this political evolution also necessi-tated the reinvention of his own personal history, and he was arguing in 1886, in 'The history of an idea' and in 1893 (much to the choked amusement even of John Morley) that against all the evidence 'he had been open to the idea for the past 30 years'.[41] This 'convoluted honesty' or (to use Roy Foster's phrase) 'imposition of consistency' upon an otherwise pragmatic and convoluted polit-ical and intellectual career has had a real relevance for those more recent politicians who have had to move dramatic political distances in order to accom-modate substantial change in Ireland.[42]

## GLADSTONE AND THE LONGEVITY OF THE UNIONS

Turning from Gladstone's legacy and influence, the issue of the reformed Union, one of the GOM's central preoccupations, may now be addressed. Despite the dark murmurings of some Conservative journalists concerning his

41 Bodleian Library, John Morley Diary, 2 May 1893.  42 E.D. Steele, 'Gladstone and Ireland', *Irish Historical Studies*, 17 (Mar. 1970), 78.

(in fact very Gladstonian) preoccupation with a nationalist reading of Irish history, Tony Blair occasionally, and (so far as one can tell) sincerely, proclaimed himself to be a 'Unionist'. The affinity between Blair and Trimble and (even) Paisley doubtless says much about the devastating success of the former prime minister's personal style and accessibility, and much about the vanities and susceptibilities of provincial Unionism (even in its Democratic Unionist plumage) to the blandishments of metropolitan political leaders; but it also arguably reflects some overlap between their respective political fundamentals. Each of these particular actors was interested in a reformed and therefore possibly more workable Union, even if the investment of (particularly) Paisley in this project had sometimes hitherto been in doubt. As John Vincent argued more than thirty years ago, however else he may be judged in terms of the British-Irish connection, Gladstone has to be seen firmly in the context of the preservation of Union (Vincent proclaimed provocatively that 'Gladstone [was] the most masterly upholder of Unionism since Pitt, one who with a minimum of real concession put the United Kingdom on a satisfactory basis which could, so far as Ireland went, have lasted well beyond 1922'); but, more than that, he should be seen firmly within the context of explanations for the longevity of the British-Irish and Anglo-Scots Union.[43] One of the central (and neglected) questions in British, Irish and Scottish political history revolves around the survival of these two Unions; and, certainly in the Irish case, Gladstone's contribution is highly relevant to any process of explanation.

This deficit in Irish and Scots political historiography may be touched upon, before Gladstone's position within a corrective literature is revisited. In 2000, Louis Cullen, the patriarch of Irish social and economic history, judged that 'the [Irish] Union has been little studied; its undoing on the other hand has been much debated'.[44] This judgment is complemented by that of the late Conrad Russell who, writing in 1995 of the unions of Britain and the United Kingdom, has observed that

> we are not used to thinking of the British and Irish example as a success ... yet the different and equally valid teleology of the Act of Union of 1707 leads to a search for things which were right. The search for problems should not blot out the successes. The most remarkable success of the British and Irish union is that so many parts of it are still there.[45]

43 Steele, 'Gladstone and Ireland'; J.R. Vincent, 'Gladstone and Ireland', *Proceedings of the British Academy*, 62 (1977), 232. McCarthy, 'Gladstone's Irish questions' vigorously interrogates Vincent's emphasis upon the 'minimalist' nature of Gladstonian Home Rule.  44 Louis Cullen, 'Alliances and misalliances in the politics of the Union', *Transactions of the Royal Historical Society*, 6th ser., 10 (2000), 221.  45 Conrad Russell, 'Composite monarchies in early modern Europe' in Alexander Grant & Keith Stringer (eds), *Uniting the kingdoms: the making of British*

Now, while there is clearly a very sharp distinction to be drawn between 'success' and 'longevity', there is still a challenge in Irish historiography to understand more fully the survival of the Union settlement.[46]

A related challenge exists for Scottish historians; and indeed here (as in so many other respects) there are some similarities between the historiographical contours of the two countries. But if the historiography of the Irish Union is disproportionately the story of its collapse between 1916 and 1922, then the historiography of the Scots union is predominantly the historiography of its creation in 1707. Most Scots (as with Irish) historians with an interest in the relationship between their nation and the Union have tended to pursue this interest through focusing upon the challenge presented in the nineteenth century and after by an emergent nationalism.[47] But there are some exceptions to this rule, as evidenced in the Scottish case by (for example) two pioneering University of Edinburgh historians, Gordon Donaldson and Richard Pares, and by some more recent corrective work.[48] Donaldson's teasing lecture ('a kind of final entertainment') on 'The anglicization of Scotland' ('anglicization of the country we now call Scotland started in the sixth century') emphasized, inter alia, educational exchange, improved transport and communications, the labour movement, English immigration, the Empire, and soldiering and warfare; and his listing has a relevance for Irish historians of the Union.[49] His Edinburgh contemporary, Richard Pares' essay on 'A quarter of a millennium of Anglo-Scottish Union', originally delivered as a lecture in 1954, is also implicitly an exploration of some of the bolsters of this critical constitutional relationship.[50]

It is not the purpose of this essay to set out at length the explanations for the mouldering survival of the two unions, still less to sustain a detailed comparison between the two: of greater interest and relevance is Gladstone's role in defining a reformable and malleable union.[51] The limited malleability of Union is one aspect of its relative longevity: the survival of the Irish Union lay partly in its capacity for periodic reinvention, and its ability to absorb *some* political challenge. Scottish historians have sometimes made a more emphatic version of the same point in relation to the Anglo-Scots Union – that (in the words of Ewen Cameron) 'a key element in the development of the government of Scotland has

*history* (London, 1995), p. 135.   46 See Brian Girvin, *From union to union: nationalism, democracy and religion in Ireland – Act of Union to EU* (Dublin, 2002), pp 1–28 ('Why the Irish did not become British!').   47 For example, Christopher Harvie, *Scotland and nationalism: Scottish society and politics, 1707–1994*, 2nd ed. (London, 1994).   48 For example, Catriona Burness, *'Strange association': the Irish Question and the making of Scottish Unionism, 1886–1918* (East Linton, 2003); Catriona MacDonald (ed.), *Unionist Scotland, 1800–1997* (Edinburgh, 1998); Colin Kidd, *Union and Unionisms: political thought in Scotland, 1500–2000* (Cambridge, 2008). 49 Gordon Donaldson, *Scotland's history: approaches and reflections* (Edinburgh, 1995), pp 118–35. 50 Richard Pares, 'A quarter millennium of Anglo-Scottish Union', *History*, 39 (1954), 98.   51 See Alvin Jackson, *The two unions: Ireland, Scotland and the United Kingdom, 1707–2007* (Oxford, forthcoming).

been the ability of the Union to adapt and accommodate nationalist sentiment' and that 'one of the most important characteristics of the Union is its inherent flexibility. It has proved possible to accommodate Scottish distinctiveness throughout its history'.[52] This, in fact, is the essence of Graham Morton's concept, 'unionist nationalism'.[53] It is evinced by (for example) the Union government's legislative responses to Scottish land agitation, by the creation of the Scots Office in 1885, by the Crofter Act of 1886, by the seriousness with which the issue of Scots Home Rule was taken in the 1890s and after, and ultimately by the extent of the administrative devolution granted to the Scots, beginning in the inter-war years.

The British-Irish Union, as is well known, was originally and unsuccessfully defined by William Pitt in relatively inclusivist terms, and was immediately recast as an instrument of Protestant ascendancy. Gladstone's achievement, or effort, was directed towards seeking to make the Union capable of accommo-dating Irish 'distinctiveness'. Though Gladstone famously emphasized that he was not responding to violence, popular mobilization in support of the Fenian martyrs and prisoners clearly indirectly inspired him in a succession of far-reaching reforms, or attempted reforms. By 1869, through the Irish Church Act, he was prepared to amend the Act of 1801 by breaking the ecclesiastical union of the two kingdoms (through which the Church of Ireland was disestablished, and the United State Church of Britain and Ireland – created under the Union settlement – formally dissolved). By 1885, he was prepared to restore a subordi-nate Irish parliament in the interests of preserving what he saw as the essence of the Union settlement – the supremacy of Westminster, the economic unity and military security of the two islands, the social leadership of the landed classes. Scholars tend to concentrate upon the failure of Home Rule in 1886 and 1893, and to ignore the wide sense of probability, even inevitability, that Home Rule now possessed, with Gladstone's conversion. The Union was ultimately 'greened' (to use the label of the late Lawrence McBride) at the end of the nineteenth century in preparation for Gladstonian Home Rule – that is to say, redefined and (in terms of the higher civil service and judiciary) slowly if incon-sistently repeopled in a manner more accessible to Irish nationalists.[54] This certainly was Gladstone's specific aspiration: writing to Earl Spencer from Edinburgh in July 1892, he alluded to the celebrated Scots Benthamite, in arguing that 'the main portion of our plan [for government] must ... evidently be to *Drummondize* (so to speak) the administration of Ireland. The operation of

---

52 Ewen Cameron, 'The politics of union in an age of Unionism' in T.M. Devine (ed.), *Scotland and the Union, 1707–2007* (Edinburgh, 2008), p. 130.   53 Graham Morton, *Unionist nationalism: governing urban Scotland, 1830–60* (East Linton, East Lothian, 1999).   54 For example, Lawrence McBride, *The greening of Dublin Castle: the transforming of bureaucratic and judicial personnel in Dublin Castle in Ireland, 1892–1922* (Washington, DC, 1991); see the critique by Fergus Campbell, *The Irish establishment, 1879–1914* (Oxford, 2009).

this method under the Melbourne government was wonderful'.[55] Gladstone's efforts towards Home Rule failed indeed; but this should not detract from the fact that he represented a tradition of pragmatic constitutional thought or 'democratic elitism' which has been prepared to jettison the traditional forms of Union in order to preserve a measure of its substance.[56] Moreover, Gladstone's commitment to Home Rule, however problematic, helped to encourage an accommodation between Irish nationalism and the United Kingdom parliament which lasted until the eve of the revolution: the mere promise of Home Rule, in the words of W.C. Lubenow, 'domesticated these new forces' in Irish and British politics, and kept constitutional nationalists at Westminster for thirty-five years.[57] Starting belatedly with Gladstone, the Union may be seen as a mechanism through which successive British governments were undertaking social and political experiments of a much more daring variety than they would ever have countenanced in England.

Of course, this argument cannot be pushed too far. The malleability of the Union has to be viewed clearly alongside British military, policing and judicial supremacy in nineteenth-century Ireland. It should also be interpreted as, in part, an expression of the fluid local alliances and encouragement of local division that were the generic hallmarks of British imperial rule. It is arguable that the British shift from working in partnership with the old Ascendancy interest in the eighteenth and early nineteenth centuries to a more direct engagement with the developing elites of Catholic society was in line with wider patterns of colonial government (in, for example, India or Malaya). In the Ireland of the late nineteenth century, as in the formal colonies, British attention was turning to the patronage and sponsorship of indigenous elites.[58]

Moreover, while a panoramic view of the Union reveals some malleability, particular critical episodes illustrate the abiding potential for ideological rigidity first perceptible with the birth of the Union and the 'emancipation' issue. Recent scholarship (work by K.T. Hoppen) has characterized the Union before emancipation as being vitiated by metropolitan over-confidence, ignorance and incomprehension.[59] Scholars also now routinely emphasize the profound limitations of British relief policy during the Irish Famine (1845–51), as well as the failure of imagination and humanity within Whitehall and Westminster. The severities of liberal economic thought have traditionally been stressed; more recent work, following in the wake of Boyd Hilton, has tended to underline the providentialist outlook of those senior British officials who were characterized

55 Peter Gordon (ed.), *The Red Earl: the papers of the Fifth Earl Spencer*, 2 vols (Northampton, 1982–5), ii, 207. 56 Biagini, 'Gladstone's legacy'. 57 W.C. Lubenow, *Parliamentary politics and the Home Rule crisis: the British house of commons in 1886* (Oxford, 1986), pp 323–4. 58 Alvin Jackson, 'Ireland, union and empire, 1800–1960' in Kevin Kenny (ed.), *Ireland and the British Empire* (Oxford, 2006 ed.), pp 130–1. 59 K.T. Hoppen, 'An incorporating union: British politicians and Ireland, 1800–30', *English Historical Review*, 123:501 (Apr. 2008) 345.

by a narrow form of evangelical religious outlook.[60] There is little doubt that this case has power: nor can there be any doubt that perceptions of, and the reality of, official neglect or even occasionally malevolence shaped the militant nationalism of the later nineteenth century.

Still, the failure of the British government during the Famine years was all the more problematic, because the Union could be used as a framework within which fundamental and otherwise unassailable issues such as property rights might be addressed. Gladstone emphatically demonstrated that neither the Union structure or his own previous convictions precluded 'advanced' reforms such as the independent arbitration of rent, the legal recognition of effective joint ownership, land purchase and (ultimately, after his death), in certain instances, compulsory land purchase. As John Morley commented, 'The Bessborough Commission on Irish Land Tenure reported in favour of the three Fs. What did Mr G. do? He denounced it in private as monstrously inequitable, and two months later he introduced a bill to that effect'.[61]

### IRELAND AND SCOTLAND

The Scottish Union, and comparisons between the two unions, Anglo-Scots and British-Irish, is also relevant in these calculations. Just as at the end of the nineteenth century, so at the beginning of the twenty-first, the common experience of Ireland and Scotland under the Union has attained a growing political relevance. Certainly before the financial crisis of 2008–9, the nationalist government of Scotland regularly looked to Ireland as a polity that had also experienced union, but (unlike Scotland) had broken free, and had accordingly prospered while the Scots remained constricted and impoverished. For example, speaking at Trinity College Dublin on 13 February 2008, Alex Salmond, the first minister of Scotland, approvingly quoted Parnell ('no man has the right to fix the boundary of a nation'), while observing that 'Scotland has a different history and a different constitution. But our aspirations for our nation are no different from those that inspired generations of Irish people to the independence and prosperity that you [Irish] enjoy today'.[62]

Gladstone's contemporaries were also frequently drawn to make analogies of this kind. Albert Venn Dicey, the Victorian jurist, writing in the *Fortnightly Review* in 1881, essayed a brief comparison of the making and embedding of the two unions.[63] For Dicey, the evidently happy Scots' experience of Union

60 For example, Boyd Hilton, *The age of atonement: the influence of evangelicalism on social and economic thought, 1785–1865* (Oxford, 1988); Peter Gray, *Famine, land and politics: British government and Irish society, 1843–50* (Dublin, 1999); Christine Kinealy, *'This great calamity': the Irish Famine, 1845–52* (Dublin, 1994). 61 J.H. Morgan, *John Viscount Morley: an appreciation and some reminiscences* (London, 1924), p. 104. 62 For example, *Daily Telegraph*, 13 Feb. 2008. 63 A.V. Dicey, 'The two Acts of Union: a contrast', *Fortnightly Review*, 30, 176 (Aug. 1881), 168.

informed a reading of 'the failure or partial failure' of the Union between Britain and Ireland: by identifying the keystones of Scottish success, the reasons for Irish failure would become self-evident.[64] With typically bold and historicist precision, Dicey ascribed the solidity and longevity of the Scots' Union, not to any superiority of their national 'character' over that of the Irish, but rather to three cardinal 'facts' – that the Scots' Union was a treaty negotiated between equal, consenting partners, that it embodied an unusually disinterested and strategic English statesmanship, and that it protected the central institutions of the Scottish nation.[65] Writing in 1881, against the backdrop of the Land War in Ireland, and a tranquil and prosperous Scotland, Dicey believed that 'English policy has achieved no triumph so great as the union between England and Scotland' (a belief that he retained until the end of his life, and expressed at greater length in *Thoughts on the Union* (1920)).[66]

As with so much of his historical commentary (indeed, as with so much historical commentary on the Unions more generally), Dicey was tacitly seeking to highlight a particular contemporary moral from his ruminations in 'the two Acts of Union': just as Scots' animosity towards the English had been (in his analysis) mitigated by creative statesmanship, so (even in the unpropitious circumstances of 1881) Irish animosity and violence were susceptible to enlightened English statesmanship. Dicey's emphasis on the 'fair and equal deal' of 1706, on the magnanimity of English statesmanship, and upon the sensitive treatment of Scottish national institutions were evidently designed as policy indicators for the 1880s; and they certainly informed interpretations of the survival of the Scots' Union, and of the condition of its Irish counterpart, from the Gladstonian era until effectively the present day.

The divergent but interlinked Irish and Scots experience of Union was a commonplace of the intellectual context against which Home Rule was devised and debated in the 1880s and 1890s. It is probable that both Gladstone and the Conservative leader, the marquess of Salisbury, read the Dicey article (though the evidence is admittedly ambiguous): both certainly shared much of the conceptual framework supplied by Dicey, viewing the Irish Union clearly in the comparative context supplied by Scotland (however much the genesis of 1801 was to be distinguished from that of 1707), and using some of the same language (as with, for example, the notion of 'moral union').[67] Salisbury accepted one of the central presumptions of Dicey's reasoning, namely that Scottish acquiescence in Union legitimized the expectation that the Irish, too, could be eventually won to its cause.[68] Gladstone accepted that, while both the Unions

---

64 Ibid., p. 176. 65 Ibid., p. 169. 66 Ibid., p. 168. 67 It is not clear whether Gladstone read Dicey, 'Two Acts of Union', though on 2 Sept. he records reading 'articles in Fortnightly': M.R.D. Foot & H.C.G. Matthew (eds), *The Gladstone diaries, with cabinet minutes and prime ministerial correspondence*, 14 vols (Oxford, 1968–94), xi (July 1883–Sept. 1886; Oxford, 1990), p. 118. W.E. Gladstone, *Special aspects of the Irish Question* (London, 1892), p. 103. 68 Gladstone,

were rooted in corruption, the level of immorality entombing the measure of 1801 was greater, and that the Scots Union was at least the result of an equal bargain. He read other work that was critical of the Scots Union, and of its origins (curiously, George Lockhart of Carnwath on the Scots Union was absent from this reading, in contrast to Jonah Barrington on the Irish): but he was also clearly impressed and persuaded by the Unionist scholarship of John Hill Burton, Scotland's 'latest and most authoritative historian', who 'denies that bribery has been proved'.[69]

Dicey's comparison of Ireland and Scotland was intended to prove that the Irish Union, whatever its manifold failings, might yet attain the solidity of its Scottish counterpart: Gladstone accepted the legitimacy of making the comparison; but he sought to turn the analogy on its head by demonstrating both that Scotland was no exemplar for Ireland, and that Ireland might in fact prove to be a paradigm for the Scots. Scotland's debt to the Union of 1707 was, in Gladstone's argument, exaggerated; the independence of pre-Union Scotland was infinitely greater than that characterizing pre-Union Ireland, while the circumstances of Union in each polity were thoroughly distinct. The Unionist comparison of the two Unions was inevitable, but misconceived: 'there was a Union in Scotland and a Union in Ireland, just as there was a river in Monmouth and a river in Macedon'.[70]

But, if the two unions were morally and politically at different ends of the continent, then the two nationalities, Scots and Irish, were altogether closer concepts in Gladstonian epistemology. Gladstone clearly envisioned that Scots (and Welsh) nationality would be boosted by the epiphany of Irish Home Rule; and indeed he claimed that his definition of Irish Home Rule was wholly dependent upon its applicability within Scotland ('nor was it, in my view, allowable to deal with Ireland upon any principle, the benefit of which could not be allowed to Scotland in circumstances of equal and equally clear desire').[71] Scotland, whose opposition to the Treaty of Union might have been overblown, had gone now to the opposite extreme, and was unreasonably supportive of Union. Gladstone looked with equanimity, indeed favour, upon the probability that Welsh and Scottish nationalism would be 'set astir' by the Irish Home Rule controversy, and that the scene would be set for the wider federation of the United Kingdom: 'Scotland, which for a century and quarter after her union was refused all taste of a real representative system, may [now] begin to ask herself when if at the first she felt something of an unreasoning antipathy, she may not latterly have drifted into a superstitious worship, or at least an irreflective acquaintance'.[72] Home Rule, in other words, was not only a providentially

*Special aspects*, p. 216. **69** Ibid., p. 101. Foot & Matthew (eds), *Gladstone diaries*, xiv, 303; McCarthy, 'Gladstone's Irish Questions', p. 261, quoting W.E. Gladstone, *Remarks on the Royal Supremacy* (London, 1850), p. 62; John Hill Burton, *A history of the reign of Queen Anne*, 3 vols (Edinburgh, 1880). **70** Gladstone, *Special aspects*, p. 101. **71** Ibid., p. 3. **72** Ibid., p. 35

ordained opportunity for the Irish: it promised to provide a lasting constitutional architecture for Scotland and for the entire United Kingdom.

If Gladstone, like other contemporaries, defined Irish Home Rule partly in terms of the comparison between 1707 and 1801, then the implications of his Irish proposals were keenly felt by Liberals in Scotland and Wales, and have been commonly observed by historians. Gladstone's colleague, Stuart Rendel, sententiously remarked in 1886 that 'the Irish Question is helping Wales by helping to make a Welsh question'.[73] It might equally be suggested that 'the Irish Question helped Scotland, by helping to make a Scottish question'. Even before the advent of Home Rule, Gladstone had readily understood that his Irish plans had Scottish implications: for example, he sought to keep the earl of Rosebery within the loop of his thinking on Ireland because (as he told him in May 1885) 'Ireland has so important a bearing on Scottish affairs'.[74] In proposing a Grand Committee for Ireland in 1880, he felt the need to outline a similar provision for Scotland.[75] Gladstone was formally responsible for the initiatives which eventually resulted in the creation of the Scottish Office, and the Secretaryship for Scotland in 1885, modelled to some extent upon the Irish Office and the Chief Secretaryship for Ireland (although it should be said that Rosebery's most recent biographer claims much of the reforming credit here to the brinkmanship of the earl (in 1883)).[76]

As is well known, some of the Gladstonian land reforms for Ireland were subsequently adapted and applied to Scotland, with the passage of a Crofters' Act in 1886, the creation of a Crofters' Commission (with similar powers to the Irish Land Commission of 1881), and a Congested Districts Board and Board of Agriculture for Scotland (both modelled partly on Irish precursors).[77] After 1886, the Liberal Party moved swiftly towards Home Rule for Scotland, and adopted this as party policy in 1888.[78] Indeed, as Ian Hutchison has argued, promoting Scottish Home Rule had a number of real advantages for Ireland – not least in 'placing Irish Home Rule in a more acceptable framework for effecting constitutional change'.[79] The impact on Scotland of Gladstone's conversion to Irish Home Rule was multifaceted. Reginald Coupland argued that the 'effect of this Irish quarrel on Scottish nationalism was profound; for it made it a party question. The nationalist movement of 1853 had been non-party ... but from 1885 on it was a purely Liberal movement'.[80] This should be qualified by the observation that the chief protagonists of the Scottish Home Rule

73 John Davies, *A history of Wales* (London, 1993), p. 454.   74 Leo McKinstry, *Rosebery: statesman in turmoil* (London, 2005), p. 139.   75 J.L. Hammond, *Gladstone and the Irish nation* (London, 1964 ed.), pp 183–4.   76 McKinstry, *Rosebery*, p. 112.   77 Ewen Cameron, *Land for the people? The British government and the Scottish Highlands, 1880–1925* (Edinburgh, 1995); Andrew Newby, *Ireland, radicalism and the Scottish Highlands, 1870–1912* (Edinburgh, 2006). 78 I.G.C. Hutchison, *A political history of Scotland, 1832–1924: parties, elections and issues* (Edinburgh, 1986), pp 171–2.   79 Ibid., p. 172.   80 Reginald Coupland, *Welsh and Scottish nationalism: a study* (London, 1954), p. 298.

Association, far from being stimulated into the kind of pan-Celtic sympathies that Gladstone envisioned, adopted an increasingly hostile attitude towards what they misinterpreted as Gladstone's partiality for the Irish, and slowness to respond to Scottish needs.[81]

This apparent discrimination had been evident, not just with Home Rule, but with the issue of the Church establishment. In both Scotland and Wales, Gladstone was much less convinced about the necessity for disestablishment than he had been for Ireland by 1869; but while in Scotland he continued to hesitate, at least in Wales he recognized the significance of non-conformist sentiment on this score, and indeed (after 1886) the disproportionate significance of Welsh Liberalism within the national party. In any event, Gladstone became a (reluctant) convert to the disestablishment of the Welsh Church (Welsh disestablishment was highlighted in the Newcastle Programme, second only to Irish Home Rule). John Davies talks more widely of

> the exceptional allegiance which Gladstone had won among the people of Wales. He lived in Flintshire ...; the firm morality which characterized his rhetoric and his statesmanship appealed strongly to the Welsh; he attended *eisteddfodau*, at which he referred with sympathy to the attributes of the Welsh; time and again he expressed his readiness to give consideration to Welsh public opinion.[82]

While some of this commentary might be applied and adapted to Scotland, it is also the case that Gladstone kept a stern distance from the highly influential and officially endorsed reading of Scottishness associated with Queen Victoria and her highland residence, and labelled as 'Balmorality'. It is indeed possible that Gladstone's increasingly great and public identification with Ireland – and Wales – should be seen as a key complement, or counterweight, to the monarchy's embrace of a version of Scottish highland tradition.

However, while it is wholly conventional to argue that Gladstone's Irish strategies had manifold implications for Scotland, it is less frequently suggested that Gladstone's understanding of Scotland (and Wales) under the Union were defining features of his approach to Ireland. Scholars have pointed to a range of earlier stimuli for Gladstone's Irish thought, including the place of Bulgaria within the Ottoman Empire (Richard Shannon) and the Ionian Islands (and enosis with Greece) (E.D. Steele); but the closer analogy of Scotland has been largely neglected. Indeed, it is striking that, while both of Gladstone's parents were Scots, while contemporaries such as James Bryce talked of the essential Scottishness of his outlook and intellect, while the family had – and still has –

81 See, for example, William Mitchell, *Is Scotland to be sold again? Home Rule for Scotland* (Edinburgh, n.d. [1893]), pp 95–8.  82 Foot & Matthew (eds), *Gladstone diaries*, xiv, 819; Davies, *Wales*, p. 451.

estates in Scotland, while he represented a Scots constituency, while he lauded the character and achievements of the Scots, so very little has been written on Gladstone and Scotland.[83]

It has been said that 'Gladstone idealized the Waldenses in youth, the Italians in middle age, the Montenegrins in old age, and the Scots always'.[84] As he told an audience at Southport in December 1867, 'what we want is to have Ireland like Scotland, that union of heart and spirit which is absolutely necessary for the welfare of the country has not yet been brought about'.[85] Gladstone's earliest allusions to 'local government' reform in Ireland were generally uttered not only in the context of parallel Scottish ideas, but often actually in Scotland itself (for example his speeches of 1871 in Aberdeen and of 1879 in Dalkeith).[86] One critical issue that occupied time and correspondence with Earl Spencer, the lord lieutenant of Ireland, during Gladstone's first administration was the possibility of an Irish royal residence; and this was of course largely defined in the context of the success, perhaps too great success, of Balmoral in forging a link between the royal family and Scotland: in October 1871, Gladstone spoke to Earl Spencer of 'the difficulties of arrangements in case of an Irish Balmoral, which in Scotland the queen settled of her own account and at her own expense. And she was too much attracted to Scotland as it was. In Ireland the difficulty would be the other way'.[87] This resonant passage indicates that Gladstone saw the intensity of Victoria's attraction to Scotland as problematic; and it permits the suggestion that he saw the need to address Irish patriotic sensitivities in the same, or similar, ways in order to preserve the stability of the kingdom.

Gladstone devoured the novels of Sir Walter Scott: Ruth Clayton Windscheffel has argued recently that Gladstone 'read no works in English (except the Bible) so consistently or completely over such a length of time', and has convincingly suggested that Gladstone shared Scott's patriotic Caledonian Unionism.[88] Gladstone also read extensively among the (by Irish standards) relatively moderate Scottish critiques of the union and its operations, taking on board work by (for example) John Stuart Blackie, Professor of Greek at Edinburgh, and Charles Waddie, or William Mitchell, each of whom advocated a Scottish patriotic agenda, and eventually Home Rule for Scotland in the 1880s.[89] He was a careful critic of the work of Dicey, which (as has been noted)

83 James Bryce, *Studies in contemporary biography* (London, 1903), pp 402–3. 84 Vincent, 'Gladstone and Ireland', p. 231. 85 Ibid. 86 Steele, 'Gladstone and Ireland', p. 86. 87 Gordon (ed.), *The Red Earl*, i, 99. For discussion of the royal residence issue, see Loughlin, *British monarchy and Ireland*, pp 129, 149, 160. Loughlin sees Gladstone using the issue in the early 1870s as a diversion from the emerging Irish demand for Home Rule. 88 Ruth Clayton Windscheffel, 'Gladstone and Scott: family, identity and nation', *Scottish Historical Review*, 86 (2007), 69–95. 89 Charles Waddie, *How Scotland lost her parliament, and what came of it* (Edinburgh, 1891); John Stuart Blackie, *The Union of 1707 and its results: a plea for Scottish Home Rule* (Edinburgh, 1892); William Mitchell, *Is Scotland to be sold again? Home Rule for Scotland* (Edinburgh, 1893). See also Foot & Matthew (eds), *Gladstone diaries*, xiv, 307, 484, 590.

included reflections on Scots and Irish unions.[90] It is striking and significant that (on the strength of this varied reading) he criticized Parnell in 1885 for alleging that under the Union the Scots had lost their nationality, remarking that 'Mr Parnell is a very thoughtful man, and, as a rule, measured in his language, but he never said a sillier thing than that'.[91]

In fact, the Scots Union was widely seen as a success; and this in turn was regularly credited to the religious settlement in 1706, as well as to the maintenance of a gamut of indigenous institutions wherein it was possible to express a Scottish patriotic identity, while working within the framework of union. In addition to these – the law, the universities, local government, the Kirk – Graham Morton has highlighted a strongly Scottish associational culture, which fulfilled broadly the same function: this aspect of civil society permitted the articulation and celebration of Scottishness, while remaining within the structure of union.[92]

The differences with Ireland in the nineteenth century were clear. Not only had the majority faith, Catholicism, not been given the same treatment in 1801 as the Kirk had enjoyed in 1706, a United State Church of England and Ireland had supplied a bolster to Anglicanism in Ireland. The Ascendancy's domination of much of Irish civil society through the early and mid-nineteenth century meant that there were fewer media for the articulation of an Irish patriotic identity inside a union constitutional framework. Irishness was defined in institutions that stood in opposition to the Union state, as opposed to the condition of Scottishness and Union. Gladstone's strategies, accordingly, were to address the issue of the Church establishment, bringing Ireland closer to the model of Scotland; and Home Rule was deployed to create a broadly representative Irish assembly which would provide the needed focus for patriotic feeling within the structure of an ongoing constitutional bond with Britain. Successive land reform, including (ultimately) land purchase, was designed to free the Irish landed classes to assume the leading role in society which their Scottish counterparts enjoyed with (relative) freedom. In part, therefore, while Ireland certainly provided a possible Home Rule agenda for the Scots, Scotland had earlier helped to shape a Gladstonian agenda and model for Ireland.

CONCLUSIONS

Gladstone's vision of the union has had a lasting and contemporary relevance, mediated through the official record, and contemporary or near-contemporary print and material culture. The comparative experience of Scotland and Ireland

**90** Foot & Matthew (eds), *Gladstone diaries*, xi, 118.    **91** Ibid., 388, n. 4.    **92** See Morton, *Unionist nationalism*.

under the Union, so relevant to Gladstone, has a similarly continuing importance: Irish Home Rule impacted of course upon Scotland, but the Scottish experience of the Union was also relevant to Gladstone's thoughts on Ireland.

Home Rule resonates still: Gladstone provided, through Home Rule, a template and a political agenda that would be revisited with the measure of 1912, and to a lesser extent in 1920 and subsequently. Debate on an exclusion from Home Rule began (albeit quietly) at least as early as 1886, was recognized by Gladstone himself (if Paul Bew's arguments are correct) in 1892, became more focused in 1910–11 and was rehearsed in parliament for the first time in 1912.[93] In 1893, with the second Home Rule Bill, Gladstone suggested that Irish representation at Westminster be retained, albeit at the reduced level of 80 MPs, a number said to be proportionate to the Irish population. The Gladstonian 'in and out' proposal of 1893 was considered as late as 1965–6, when Harold Wilson was angrily trying to rid himself of what he considered to be the 'Tory' MPs from Northern Ireland.

Gladstone provided a beacon for subsequent generations of British politicians seeking to navigate the British-Irish relationship. Gladstone, like Tony Blair, invested reform of the union with a strong moral and providentialist tone. He devised a constitutional proposition that still has an importance – the paradox that the United Kingdom could best be sustained through devolution. He also defined, through Home Rule, a form of 'variable geometry' for the government of the United Kingdom, which has been an underpinning principle of the Blair government's constitutional reform. In all of these senses, Gladstone's flexible vision of Union seems to have left a greater impact upon contemporary politicians than some at least would care to acknowledge.

93 Bew, *Ireland*, p. 362.

# Gladstone, Salisbury and the end of Irish assimilationism

## K. THEODORE HOPPEN

It is conventional – and by no means mistaken – wisdom to see the 'Question of Ireland' furnishing perhaps one of the most obvious dividing lines between the two main political alignments of late-nineteenth-century Britain. After all, one party renamed itself in honour of the Irish difference; the other, not always consistently or enthusiastically, adopted the blazon of Home Rule as its most recognizable heraldic device. Yet behind the rhetorical cannon roars and beneath the contingent surface of events, there lay a growing convergence generated by a shift away from a certain conjuncture of attitudes concerning the Anglo-Irish relationship which had provided the dominant template for analysis and action throughout the period from the 1830s to the 1860s. These decades had been marked by an insistence that Ireland's manifold 'problems' could best be addressed by aligning Hibernian to British values, institutions, and economic and social structures, by, if you like, trying to render Mayo and Leitrim into Celtic versions of Sussex and Kent. Indeed, in 1849, the prime minister, Lord John Russell, looked to a time when Englishmen might 'take the same interest in a question from Galway as a question from Gloucester'.[1] While microscopic examinations of phenomena like the Irish Poor Law of 1838 nibble away at the notion that these were unambiguous anglicizing impositions,[2] it would be difficult to deny that mid-century administrations pursued a broadly assimilationist agenda when contemplating the sister island to the west. In part, this flowed from the impact of utilitarian universalism,[3] in part from a variety of theological postulates, in part from the failures of earlier post-union attempts to govern Ireland as a remote entity requiring the harsh treatment suitable for psychologically distant provinces.[4]

While few went so far as Viscount Howick (in Melbourne's cabinet 1835–9 and, as 3rd earl Grey, in Russell's 1846–52) when suggesting that Roman

---

1 Russell to Clarendon, 13 Sept. 1849, Clarendon papers, Bodl[eian Library] Irish Deposit 26.
2 P. Gray, *The making of the Irish poor law, 1815–43* (Manchester, 2009), p. 8.   3 See Russell to Morpeth, 11 Feb. [1838], Carlisle papers, C[astle] H[oward] J19/1/17 (cited with the kind permission of the Hon. Simon Howard): 'Surely a man who understands physic is as well qualified to prescribe to an Irishman, as a man who knows Irishmen, but does not know physic'.
4 B. Hilton, *The age of atonement* (Oxford, 1988), pp 108–14, 248–50, 270–1; K.T. Hoppen, 'An incorporating union? British politicians and Ireland, 1800–1830', *English Historical Review*, 123 (2008), 328–50.

Catholicism become the established church in Ireland 'since the Establishment in each of the three divisions of the United Kingdom would then be supported on the irresistible grounds of their practical utility',[5] the overall tendency was clear enough. Persistent attempts – some more successful than others – were made to replicate English municipal reform in Ireland, to transplant the English poor law, to transform Irish county 'governors' into English-style lords lieutenant, to align the criminal and civil law of the two countries, and to prevent the Irish franchise from drifting into even more remotely incomprehensible realms of its own.[6] Indeed, mid-century prime ministers generally followed the edict laid down by Duncannon in a letter to Grey to the effect that governments should proceed 'by doing that in Ireland which you did in England',[7] a notion that soon acquired a mantra-like resonance. 'You say justly that we must deal with Ireland as with England' Ebrington told his predecessor as Irish viceroy in 1840.[8] Four years later, Peel insisted that only a rugged adherence to the precept of uniformism along English models would prevent a 'retrocession to Barbarism'.[9] By 1850, Disraeli praised the Whig policy for its acknowledgment 'that there shall be no distinction between England and Ireland', while, two years later, his party leader, Derby, warned against listening to the siren voices of those in Ireland who had become '*Hiberniores ipsis Hibernis*'.[10]

   The matter that generated the most urgent and persistent attempts at assimilation was that of land and its implications for social organization and economic success. In the first post-union decades the Irish rural economy seemed to metropolitan politicians exotic, remote, different, incomprehensible and, above all, hugely complicated.[11] In the 1830s, voices began to call for modernity and

---

5 Howick to Graham, 9 Mar. 1835, I. Newbould, *Whiggery and reform, 1830–41* (London, 1990), pp 284–5.  6 A. Macintyre, *The Liberator: Daniel O'Connell and the Irish party, 1830–1847* (London, 1965), p. 260; Morpeth to Russell, 27 Sept, 1836 and Nicholls to Morpeth, 23 Sept. 1839, Russell papers, T[he] N[ational] A[rchives] PRO30/22/2C; Gray, *Irish poor law*, p. 133 (citing Nicholls' memorandum of 21 Jan. 1836); Melbourne to Anglesey, 28 Dec. 1830, Melbourne papers, R[oyal] A[rchives: on microfilm at Bodl.] MP 93; Grey to Anglesey, 29 Dec. 1830, Grey papers, D[urham] U[niversity] L[ibrary] GRE/B3/33; Memorandum by Clanricarde of Apr. 1848 in TNA Russell papers PRO30/22/7B; Derby to Eglinton, 2 Oct. 1852, Derby papers, L[iverpool] R[ecord] O[ffice] 181/1; G. Grey to Carlisle, 2 & 4 Feb. 1858, CH Carlisle papers J19/1/77; Cardwell to Carlisle, 12 Nov. 1859, ibid., J19/1/85; Graham to Eliot, 12 Dec. 1842, Graham papers, Bodl. [microfilm: originals now in British Library and resorted] Ir/6; Clarendon to Russell, 14 Jan. 1848, Bodl. Clarendon papers Irish deposit letter-book I; Russell to Clarendon, 7 Jan. 1850, ibid., 26.  7 Duncannon to Grey, 10 Sept. 1832, DUL Grey papers GRE/B7/7/55.  8 Ebrington to Normanby, 8 Sept. 1840, Normanby papers, M[ulgrave] C[astle] V/198.  9 Peel to Heytesbury, 17 Oct. [1844], Peel papers, B[ritish] L[ibrary] Add. MS 40479.  10 Disraeli to Carrington, 8 Nov. 1850, J.A.W. Gunn, J. Matthews, M.G. Wiebe & others (eds), *Benjamin Disraeli letters*, 8 vols to date (Toronto, 1982–), v, 371; Derby to Napier, [29 Oct. 1852], LRO Derby papers 181/1.  11 J.S. Donnelly Jnr, *The land and the people of nineteenth-century Cork* (London, 1975), pp 9–72; C. Ó Gráda, 'Poverty, population and agriculture, 1801–45' in W.E. Vaughan (ed.), *A new history of Ireland V: Ireland under the union I: 1801–70* (Oxford, 1989), pp 108–36; G. Broeker, *Rural disorder and police reform in Ireland,*

simplification along English lines: the introduction of a capitalist tripartite rural structure consisting of landless waged labourers, tenant farmers and investing landlords in place of the hugger-mugger presence of conacre renting cottiers, sub-letting tenants, middlemen, bankrupt landowners, chancery estates and, it was (not always correctly) thought, inefficiency abounding. In 1836, English 'experts' like Cornewall Lewis and George Nicholls called for 'capitalist cultivators', the 'consolidation of holdings', a move to 'day-labour for wages', and the inauguration of a 'transitory period' which, though painful ('it was so in England'), could alone rescue Ireland from its benighted individuality.[12] Eight years later, Peel's Tory cabinet was presented with a long printed memorandum, which, using the recent report of the Devon Commission, argued along the same lines, attacking Irish 'customary practices' and the economic opaqueness of landlord-tenant relations, which, 'unless they be distinctly defined and respected', would yield ever increasing doses of 'social disorder and national inconvenience'.[13]

The famine of 1845–9 furnished a dramatic opportunity for such nostrums to move further from theory to practice. Politicians needed little encouragement to detect a silver lining in the possibility that Ireland might, much more rapidly than could otherwise have been anticipated, be dragged from complex rural inefficiency into straightforward English capitalism or, to put it another way, from poverty into comparative plenty. Already in 1846 the well-meaning viceroy, Lord Bessborough, rejoiced that cottiers were becoming labourers *tout court*.[14] The following year, his successor, Lord Clarendon, announced that 'conacre is no more, the middleman is no more, the squireen is becoming extinct ... the system of subdividing land ... is no more', that, indeed, 'a great social revolution is now going on in Ireland'.[15] As prime minister, Russell was equally convinced that all was becoming 'natural' (that is, English).[16] Nothing, he believed, could or should be done to stop this process or to protect those who clung to outmoded practices: 'You might as well propose that a landlord should compensate the rabbits for the burrows they have made on his land'.[17] Many others thought the same, among them Palmerston, Wood, Graham, Horsman and not least the senior administrator of famine relief, Trevelyan.[18] Although

*1812–36* (London, 1970), passim. **12** M. Beames, *Peasants and power: the Whiteboy movements and their control in pre-famine Ireland* (Brighton, 1983), pp 183–4; P. Gray, *Irish poor law*, pp 137–8; R.B. McDowell, *Public opinion and government policy in Ireland, 1801–1846* (London, 1952), pp 194–5. **13** 'Memorandum-Ireland' (48pp) in LRO Derby papers 36. **14** Bessborough to Russell, 18 & 22 Dec. 1846, TNA Russell papers PRO30/22/5F & G. **15** Clarendon to Brougham, 10 Aug. 1847, Bodl. Clarendon papers Irish Deposit Letter-Book I; to Russell, 10 Oct. 1847, ibid. **16** Russell to Bessborough, 6 Nov. 1846, TNA Russell papers PRO30/22/5E; and 28 Feb. 1847, ibid., PRO30/22/6B. **17** Russell to Clarendon, 10 Nov. 1847, TNA Russell papers PRO30/22/6G. **18** Palmerston's memorandum on 'State of Ireland', 31 Mar. 1848, TNA Russell papers PRO30/22/7B; Wood in *Hansard* 3: 89, 1249 (12 Feb. 1847); Graham in *Hansard* 3: 91, 347 (23 Mar. 1847); Horsman in *Hansard* 3: 107, 846 (23

what was happening was seen by some as a 'natural process',[19] most felt that governmental encouragement might be required lest the inscrutable hand of God or the hidden hand of economic self-adjustment proved unequal to the task.

The two sovereign remedies hit upon were the so-called Gregory clause in the 1847 Poor Law Amendment Act and the Encumbered Estates Act of 1849. The former denied relief to all those holding more than a quarter of an acre of land and was designed simultaneously to prevent fraud and to turn smallholders into labourers.[20] The Encumbered Estates Act addressed the problem from the other extreme and provided machinery for the expeditious sale of bankrupt estates, in the hope that more economically literate and predominantly British entrepreneurs would enter the market and introduce efficient management techniques. Clarendon described it as correcting 'four years of famine … 400 of malversation' by means of 'rough but indispensible treatment' that would 'eventually save the patient'.[21] As it turned out, the majority of new purchasers – few of whom came from outside Ireland – proved to be, not keen-eyed innovators, but Irish landlords who had managed to survive the famine in relatively good shape.[22]

The crowning glory of this volley of anglicizations proved to be the legislation of 1860 generally known as Cardwell's and Deasy's Acts, which swept away all relics of customary land tenure in Ireland, placed everything upon a basis of contract or, as Cardwell put it, 'business-like written engagements between landlord and tenant with respect to the occupancy and improvement of land', thus completing 'what the Encumbered Estates Act' had begun.[23] However, it soon became obvious that, while the poorest agriculturalists had undoubtedly suffered the greatest numerical attrition during and after the Famine,[24] the high hopes that all would henceforth be changed utterly had entirely failed to take root or indeed flight. Deasy himself lamented that it was still not possible 'to govern Ireland as you do Yorkshire or Devon', while already by 1865 the supposedly crucial legislation of 1860 was being declared an utter failure in almost every respect.[25]

With one important exception, Gladstone's involvement in these developments had been minimal. For reasons that remain obscure, he had expected Peel

July 1849); Trevelyan to Burgoyne, 8 Apr. 1847, Trevelyan papers, N[ewcastle] U[niversity] L[ibrary] CET18/13/289–94.  **19** Clarendon to Lansdowne, 15 Nov. 1848, 3rd marquess of Lansdowne papers, BL B85 (temporary reference).  **20** P. Gray, *Irish poor law*, p. 278. By the week ending 4 July 1847, of 681,794 persons being relieved, 335,535 fell into the Gregory clause category: see J. Prest, *Lord John Russell* (London, 1972), p. 251.  **21** Clarendon to Lansdowne, 19 June 1851, BL 3rd marquess of Lansdowne papers B86.  **22** J.S. Donnelly Jnr, 'Landlords and tenants' in W.E. Vaughan (ed.), *A new history of Ireland V: Ireland under the union I*, p. 348; also *Land and people of nineteenth-century Cork*, p. 131.  **23** Cardwell in *Hansard* 3: 157, 1565 (29 Mar. 1860); Cardwell to Carlisle, 25 Aug. 1860 CH Carlisle papers J19/1/90.  **24** K.T. Hoppen, *Elections, politics and society in Ireland, 1832–1885* (Oxford, 1984), pp 89–116.  **25** Memorandum by Deasy, 25 Oct. 1860, CH Carlisle papers J19/11/13; W.E. Forster in *Hansard* 3: 178, 586 (31 Mar. 1865).

to offer him the post of chief secretary for Ireland in 1841.[26] Some months after his resignation in 1845 over the Maynooth grant (for him a religious rather than an Irish issue), Gladstone produced the famous declaration about Ireland as 'that cloud in the west, that coming storm, the minister of God's retribution'.[27] But this was no more than an outburst without context. Indeed, seven years later he was telling the prime minister that he (Gladstone) 'ought not to meddle with Irish matters of which I know so little'.[28] Meddle, however, he did in his famous budget of 1853, which, in complete accord with the contemporary push towards assimilation, extended the income tax to Ireland. When in 1842 Peel and Goulburn had reintroduced the tax, they had exempted Ireland, not least because of deficiencies in its collection and assessment machinery.[29] The expense of famine relief had, however, generated complaints.[30] In 1852, Disraeli, as chancellor, had proposed some modest tax extensions to Ireland; in 1853, Russell and most of the cabinet enthusiastically supported Gladstone's plans (required, he claimed, by 'the strongest demands of justice') to remit certain famine debts in return for the extension to Ireland of an income tax that would, he declared, be altogether abolished within a decade.[31] Although abolition proved illusory, Gladstone remained convinced for the rest of his long career that Ireland had been, was and would probably (despite his best efforts) continue to be treated with unwarranted fiscal generosity, that 'establishments and expenditure are maintained there … in excess of all real wants, simply because they are Irish'.[32] Indeed, if parsimony in general proved to be Gladstone's most obvious political motivation, resentment at what he considered Ireland's extravagance constituted a key element within his overall mission to save public money.

None of this, however, prevented a dramatic *bouleversement* from taking place during the late 1860s in the attitudes of British politicians (Gladstone prominent among them) towards Ireland. As a result, the earlier agenda of treating Ireland as if it were (or could rapidly be transformed into) a sort of smaller version of England was entirely abandoned. The reasons for this are complex and not yet fully understood. Certainly, as Clive Dewey showed in a brilliant essay, shifts in

**26** Memorandum of 16 Sept. [1841], BL Gladstone papers Add. MS 44819 printed in J. Brooke & M. Sorensen (eds), *The prime ministers' papers: W.E. Gladstone*, 4 vols (London, 1971–81), ii, 162–3; also M.R.D. Foot & H.C.G. Matthew (eds), *The Gladstone diaries*, 14 vols (Oxford, 1968–94), iii, 140 (16 Sept. 1841).    **27** H.C.G. Matthew, *Gladstone, 1809–1874* (Oxford, 1986), pp 65, 68–9.    **28** Gladstone to Aberdeen, Christmas 1852, BL Aberdeen papers Add. MS 43070.    **29** *Hansard* 3: 61, 443–50 (11 Mar. 1842).    **30** See, for example, Clarendon to Wood, 2 Feb. 1848, Hickleton papers B[orthwick] I[nstitute, York] A4/57; Clarendon to Wood, 13 Feb. 1848, Bodl. Clarendon papers Irish Deposit Letter-Book I; *Hansard* 3: 102, 801–3 (16 Feb. 1849).    **31** J.A.W. Gunn et al. (eds), *Benjamin Disraeli letters*, vi, 236–7; Russell to Gladstone, 30 Mar. 1853, BL Gladstone papers Add. MS 44291; Gladstone's memorandum of 11 Apr. 1853, ibid., Add. MS 44778; *Hansard* 3: 125, 1350–1427 (18 Apr. 1853) & 127, 522 (23 May 1853); Gladstone to Aberdeen, 30 Apr. 1853, BL Aberdeen papers Add. MS 43070; J.B. Conacher, *The Aberdeen coalition, 1852–1855* (Cambridge, 1968), pp 58–78.    **32** Gladstone to Wodehouse, 17 Dec. 1864, Kimberley papers, Bodl. MS 4016.

the intellectual weather played a part, in particular a move away from classical political economics and utilitarian universalism (with their emphases upon immutable general principles) and towards a greater sympathy for historicist views that stressed cultural relativism, envisaged social phenomena as historically determined, and displayed a respect for traditions of every kind.[33] Not only did this help to transform attitudes towards Ireland as a whole, it helped, together with contingent phenomena such as Fenian violence[34] and the power of Irish voters, to raise Ireland to a prominence in political minds that it had not occupied since the Famine of the 1840s. Already by 1867 Gladstone had discovered an 'Irish question which in its several branches is gradually overshadowing every other'.[35] He had also concluded that in all matters it was now best to cease 'making the opinion of one country overrule and settle the questions belonging to the others' and to deal instead with 'the interests of each as nearly as we can in accordance with the views and sentiments of the natives of that country'.[36] He even went so far as to demand a new kind of psychological empathy in which 'each of us' might 'individually make a mental effort to place himself in the position of an Irishman ... under the influence of their traditions'.[37]

Gladstone, always a great bookman, now began to read voraciously about Ireland with (as he put it) the advantage of ignorance and a lack (or so he claimed) of preconceptions.[38] In part, his sources were 'historical', such as the writings of W.N. Hancock (editor of two volumes of early Irish law tracts published in 1865), who had turned 180 degrees from supporting the contract-based land law of 1860 to demanding 'special' Celtic legislation ten years later, in part 'historico-contemporary' like George Campbell's 'little book' *Irish land* published in 1869, which, using Indian analogies, argued that the assimilation of Irish land legislation to English models had failed and that instead Ireland required a different and localist approach.[39] Gladstone began to talk of 'old customs', of 'tribal property', of 'historical and traditional rights', all of which appeared reassuringly conservative tropes to one who was later to insist on being 'a firm believer in the aristocratic principle ... I am an out-and-out *inequalitarian*'.[40] Placing Ireland, whether in its religious (disestablishment) or agrarian

33 C. Dewey, 'Celtic agrarian legislation and the Celtic revival: historicist implications of Gladstone's Irish and Scottish land acts, 1870–86', *Past & Present*, 64 (1974), 30–70. 34 While Gladstone later denied that Fenianism had directly influenced his change of mind, he allowed that it had brought Irish affairs 'under the impartial action of the national judgment and conscience': to D.H. Macfarlane, 28 Nov. 1880, in Foot & Matthew (eds), *Gladstone diaries*, ix, 624. 35 Gladstone to O'Hagan, 12 Dec. 1867, O'Hagan papers, P[ublic] R[ecord] O[ffice of] N[orthern] I[reland] D2777/9/42/3. 36 *Hansard* 3: 181, 272 (8 Feb. 1866). 37 *The Times*, 20 Dec. 1867 (reporting Gladstone's Southport speech of 19 Dec.). 38 R.D. Collison Black, *Economic thought and the Irish question, 1817–1870* (Cambridge, 1960), pp 62–3. 39 C. Dewey, 'Celtic agrarian legislation', pp 45–9; R.D. Collison Black, *Economic thought*, p. 63. Isaac Butt, in *The Irish people and the Irish land* (1867), had also put forward 'Indian' arguments. Twelve years later, Campbell, then an MP, bemoaned the fact that 'excessive liberty' had been bestowed upon the Irish: *Hansard* 3: 258, 325–7 (7 Feb. 1881). 40 Gladstone's memorandum of 11 Dec. 1869,

(land legislation) mode, into a separate self-contained box also had the advantage of preventing the Hibernian bacillus from attacking the glowingly healthy state of things in England and Scotland.[41] Preparing himself for what became the Irish Land Act of 1870, he urged colleagues to follow a similar course of historicist immersion, and was delighted when some of them began to respond to the same intellectual and political vibrations and to accept that Ireland be treated 'according to Irish views'.[42] Although the Disestablishment Act (which prescribed remedies even now unknown to England) constituted the first shot in the campaign, it was the Land Act which marked the real beginning of that process of Irish differentiation that was to dominate the next fifty years. Under the eyes of eternity, the actual provisions of the act might seem modest enough, but the privileges it conferred upon tenants were to lead – almost inexorably – to greater things: among much else, compensation for improvements made without the landlord's consent, restrictions on the power to evict, and statutory endorsement of the right of tenants to sell 'interests' in their holdings.

Gladstone was far from alone in his new insistence that Ireland should now be treated differently. Spencer, the newly-appointed viceroy and later to become a key member of Gladstone's Irish 'team', told the Statistical Society of Ireland in 1869 of his dislike of 'abstract theories' with their allegedly 'universal application'.[43] And while this species of discourse was pursued most comfortably among Liberals (where writers like J.S. Mill possessed some force),[44] Tories too were beginning to sing similar tunes, if not always in the same key. Northcote (never entirely able to shake off Gladstone's tutelage) addressed the Social Science Association in 1869 in words that could have come straight from his master's mouth: 'The facts are stubborn and cannot be bent ... The [Irish] national idea of the relations between landlord and tenant is something totally different from the national idea in England ... If that be the case, you must provide accordingly'.[45] Disraeli, who may have encouraged Northcote, told parliament, in a speech containing what even for him was a high quotient of

in BL Gladstone papers Add. MS 44758; *Hansard* 3: 199, 339–40 (15 Feb. 1870); Gladstone to Granville, 27 Dec. 1869, TNA Granville papers PRO30/29/57; J. Morley, *The life of William Ewart Gladstone*, 3 vols (London, 1903), ii, 582.   41 E.D. Steele, *Irish land and British politics: tenant-right and nationality, 1865–1870* (Cambridge, 1974), p. 214; P. Gray, 'The peculiarities of Irish land tenure, 1800–1914' in D. Winch & P.K. O'Brien (eds), *The political economy of British historical experience, 1688–1914* (Oxford, 2002), pp 155–6.   42 Gladstone to Argyll, 4 Dec. 1869, 5 & 8 Jan. 1870, BL Gladstone papers Add. MSS 44538 & 44101; Fortescue to Gladstone, 30 Nov. 1869 & 14 Dec. 1867, ibid., Add. MSS 44122 & 44121; Fortescue to Wodehouse, 24 Dec. 1866, Bodl. Kimberley papers MS 4043. See also Wodehouse to Clarendon, 27 Jan. 1865, ibid., MS 4018.   43 T.A. Boylan & T.P. Foley, *Political economy and colonial Ireland* (London, 1992), pp 137–8: 'You must consider the position of the country, the state and progress of the people'.   44 E.D. Steele, 'J.S. Mill and the Irish question', *Historical Journal*, 13 (1970), 216–36, 419–50; B.L. Kinzer, *England's disgrace? J.S. Mill and the Irish question* (Toronto, 2001), passim.   45 E.D. Steele, 'Ireland and the empire in the 1860s', *Historical Journal*, 11 (1968), 77. Northcote had once been Gladstone's private secretary.

waffle, that the organic and historical approach was the one to take, that, indeed, 'Irish policy is Irish history'.[46] Salisbury, newly succeeded to the marquessate and not long after resigning from the Tory cabinet over parliamentary reform, now also proclaimed Ireland to be a different place no longer amenable to anything like assimilation, though his particular point of approach came from a very different part of the political compass. For him, the English were 'Teutonic' (good), the Irish 'Celtic' (bad) and 'of a lower civilization', the conclusion being that while Ireland certainly needed 'special' treatment, its distinctiveness demanded harsh measures that alone could lift it out of 'the very depths of barbarism'.[47] Yet this, no less than the Gladstonian mode, marked a distinct end to the integrative approach of earlier years. For Gladstone, legislative acknowl-edgment of Irish difference implied disestablishment and land reform, leading, he believed, to a strengthening of the union.[48] For Salisbury, no less convinced that Irish distinctiveness demanded recognition, the solution lay along different, though in the end parallel and sometimes even convergent, lines.

The anti-assimilationist discourse that began to emerge in the late 1860s took wing in the decades that followed, with only a few brave heretics such as the 3rd earl Grey and the 8th duke of Argyll (a keen, if eccentric, student of evolution in all its forms) doggedly holding out for older truths. For Grey, 'economic laws' remained 'fixed by Divine wisdom' and therefore universally applicable; for Argyll, cultural relativism was a snare and delusion, English models were best, and Ireland could only become a better place if old Celtic customs were entirely smitten into dust.[49] Arthur Balfour, a less marginal figure, also had doubts about historicism, regretting in 1882 that 'they had deliberately turned back the course of civilization by substituting status for contract',[50] but he never pushed these views strongly and certainly never sought to undermine the land policies of his uncle (Salisbury) and of the Tory party as a whole.

Although the question of Ireland rather faded from view in the mid-1870s, Gladstone took the opportunity to organize a visit to the country in 1877 (his only significant tour), during which he turned his mind towards rendering 'the Ireland of a thousand and twelve hundred years back ... an object of just vener-ation'.[51] More pertinently, it was during the first half of the 1880s that the acceptance of the concept that Ireland was a separate and distinct place

46 Hansard 3: 190, 1771–92 at 1791 (16 Mar. 1868). 47 Hansard 3: 200, 825 (22 Mar. 1870) & 206, 32–3 (2 May 1871). 48 Hansard 3: 194, 412–66 (1 Mar. 1869). He even thought it right to allow the flying of 'the green flag ... for after all it is the national flag of Ireland' to Spencer, 27 Aug. 1872, BL Spencer papers Add. MS 76851. 49 For Grey, see Hansard 3: 254, 1857 (2 Aug. 1880); for Argyll ibid., 308, 40 (19 Aug. 1886) also his Irish nationalism (London, 1893), p. 71: 'The law and usages of England, if universally established and resolutely enforced, would have been the salvation of Ireland'. 50 Hansard 3: 266, 1771 (27 Feb. 1882). 51 Gladstone to Granville, 31 Oct. 1877 in A. Ramm (ed.), The political correspondence of Mr Gladstone and Lord Granville, 1876–1886, 2 vols (Oxford, 1962), i, 56. See the essay by Kevin McKenna in this volume.

demanding, on historical as well as contemporary grounds, *sui generis* treatment, more or less completely hypnotized British political minds. Thus the Land Act of 1881 involved, according to Gladstone, 'a perfectly frank acceptance of Irish custom'.[52] In a famous phrase, he mocked any individual who would apply 'the principles of abstract political economy to the people and circumstances of Ireland exactly as if he had been proposing to legislate for the inhabitants of Saturn and Jupiter'.[53] In the event, politicians, whatever their views on the details of the Land Bill, queued up to announce a commitment to Irish distinctiveness. The strongly Tory duke of Richmond (who had chaired an important royal commission on the land question) was astonished to discover how much Ireland differed from England, while the equally strongly Liberal earl of Kimberley (who had served as Irish viceroy in 1864–6) dismissed those who would 'apply to Ireland the same principles we applied to England'.[54] And, during the debates on the bill, prominent figures from both parties – among them Forster, Hartington, Carlingford, Northcote and Selborne, as well as smaller fry like William Summers, Sir John Holker and Benjamin Rodwell – were all to be found singing from the same distinctivist/historical hymn sheet.[55]

Salisbury, for his part, after making a few jokes about Saturn and Jupiter, confined his comments to complaints that the proposed legislation was altogether too timid in its provisions for state-assisted purchase by tenants.[56] Having (upon Disraeli's death) become, with Northcote, dual leader of his party, he was to devote the next years to fine-tuning a refrain that the dual system of land ownership set up by Gladstone's 1881 act was unnatural, inefficient and productive of rural violence. Henceforth, the Tory policy of distinctiveness towards Ireland was to take a specific shape: the ending of dual ownership by a tolerably rapid transfer of farms into tenant (or 'peasant') hands with the help of cartloads of government cash. By the time Salisbury had pushed Northcote aside and been appointed prime minister for the first time in mid-1885, he had become entirely convinced of the 'hopelessness of managing England and Ireland together' and of the 'labyrinth of difficulties' any attempted assimilationism would automatically produce.[57] By the time, therefore, that Gladstone

---

52 *Hansard* 3: 261, 601 (16 May 1881).  53 *Hansard* 3: 260, 895 (7 Apr. 1881).  54 Richmond to Cairns, 11 July 1880, TNA Cairns papers PRO30/51/4; Kimberley: *Hansard* 3: 254, 1932 (2 Aug. 1880).  55 Forster: *Hansard* 3: 260, 1155 (25 Apr. 1881); Hartington: *Hansard* 3: 261, 920 (19 May 1881) 'The law in Ireland has too long neglected to recognize the customary and equitable rights of the tenants'; Carlingford (the former Fortescue): *Hansard* 3: 264, 237, 253 (1 Aug. 1881); Northcote: *Hansard* 3: 261, 901–3 (16 May 1881); Selborne: *Hansard* 3: 264, 517 (2 Aug. 1881) 'It is pedantic to insist upon theoretical and abstract ideas'; Smaller fry: *Hansard* 3: 261, 81, 86, 622 (9 & 10 May 1881).  56 *Hansard* 3: 264, 254–70 (1 Aug. 1881).  57 Salisbury to Carnarvon, 22 July 1885, BL Carnarvon papers Add. MS 60762. Carnarvon (viceroy 1885–6), in this respect at least, enthusiastically echoed his master's voice: to Hicks Beach, 21 July 1885, TNA Carnarvon papers PRO30/6/63; to the queen, 3 Aug. 1885, ibid., PRO30/6/53; to H. Ponsonby, 17 Oct. 1885, ibid., PRO30/6/53.

was moving towards a final acceptance of Home Rule in the autumn of 1885 ('What I do think of is the Irish nation, and the fame, duty and peace of my country'),[58] Tories too were developing an engagement with Ireland informed by an equally strong adherence to the view that English norms ineluctably lost their salience once transferred across the Irish Sea. For Northcote, this was expressed in the feebly emollient terms of hoping 'to meet the wants and to consider the feelings, and even the susceptibilities, of the Irish people, treating "Irish ideas" with great tenderness'.[59] For the carnivorous Salisbury, it meant something rather different, though for him too the notion of Irish distinctiveness had quickly become a standard analytical tool. Already in 1870, he had sneered at Irish landlords 'for not holding their own in the open fight of politics' against Gladstone's first Land Act.[60] Fifteen years later, he had also come to formulate a poor opinion of Ulster's Protestant Conservatives, whose support for the 1881 Land Act and admiration for Northcote annoyed him in more or less equal measure.[61] And as for the rest of the Irish – the Hottentots as he called them[62] – well, they might indeed be savages, but curiously privileged ones all the same, privileged in the sense that Salisbury believed that the state should furnish mountains of money to help them buy the properties they occupied and of which Gladstone had already (to Salisbury's great annoyance) made them dual 'owners' since 1881.

By contrast, the Liberal mode for expressing the accepted 'fact' of Irish difference now took the form of support for some measure of political devolution or Home Rule. Already in 1877, Gladstone (who in 1871 had famously scorned Home Rule in a speech at Aberdeen)[63] had begun to talk of going 'much further than the "average" Liberal'. By 1881, he was refusing to fix any 'limits' to Irish devolution 'except the supremacy of the imperial parliament'.[64] In this he was plugging into a wider Liberal attack on the centralization of the Irish administration and a growing support for the establishment of local bodies to control education, railways and similar matters.[65] Individual Liberal leaders began to use a limited and common word-kitty when talking of Ireland 'being governed in Ireland', though what such phrases actually meant was never entirely clear.[66] In 1882 and 1883, Trevelyan (then chief secretary) wanted

---

58 Gladstone to Rosebery, 10 Sept. 1885, Rosebery papers, N[ational] L[ibrary of] S[cotland] MS 10023.   59 Northcote (now earl of Iddesleigh) to Carnarvon, 7 Sept. 1885, BL Carnarvon papers Add. MS 60825.   60 *Hansard* 3: 202, 76 (14 June 1870).   61 K.T. Hoppen, *The mid-Victorian generation, 1846–1886* (Oxford, 1998), p. 676.   62 *The Times*, 17 May 1886.   63 *The Times*, 27 Sept. 1871. However, in the following month, Gladstone 'heartily wished that the Irish government could be decentralized': see Memorandum by Spencer of a conversation with Gladstone, 14 Oct. 1871, BL Spencer papers Add. MS 76856.   64 Gladstone to Granville, 20 Nov. 1877 & 16 Sept. 1881, in A. Ramm (ed.), *Political correspondence of Mr Gladstone and Lord Granville, 1876–1886*, i, 58 & 293.   65 See Spencer to Granville, 1 Feb. 1869, TNA Granville papers PRO30/29/29; Hartington to Granville, 13 Nov. 1877, ibid., PRO30/29/22A/2/.   66 Hartington to Spencer, 24 June 1882, and Trevelyan to Spencer, 24 June 1882, BL Spencer

something 'very big' in order to 'engage the people in the management of their own affairs'.[67] Gladstone claimed to have developed 'elementary and fixed ideas', Forster wanted a 'measure of local government', Argyll, 'quite spontaneously', spoke of 'some kind of Irish legislature', while Lowe (according to Gladstone 'a person sufficiently conservative') proposed a 'larger allowance of local government for Ireland' than had been given to Canada.[68] Chamberlain, whose ideas were very advanced, was driven, above all, by a hatred of the 'Dublin Castle' machine and by a desire to cut it down to size.[69]

So long as everything remained predominantly rhetorical, the Liberal ship continued fully crewed. Yet Gladstone, even before his definite conversion to Home Rule became public as a result of the so-called 'Hawarden kite' of mid-December 1885, was mighty busy in regaling his party with arguments for movement, in which 'special' Irish 'circumstances', the singular nature of the 'Irish character', the historical context of the Anglo-Irish relationship, and the importance of a general plan that could not be perceived as an 'English' plan were repeatedly emphasized as necessary for political settlement.[70] By the end of 1885, even Rosebery had briefly been persuaded that, however 'wrong' Home Rule might be as an 'abstract principle', its 'practical necessity' had become 'certain'.[71]

One of Gladstone's recognized traits was a disposition to clothe complex notions in words of gnomic obscurity. This was usually a sign of self-doubt, and it is significant that only weeks before the 'Hawarden kite' he was to be found declaring that the setting up of a legislature for Ireland 'will cause a mighty heave in the body politic ... It may possibly be done, but only by the full use of great leverage. That leverage can only be found in their equitable mature consideration and what is due to the fixed desire of a nation, clearly and constitutionally expressed'.[72] Though this could be interpreted as meaning pretty well anything, Gladstone did remain much clearer about two aspects of his proposals that he

papers Add. MS 76945. **67** Trevelyan to Gladstone, 23 Dec. 1882, BL Gladstone papers Add. MS 44335; to J. Chamberlain, 7 Jan. 1883, J. Chamberlain papers, B[irmigham] U[niversity] L[ibrary] JC5/70/4. Campbell-Bannerman too had no fears (as chief secretary) in Apr. 1885 'of going great lengths': to Spencer, 30 Apr. 1885, BL Spencer papers Add. MS 76871. **68** Gladstone to Hartington, 3 Feb. 1883, BL Gladstone papers Add. MS 44146; Spencer to Gladstone, 25 May 1883, ibid., Add. MS 44310. **69** See his speeches at Holloway on 17 June 1885 and at Islington on 18 June 1885 in BL Gladstone papers Add. MSS 44126 & 44258. **70** Gladstone to Spencer, 3 Feb. 1883, BL Gladstone papers Add. MS 44310; to Hartington, 8 Sept. 1885, ibid., Add. MS 44148 ('give to the Irish a really historical consideration') and 11 Sept. 1885, ibid., Add. MS 44148 (demands a 'historical and therefore a comprehensive view of the Irish question'). See also Gladstone to Forster, 12 Apr. 1882, ibid., Add. MS 49545; to Trevelyan, 5 Dec. 1882, ibid., Add. MS 44546; also Gladstone's extensive historical reading (ibid., Add. MS 49770) and the retrospective memorandum on 1885–6 of 28 Sept. 1897 in J. Brooke & M. Sorensen (eds), *Prime ministers' papers: W.E. Gladstone*, i, 108. **71** Rosebery to Spencer, 31 Dec. 1885, BL Spencer papers Add. MS 76866. **72** Gladstone to Rosebery, 13 Nov. 1885, BL Gladstone papers Add. MS 44288.

felt rendered them especially necessary and indeed attractive. Both chimed in with deeply-held and long-term convictions. The first was that Home Rule was a profoundly conservative phenomenon, which, far from implying separation, would bind Ireland more closely to Britain and hence strengthen imperial unity. As he told Hartington, Home Rule would 'consolidate the unity of the empire on the combined basis of imperial authority and mutual attachment'.[73] It was a belief that grew stronger with the passage of time, so that by 1892 Gladstone was insisting (to the queen) that Home Rule was 'a proposal eminently conservative in the highest sense of the term, as tending to the union of the three countries'.[74]

What mattered almost as much was that Home Rule would, Gladstone believed, save money. This, for the great proponent of the minimal state, was, if not a primary motivation, certainly a very attractive potential consequence of any devolutionary plan. 'Public expenditure' would be 'thrown on local rates' and thus force the Irish to pay for their own extravagances. There would be a stop to that waste of public treasure 'involved in the present system of government and legislation in Ireland'. Above all, 'the chapter of … material aid, eleemosynary aid' to Ireland would be brought to a very satisfying halt.[75]

With regard to the abandonment of Irish assimilationism, it matters not whether Gladstone's motives were high-minded and based upon sustained thinking about the Anglo-Irish relationship or shaped by short-term contingencies and an urgent desire to tighten his control over the Liberal party by effectively expelling those who took a different view. What matters is that the party's mode of discourse about Ireland changed to one based upon a general acceptance of Irish difference and that this was now expressed in terms of Home Rule. It goes without saying that attachment to such an approach was never consistent in either content or intensity. Even true believers like Morley saw Gladstone's claims at the time of his second Home Rule Bill of 1893 that he had never deviated regarding Ireland over 'the last 30 years' as hokum.[76] And, indeed, most Liberals spent the years immediately after 1893 shelving the whole issue, some with pleasure, others with weary relief.[77] They fought the 1906

73 Gladstone's Statement of 30 Jan. 1886 in Devonshire papers, Ch[atsworth] H[ouse] 340.1921; Gladstone to Hartington, 3 Feb. 1883 & 18 Nov. 1885, ibid., 340.1320 & 1833; to Forster, 25 Oct. 1880, BL Gladstone papers Add. MS 44157; to Queen Victoria, 13 May 1885, TNA Royal Letters CAB41/19/38; Edward Hamilton's Diary for 6 Feb. 1886 in J. Brooke & M. Sorensen (eds), *Prime ministers' papers: W.E. Gladstone*, iv, 116. **74** Gladstone's memorandum of 28 Oct. 1892 in Foot & Matthew (eds), *Gladstone diaries*, xiii, 125–6. He was not alone in this view, see *Hansard* 3: 302, 229 (22 Jan. 1886). **75** Gladstone to Hartington, 10 Dec. 1882, ChH Devonshire papers 340.1287; *Hansard* 3: 304, 1084 (8 Apr. 1886); see also Shaw Lefevre's similar argument in ibid., 305, 1021 (13 May 1886); Gladstone to Knowles, 5 Aug. 1885 in J.L. Hammond, *Gladstone and the Irish nation* (London, 1938), p. 410; Gladstone to Forster, 8 May 1885 in Foot & Matthew (eds), *Gladstone diaries*, ix, 518; J. Brooke & M. Sorensen (eds), *Prime ministers' papers: W.E. Gladstone*, iii, 269–70. **76** Morley's diary for 2 May 1893, Morley papers, Bodl. MS Eng.d.3454. **77** P. Jalland, *The Liberals and Ireland: the Ulster question in British politics to 1914* (Brighton, 1980), pp 22–4; H.W. McCready, 'Home Rule and the Liberal

election without any pledge to introduce Home Rule,[78] and their huge majority allowed them to concentrate on other things. Nonetheless, Home Rule had become irretrievably attached to the Liberal party, not least because of the path taken by their opponents, but also because 'Home Rule' had established itself as the phrase in which Liberals characteristically expressed their particular acknowledgment of a truth now universally acknowledged, namely, the 'fact' of permanent and irremovable Irish distinctiveness. In short, for them no alternative Irish policy was viably available. The Tories had captured the unambiguously anti-Home Rule department, while the fate of the feeble devolutionary plans of 1907 – together with the mathematical discipline imposed by the elections of 1910 – demonstrated that lesser alternatives no longer possessed much political traction. Indeed, by December 1909, the show was once again on the road when Asquith publicly ditched gradualism and announced that Home Rule was back in place as the only solution to the Irish question.[79] Thereafter, even if many Liberals did not pursue Home Rule *con amore*,[80] the issue once more took its place among the party's key defining principles.

If for Conservatives the idea of Irish distinctiveness was no less central, their mode of discourse was quite different. The adoption of the title 'Unionist' might be taken to mean all sorts of things (not least a belief that Ireland 'was the best card in their hands'),[81] but what it did not imply was any desire to resurrect or pursue the assimilationist policies of the years between 1830 and 1868. Instead, Unionist leaders proclaimed their conviction that Ireland must be recognized as possessing distinct and different characteristics and that the best way of dealing with these was by developing a land policy capable of generating a dramatic transfer of property from landlords to tenants underpinned by massive financial support from the United Kingdom government. If a central characteristic of Gladstone's Irish policy was parsimony, his opponents were ever ready to put their hands into the pockets of the tax payer.

All of this mattered so much because the land question constituted a key – perhaps the key – element in the Anglo-Irish relationship. For Conservatives, its proper handling might furnish the ace with which to trump the devolutionary king and thus produce (as Arthur Balfour put it in 1887) 'the only final solution' to Irish problems.[82] For Liberals, agrarian agitation certainly demanded some

party, 1899–1906', *Irish Historical Studies*, 13 (1963), 316–48.   78 Asquith to Herbert Gladstone, 22 Oct. 1905, Herbert Gladstone papers, BL Add. MS 45989.   79 D. Gwynn, *The life of John Redmond* (London, 1932), p. 169.   80 But then neither really had Gladstone, who never developed much affection for the Irish and always regarded them with less enthusiasm than he did the English, Welsh and (above all) the Scots. See *Hansard* 3: 305, 1363 (18 May 1886); J. Vincent, 'Gladstone and Ireland', *Proceedings of the British Academy*, 63 (1977), 230–1.   81 As Labouchere pointed out: *Hansard* 3: 308, 286 (23 Aug. 1886).   82 Balfour to Salisbury, 9 Mar. 1887, in R.H. Williams (ed.), *Salisbury-Balfour correspondence* (Hertfordshire Record Publication No. 4, 1988), p. 179; L.P. Curtis Jnr, *Coercion and conciliation in Ireland, 1880–1892* (Princeton, NJ, 1963), pp 348–55; A.B. Cooke & J.R. Vincent (eds), 'Ireland and party politics, 1885–7: an

kind of dramatic reaction, but also necessarily required Home Rule in order to render expenditure 'safe'.[83] But, while the first (very small-scale) legislative steps along the purchase road were indeed taken by Liberal administrations in 1869, 1870 and 1881,[84] only the Tories ever adopted the policy with real enthusiasm. Salisbury's support went back to 1870, when he had also mischievously pointed out that the part of Ireland where agriculture flourished best was that part (Ulster) where 'free contract has been most violated'.[85] From then on, his support for purchase remained constant and his admiration for Irish landlords (who, he believed, had cravenly failed to fight their corner) steadily and steeply declined.[86] While, therefore, Liberals regularly accused Tories of pushing purchase primarily as a means of bailing out their landed friends, this was never more than partially true.[87] Indeed, if any one strand of thinking runs consistently through nineteenth-century British political attitudes towards Ireland, it is that of outright distaste for Irish landlordism, an attitude found hardly less in the Conservative than in the Liberal party.

Salisbury and the Tories supported purchase above all because they believed that it alone might prove capable of producing a rural Ireland dominated by a truly 'conservative' class of small proprietors. Expensive purchase plans might not, they unsurprisingly insisted, be appropriate for Britain, but in an Ireland distinct and different it was the only possible remedy for conditions at once singular and dangerous. Gladstone's Land Act of 1881 having created, the Tories claimed, an unsupportable system of dual ownership, the only solution was to provide sufficient finance to enable tenants to buy their holdings: to introduce, in other words, a special economic policy for a special and therefore (in a sense) already separate political entity.[88] Such an approach meant that arguments in favour of state-financed purchase can be found running through virtually all Conservative analyses of Irish problems from at least the early 1880s until the

unpublished Conservative memoir' [by Hugh Holmes], *Irish Historical Studies*, 16 (1969), 446. **83** The view that only the existence of some devolved Irish 'authority' could provide satisfactory financial guarantees for British expenditure on land purchase lay at the centre of the Gladstonian analysis. See Gladstone to Queen Victoria, 23 May 1885, TNA Royal letters CAB41/19/38; *Hansard* 3: 309, 1142 (21 Sept. 1886: Morley); 310, 358 (31 Jan. 1887: Labouchere); also Spencer's introduction to J. Bryce (ed.), *Handbook of Home Rule*, 2nd ed. (London, 1887), p. x, and p. 258 (Morley). **84** Of the 7665 tenants who purchased under the 1869–81 legislation, 79 per cent bought under the (rather tangential) provisions of the Irish Church Act of 1869. H.D. Gribbon, 'Economic and social history, 1850–1921' in W.E. Vaughan (ed.), *A new history of Ireland V: Ireland under the union I*, p. 274. **85** *Hansard* 3: 75–6 (14 June 1870). **86** *Hansard* 3: 264, 257 & 267 (1 Aug. 1881); ibid., 299, 1358 (21 July 1885). **87** For strong criticism of Irish landlords, see Salisbury to Northcote, 10 Aug. 1882, in L.P. Curtis Jnr, *Coercion and conciliation in Ireland*, p. 33; Holmes' remarks in A.B. Cooke & J.R. Vincent (eds), 'Ireland and party politics, 1885–7', *Irish Historical Studies*, 16 (1969), 446. **88** Salisbury: *Hansard* 3: 308, 69 (19 Aug. 1886) & 354, 1573–9 (26 June 1891); Hicks Beach: ibid., 310, 1339 (11 Feb. 1887); Lansdowne to Salisbury, 8 Dec. 1887, 5th marquess of Lansdowne papers, BL 'English Career' no. 15 (temporary reference); A.J. Balfour's Cabinet papers of 20 Feb. & May 1889, TNA Cabinet papers CAB37/23/5 & 37/25/31.

first decade of the next century and beyond.[89] The inevitable corollary was that Tory leaders showed no reluctance to spend taxpayers' cash. Indeed, on occasion they almost gloried in their magnificent generosity, as when Arthur Balfour (then prime minister) insouciantly informed Edward VII that the government's planned legislation for 1903 (the Wyndham Act) would indeed prove costly, but that the cabinet, despite the financial exigencies produced by the South African War, was convinced 'that in the interests of a great policy minor difficulties must be ignored'.[90] Small wonder, therefore, that virtually all of the significant purchase acts were passed by Tory administrations: 1885, 1888, 1891, 1896 and 1903 (with only 1909 – basically an inevitable extension of the 1903 Act – an exception). Put another way, taking all the relevant legislation between 1870 and 1909 into account, the Tories advanced more than £112.5m as opposed to the Liberals' £11.8m (and 90 per cent of that under the 1909 Act alone).[91] The result of all this was that by 1919 some 72 per cent of all occupiers of land in Ireland had become or were in the process of becoming owners.[92] But it was to be the Free State (and Northern Ireland) that came to reap the harvest of all these costly Tory efforts to render the countryside conservative, not only cultur-ally, but socially and politically too. Indeed, as Balfour pointed out in 1928: 'And what was the Ireland which the Free State Government took over? The Ireland that *we* made. Why – even the Land Purchase Act ... even that had gone far to save the country'.[93]

By contrast, Liberals (with Gladstone leading the way) believed that legal adjustments to tenurial relations (of course a no less specifically 'Irish' policy) were infinitely to be preferred to schemes for spending state cash. Not only that, but peasant proprietorship remained for many Liberals a potentially dangerous concept about which it was best to remain cautious if not antagonistic. In this last sense, and indeed in a desire to prop up Irish landlordism, Gladstone and his

**89** See, for example, Gorst to Lord R. Churchill, 9 Oct. 1880, Lord R. Churchill papers, C[ambridge] U[niversity] L[ibrary] Add. MS 9248/1/23 (reporting the views of Beaconsfield & Salisbury); Northcote to Ashbourne, 18 Dec. 1880, Ashbourne papers, P[arliamentary] A[rchives] B71/9; W.H. Smith: *Hansard* 3: 269, 85–6 (4 May 1882); A.J. Balfour: *Hansard* 3: 280, 429 (12 June 1883); also G.D. Goodlad, 'The Liberal party and Gladstone's Land Purchase Bill of 1886', *Historical Journal*, 32 (1989), 629. **90** Balfour to Edward VII, 10 Mar. 1903, TNA Royal Letters CAB41/25/5. Balfour believed the bill would help in finally 'settling the Irish land controversy' (to Devonshire, 4 June 1903, J.S. Sandars [Balfour's private secretary] papers, Bodl. C739). His protégé Wyndham never disguised the amounts involved. See BL 5th marquess of Lansdowne papers 'Papers as foreign secretary' no. 3; and to Lansdowne, 17 Sept. 1902, ibid., 'Ireland' no. 1. **91** These figures are obtained by combining those (up to 31 Mar. 1913) in Birrell's Cabinet papers of 14 July 1914 (TNA Cabinet papers CAB37/120/86) and those in J.E. Pomfret, *The struggle for land in Ireland, 1800–1923* (Princeton, NJ, 1930), p. 307. There are small discrepancies. **92** H.D. Gribbon, 'Economic and social history' in W.E. Vaughan (ed.), *A new history of Ireland V: Ireland under the union I*, p. 274. **93** B.E.C. Dugdale, *Arthur James Balfour*, 2 vols (London, 1936), ii, 392. When Tory-inspired expenditure on exclusively Irish projects such as the Congested Districts Board and the Department of Agriculture and Technical Instruction are included, the costs run higher still.

associates were far more deeply wedded to existing arrangements than were their political opponents. As early as 1869, Gladstone had denied any desire to 'force peasant proprietary into existence' and had deplored attempts to 'bring the government into the land market'.[94] This attitude flowed, not only from his deep belief in a minimal state, but from a genuine attachment to landlords as a class, an attachment sustained as much by rose-tinted spectacles as by an informed grasp of contemporary realities.[95] That reluctance, which he rather grandly announced in his Southport speech of December 1867, to 'bribe Ireland into union with this country by the mere vulgar expenditure of doses of public money'[96] remained – with one aberrant and unsuccessful exception – the guiding light of Gladstone's policy towards Ireland.

This exception was of course the Liberal Land Purchase Bill introduced in tandem with the Home Rule Bill of 1886.[97] Under the unconvincing fig-leaf argument that Home Rule would render the supply of money to Irish tenants safe and reliable, the cabinet reluctantly signed up to the provision of potentially monstrous sums, or, as Gladstone put it, committed 'to the uttermost our finan-cial strengths', largely, he claimed, because only thus could Home Rule take flight.[98] Whether this was a considered policy or merely the result of short-term cabinet manoeuvrings[99] matters less than that it stands in splendid isolation, for in every respect the 1880s were marked by more or less continuous Liberal complaints about the costs of purchase and the profligacy of their opponents. Throughout the decade, Gladstone is to be found denouncing purchase and its related extravagances in virtually every passing year. Purchase involved 'novel principles', the Tories were spendthrifts with a weak grasp of public morality, almost anything was to be preferred, and only pressure from Bright induced him to authorize the timid introduction of very modest proposals into the Land Acts of 1870 and 1881. And this remained his firm view immediately before and immediately after the failed bill of 1886.[1] Indeed, in 1890, sliding smoothly past

---

94 Gladstone to Fortescue, 15 Sept. 1869, BL Gladstone papers Add. MS 44121. 95 H.C.G. Matthew, *Gladstone, 1875–1898* (Oxford, 1995), pp 88–9, 388–9; K.T. Hoppen, *Mid-Victorian generation*, p. 10; Gladstone to Halifax, 1 Oct. 1869, BI Hickleton papers A4/88. Gladstone's secretary, Edward Hamilton, noted in Jan. 1881 how his master 'holds very un-radical views on anything touching landed property': D.W.R. Bahlman (ed.), *The diary of Sir Edward Walter Hamilton, 1880–1885*, 2 vols (Oxford, 1972), i, 99. 96 *The Times*, 20 Dec. 1867. 97 R.T. Shannon (*Gladstone: heroic minister, 1865–1898* (London, 1999), p. 77) points to a minor 'eccen-tric and curious episode' in 1877–9 of passing sympathy for purchase. 98 Gladstone to Harcourt, 12 Feb. 1886, Harcourt papers, Bodl. Harcourt 10. On the fig-leaf, see *Hansard* 3: 304, 1786, 1795 (16 Apr. 1886). The possible sums were indeed potentially enormous. Gladstone produced one figure of £133m, then another of £50m, while opponents estimated £150m. See G.D. Goodlad, 'The Liberal party and Gladstone's Land Purchase Bill', p. 633; also W.H. Smith in *Hansard* 3: 304, 1825 (16 Apr. 1886). 99 See J. Loughlin, *Gladstone, Home Rule and the Ulster question, 1882–93* (Dublin, 1986), pp 80–94; A. O'Day, *Parnell and the first Home Rule episode, 1884–87* (Dublin, 1986), pp 183–7; A.B. Cooke & J.R. Vincent, *The governing passion: cabinet government and party politics in Britain, 1885–86* (Brighton, 1974), pp 407–8. 1 Gladstone to

his own proposals of four years before, Gladstone was still arguing 'that we are hardly competent to vote in this parliament for an English liability in respect of Irish land'.[2]

If Gladstone was the Isaiah of parsimony, there were many lesser prophets to be found in the Liberal ranks: among them Carlingford, Kimberley, Trevelyan, Spencer, Harcourt, the whole Irish administration in 1884, Chamberlain and (for a time) Morley as well.[3] In September 1885, after Ashbourne's pioneering if modest Tory Purchase Act of that year, Morley told an audience in Cambridge that

> The Tory policy in Ireland was the not very original one of ... plenty of hard cash ... The hard cash is very laboriously earned and it is yours and mine ... The notion that the payment of tribute by Great Britain to Ireland would solve all their difficulties in that distracted land was not statesmanship at all, but mere makeshift and quackery.[4]

But while remaining, in his own words, 'frugal' when chief secretary of Ireland between 1892 and 1895, Morley later became a convert to purchase, though his remained very much a minority Liberal position until Birrell was obliged to extend Wyndham's ground-breaking legislation in 1909.[5] The basic differences between the parties were laid out by the young Lloyd George in 1895.

> The Tory policy towards Ireland was the policy of giving them millions of pounds to buy land, more harbours, build railways and even to supply them with potatoes. They would give them everything except freedom ... The Liberal policy was no more subsidies, no more grants, but that of power to the people to work out their own salvation.[6]

Queen Victoria, 31 Dec. 1880, TNA Royal letters CAB41/14/36; Gladstone's Cabinet paper of 9 Dec. 1880, TNA Cabinet papers CAB37/4/81; D.W.R. Bahlman (ed.), *Diary of Sir Edward Walter Hamilton*, i, 86, 91, 151 (7 & 19 Dec. 1880 & 8 July 1881); Gladstone to Forster, 30 Apr. 1882, BL Gladstone papers Add. MS 44160; *Hansard* 3: 269, 1271 (22 May 1882); ibid., 280, 446 (12 June 1883); Gladstone to J. Chamberlain, 1 Aug. 1885, BUL J. Chamberlain papers JC5/34/37; Morley to Gladstone, 1 Aug. 1887, Bodl. Morley papers MS Eng.d.3571; Gladstone's 'Notes and queries on the Irish demand', *The Nineteenth Century*, 21 (1887), 185. 2 Gladstone to Morley, 5 Nov. 1890, Bodl. Morley papers MS Eng.d.3571. 3 Carlingford's memorandum of 14 May 1885, BL Gladstone papers Add. MS 44123; Kimberley to Gladstone, 11 June 1881, ibid., Add. MS 44226; Trevelyan to Spencer, 13 June 1883, BL Spencer papers Add. MS 76957; Spencer: *Hansard* 3: 299, 1343 (21 July 1885); Harcourt: *Hansard* 3: 310, 1325 (11 Feb. 1887); Spencer to Trevelyan, 5 Mar. 1884, BL Spencer papers Add. MS 76961 (on position of Irish administration); J. Chamberlain to Gladstone, 15 Mar. 1886, BUL J. Chamberlain papers JC5/34/88; Morley to Gladstone, 1 Aug. 1887, Bodl. Morley papers MS Eng.d.3571. 4 *The Times*, 30 Sept. 1885. 5 Morley to Harcourt, 11 Jan. 1895, Bodl. Harcourt papers 27; Morley to Campbell-Bannerman, [May 1895], Bodl. Morley papers MS Eng.c.7068. 6 *South Wales Daily News*, 18 Jan. 1895: addressing the National Liberal Federation at Cardiff.

This juxtaposition of the approaches adopted by the two main parties disguised the important fact that both were based on a firm attachment to the view that Ireland must now be governed according to Irish (that is non-English) principles. For one party this meant high spending; for the other significant devolution or Home Rule. And, indeed, this shared underpinning of seemingly divergent doctrines continued to inform political debate and to constitute a universal mode of discourse from the 1880s onwards. Just as during the thirty years immediately after the union, when British politicians had stressed the foreignness and distinctiveness of Ireland,[7] so now again (though in less consistently harsh and coercive modes) their successors did much the same. Debates might continue as to whether the Irish were or were not a 'nation' in either a present or a historical sense,[8] but agreement was universal that the island they inhabited was a far-off entity with idiosyncratic, indeed, rebarbative, customs, habits and practices. Men as different as Arthur Balfour, Hartington, Carnarvon, Brodrick, Gorst and Drummond Wolff (these last two of the so-called 'Fourth party'), Bryce, Dicey, Wyndham, Dudley, Haldane and Long, all, with varying degrees of conviction, talked this kind of language.[9] Simply put, the history of Ireland, as Morley pointed out, was 'utterly different from the history of England'.[10] Stronger still was Gladstone's admission (and coming from the great admirer of all things Caledonian this was a very powerful admission indeed) that 'the Irishman is more profoundly Irish' than 'Scotchmen' were 'Scotch'.[11]

Gladstone's role in the ending of Irish assimilationism, while important, was therefore part of a wider and more general shift in British political sensibilities. Indeed, in some ways, Gladstone's highly idiosyncratic mode of analysis and self-understanding meant that, once the machinery had been set in motion, his own direct influence proved smaller than might otherwise have been the case. His weird claim in April 1886 that 'for 42 at least of the 54 years of my public

---

7 K.T. Hoppen, 'An incorporating union?', pp 328–50.   8 See, for example, J. Chamberlain to Duignan, 17 Dec. 1884, BUL J. Chamberlain papers JC5/3/1/24 & to Morley, 21 Jan. 1885, ibid., JC5/54/599; Gladstone: *Hansard* 3: 304, 1080–1 (8 Apr. 1886); W.E. Gladstone, *The Irish question*, revised ed. (London, [1886]), pp 24–5; Memorandum by A. Chamberlain, 27 Nov. 1913, BUL A. Chamberlain papers AC11/1/21; Lloyd George: *Hansard* 5 [Commons]: 1051–4 (21 July 1919).   9 Balfour's speech of 5 July 1898 noted in TNA Balfour papers PRO30/60/23; Hartington to J. Chamberlain, 6 Mar. 1887, BUL J. Chamberlain papers JC5/22/26; Carnarvon: *Hansard* 3: 308, 54 (19 Aug. 1886); Memorandum by Brodrick, 30 Sept. 1887, in J. Chamberlain papers JC8/4/3/22; Gorst to Lord R. Churchill, 29 Jan. 1883, CUL Lord R. Churchill papers Add. MS 9248/1/105; Memorandum by Drummond Wolff, 9 Oct. 1885, ibid., MS 9248/8/961–2; J. Bryce, 'How we became Home Rulers', *Contemporary review*, 51 (1887), 736–56; Dicey to A. Balfour, 29 Apr. 1890, BL Balfour papers Add. MS 49792; Wyndham to A. Chamberlain, 4 Jan. 1903 [recte 1904], BUL A. Chamberlain papers AC16/3/35; Dudley to W. Churchill, 1 Nov. 1905, W. Churchill papers, C[hurchill] C[ollege] C[ambridge] CHAR2/23/36–7; Memorandum by Haldane, 16 Jan. 1919, in French papers, I[mperial] W[ar] M[useum] JDPF/8/1B; Memorandum by Long, 9 May 1918, Lloyd George papers, PA F/32/5/35.   10 *Hansard* 3: 306, 951 (3 June 1886).   11 *Hansard* 3: 304, 1082 (8 Apr. 1886).

life, Ireland has had a rather dominant influence over it', when placed beside his equally odd insistence that 'the less direct dealing I have with the Irish people, the more useful I shall be to them',[12] reflect a certain cloudiness of comprehension which tended to interfere with the practical impact of his thinking and behaviour. By contrast, Salisbury's acceptance of Irish peculiarism in the shape of expensive land purchase schemes and other money-draining endeavours, while no less marked, was much less opaque.

Of course it would be misleading to maintain that the obvious contrasts between Tories and Liberals, between those opposed to and those willing to grant Home Rule, were not, in some respects, important or divisive. But a failure to place these within a general context of agreement over Irish differentiation would be no less, and perhaps more, misleading. Beneath the turbulent surface waves of party conflict there flowed a deeper all-embracing current moving in a single direction. In a very different connection, Ludwig Wittgenstein (a man not without Irish connection) once drew a distinction between what he called 'surface grammar' (in which logical nonsense could not be excluded) and 'depth grammar' (which alone can prevent the predicament of our not knowing our way about).[13] In a similar way, what was, and still seems to us, an all too visible party conflict over Ireland in the late nineteenth century in fact obscures the more finely attuned and, indeed, coherent unity that lay beneath. In this sense at least, the bitter disputes between those who supported and those who opposed Home Rule in its various manifestations were always a kind of shadow-boxing involving a great deal of fury over distinctions without ultimate differences, in which – as the Argentinean writer Jorge Luis Borges put it when talking of a later conflict[14] – we are confronted with some very angry bald men fighting over a comb.

12 Gladstone to Tennyson, 26 Apr. 1881, Foot & Matthew (eds), *Gladstone diaries*, xi, 540; Reported in Morley to Dillon, 10 Oct. 1888, Dillon papers, T[rinity] C[ollege] D[ublin] MS 6798. 13 *Philosophical Investigations* (1953) §664. 14 Reported in *Time* magazine, 14 Feb. 1983.

# Gladstone's Irish Home Rule legacy: Philip Kerr and the making of the 1920 Government of Ireland Bill

## MELANIE SAYERS

This paper will consider Gladstone's Irish Home Rule legacy through exploring the role of Philip Kerr in Irish affairs during his early career, and in particular his part in drafting the Government of Ireland Act of 1920, also known as the fourth Home Rule Bill. During the course of his life, Kerr became the disciple of various influential figures, including Alfred Milner, in later years David Lloyd George, and eventually the founder of Christian Science, Mary Baker Eddy. Historians John Turner and Michael Dockrill have claimed that if Milner and Eddy were in the foreground of Kerr's thought, then there can be no doubt that Mr Gladstone towered in the background.[1] Beginning with an overview of his family's stance on Home Rule, this paper will consider Kerr's early attitude to Irish affairs before looking in some depth at his work on Ireland between 1919 and 1921. In doing so, some comparison will be drawn between Gladstonian Home Rule and the 1920 act that Kerr drafted. The aim is to consider the evolution of Kerr's thought on Ireland, and to determine what role, if any, Gladstone played in this.

Kerr, who would later become the 11th marquess of Lothian, was an interesting character in his own right and led a varied and distinguished career. He is most widely recognized, however, as having been private secretary to the prime minister, David Lloyd George, from 1916 to 1921 and as the British Ambassador to the United States in 1940. Historians have shown an interest in him for a number of reasons. As Lloyd George's secretary, Kerr drafted sections of the Treaty of Versailles following the First World War and was interested in promoting strong Anglo–American relations. In the 1930s, he interviewed Hitler and famously supported the policy of appeasement. Kerr's role in Irish affairs, however, is less well known and to date there has been no single study that deals purely with his work on Ireland. The historian Gary Peatling has acknowledged Kerr's involvement in addressing the Irish problem within a broader study of British opinion and Irish self-government.[2] The full extent of his involvement and influence is in need of further exploration.

It is possible that Kerr was exposed to the question of Irish Home Rule at an

---

1 John Turner & Michael Dockrill, 'Philip Kerr at 10 Downing Street' in John Turner (ed.), *The larger idea: Lord Lothian and the problem of national sovereignty* (London, 1988), p. 60.   2 G.K. Peatling, *British opinion and Irish self-government, 1865–1925* (Dublin, 2001).

early age. His father, Lord Ralph Kerr, was the major-general commanding the British military base at the Curragh in Ireland between 1891 and 1896. It was during this time that Lord Ralph publicly opposed Gladstone's second Home Rule Bill by signing the statement of the 'British Catholic Unionists on Home Rule' in 1893.[3] The group was led by Philip's uncle, Henry Fitzalan-Howard, the 15th duke of Norfolk, who publicly opposed Gladstone's policy. Lord Ralph Kerr was in an interesting position as he was a Scottish Catholic from an aristocratic line and had married into the most powerful Catholic family in England – the Fitzalan-Howards. His appointment in Ireland meant that he was an upperclass Catholic in a role of policing the British Empire. He therefore took an anti-Home Rule stance both as a Catholic and as an imperialist. Philip Kerr would have been 9 when the family moved to Ireland in 1891 and 14 when Lord Ralph retired from his post and moved the family back to their home near Edinburgh in 1896. At this impressionable age, he would have had some awareness of his father's anti-Home Rule stance. It is ironic that Philip would later draft the fourth and final Home Rule Act that partitioned the country and granted self-government to Ireland in 1920.

Although not openly rebellious, Kerr was not an individual who conformed to family expectations. Following an education at the Catholic Oratory School, Edgbaston, and later at New College, Oxford, Kerr worked for the British administration in South Africa following the Boer War between 1905 and 1909. During these years he became closely involved in the activities of 'Milner's Kindergarten', the group of colonial administrators who hoped to bring about the union of South Africa and ultimately a federated empire. When union was finally achieved in 1909, the Kindergarten members were inspired by what they perceived to be their own success and on their return to England founded 'The Round Table Movement for Imperial Federation'.[4] Nicholas Mansergh has argued that due to the settlement reached in South Africa, British statesmen were prompted to think of a solution to the problem of relations with national communities within the empire, such as Ireland and India.[5] This would remain a constant theme throughout Kerr's career. His experience in South Africa would shape his early attitude to Irish Home Rule just as his experience with Ireland would later influence his work on Indian federation.

On his return home, Kerr had intended to pursue a career in politics, however he actually turned down the opportunity to run for the Midlothian Unionist candidacy in April 1910. Instead, he became editor of the *Round Table*, the group's monthly magazine that aimed to spread the Round Table philosophy throughout the British Empire and its dominions. In doing so, the members

3 'British Roman Catholics and Home Rule', *The Times*, 1 June 1893, p. 7.   4 For information on the Kindergarten's role in South African Union, see Kenneth Ingham, 'Philip Kerr and the unification of South Africa' in Turner (ed.), *The larger idea* (1988).   5 Nicholas Mansergh, *South Africa, 1906–1961: the price of magnanimity* (London, 1962), p. 97.

hoped to promote the federal ideal as a means of governing the empire.[6] In 1910, this vision developed to include the idea of United Kingdom Federation in order to relieve the burden on the imperial parliament at Westminster. It was at this time that Kerr first became more concerned with Irish affairs. The situation in Ireland was potentially useful for attempting to persuade the British government of the benefits of United Kingdom devolution. In Ireland's case, it would put an end to the arguments for and against Home Rule that had interfered with parliamentary business for decades. Gladstone had also been interested in devolved government. Explaining that Gladstone 'deplored centralization', Eugenio Biagini points out that Gladstone maintained a 'Burkean theory' of 'local freedom' for the colonies, and in Ireland as much as in the colonies, self-government was the key to political stability and efficient administration.[7]

In 1910, Kerr and his colleagues were working hard to try and place federalism on the agenda to be discussed at the constitutional conference. Although Kerr understood that Ireland could help them to get federalism more widely discussed, he was not convinced that Britain was ready to implement federal schemes. Kerr urged caution in proposing a federal solution to the Irish question. His long-term vision was of imperial federation rather than devolved government for the United Kingdom. In a letter to his friend Lionel Curtis in 1910, Kerr asked 'Is Ireland to be a Canada or a Quebec?' The federalist project was deliberately vague in its aims and Kerr raised the question whether Ireland would have the autonomy of a dominion or the more limited government of a Canadian province. He asked Curtis 'what part, if any, has the present movement for federalizing the United Kingdom to play in the march to imperial unity?', he continued

> Strictly it has none, for its ostensible object is to entrust the control of 'purely Irish' affairs to local assemblies – even the Irish Nationalists only ask for this – leaving national and imperial affairs to the present imperial parliament.[8]

Gladstone had used the Canadian model when drafting the first Home Rule Bill in 1885, although the Dublin parliament was to have more limited powers than its Canadian counterpart.[9]

Kerr was fully aware of the problems of terminology in setting forth arguments for self-government. He preferred the term 'federalism' to 'Home Rule'. He said to Curtis

6 For more on the Round Table movement, see John Kendle, *The Round Table movement and imperial union* (Toronto, 1975). For the federalist project and Ireland, see John Kendle, *Ireland and the federal solution* (Kingston, Ontario, 1989).   7 E.F. Biagini, *Gladstone* (London, 2000), p. 99.   8 Philip Kerr to Lionel Curtis, 30 Sept. 1910, Lothian papers, Scottish Record Office GD40/17/2/103.   9 Biagini, *Gladstone*, p. 103.

it (Federalism) is a good fighting word. (To) begin with Devolution
has noisome associations. Home Rule all round worse, Federalism has
been a success everywhere and people will therefore not be inclined to
fight shy of the word – a great advantage.[10]

Although Kerr recognized that the Irish case could be useful in promoting the
federalist project, he did not want to taint it by association with Irish Home Rule
either. Where Gladstone had made pacifying Ireland his mission, Kerr's vision
was an imperial one. In 1910, he was thinking about Irish federation as part of a
wider scheme. Kerr never considered dominion status for Ireland, merely a
limited measure of self-government. In these earlier years of his career, his view
of Home Rule was closer to the Gladstonian model. It was not, however, his
main concern. Kerr maintained an awareness of Gladstone's importance as a
figure during the early Home Rule debates. He explained to Lionel Curtis that
only a figure of Gladstonian force could make significant headway in educating
the masses and in driving such proposals through.[11] Kerr believed that no such
figure with federal leanings existed at that time. For the time being, therefore, it
was his aim to set the groundwork for such a time when significant change could
take place or indeed ideas and proposals could be received more readily.

Kerr had very little to do with the third Home Rule Bill that the Liberal
government introduced in 1912, as he was experiencing a period of ill health at
that time and was recovering in sanatoria in Europe. He wrote to Nancy Astor in
January, saying 'I suppose you are all awaiting the Home Rule Bill. I haven't the
foggiest notion of what has been going on at home, as I have had no letters for a
month'.[12] His Round Table colleagues, however, attempted to lobby key politicians in order to urge a federal settlement for Ireland in the hope of avoiding a
potential civil war over the question of Ulster. Although Edward Carson and
Winston Churchill showed interest in such a solution, it remains unclear
whether this would have been achieved as all sides were saved by the outbreak of
war in August 1914. The Home Rule Bill had been passed and was on the statute
book, it was, however, suspended for the duration of the war. This is important
in understanding the context of Kerr's work on the fourth Home Rule Bill
between 1919 and 1920. The suspension of the 1914 act allowed a more militant
brand of Irish nationalism to seize control of the Irish psyche and the 1916
Easter Rebellion in Dublin pointed towards a growing desire for independence.
Shortly after this, Kerr took up his post as private secretary to the new prime
minister, David Lloyd George, and quickly fell under his spell. Although he
came from a unionist background, Kerr would claim to be a Lloyd George
Liberal for the rest of his life.

10 Philip Kerr to Lionel Curtis, 10 Aug. 1910, Lothian papers GD40/17/2/91. 11 Philip
Kerr to Lionel Curtis, 10 Aug. 1910, Lothian papers GD40/17/2/90/7. 12 Philip Kerr to
Nancy Astor, 27 Jan. 1912, Nancy Astor papers, University of Reading MS1416/1/4/45.

The secretariat that Kerr joined became known as the 'Garden suburb' in reference to its temporary offices in the Downing Street garden. John Turner has defined it as primarily an administrative intelligence department.[13] Its aim was to keep Lloyd George in touch with the expanding wartime administrative system. The Garden suburb was experimental and controversial from the outset as it was accused of being a 'Fabian-like Milnerite penetration' and in effect an extension of the Kindergarten that surrounded Milner in South Africa.[14] This suggests that people at the time felt threatened by the potential influence that civil servants had in the development of policy. Kerr was known to be particularly close to Lloyd George and was the only member of the Garden suburb to be kept on as the prime minister's private secretary when the secretariat disbanded at the end of the war. In an original plan, Kerr was to be in charge of labour matters, however in a later scheme it was decided that he would deal with foreign and colonial questions.[15] Although in 1917–18 W.A.S. Adams was chiefly concerned with Irish affairs, Kerr began to see the Irish problem from the perspective of the government.

Both Turner and Dockrill have claimed that the themes that dominated Kerr's work for Lloyd George were typically Gladstonian and towards these subjects he took typically Gladstonian positions. Ireland was chief among these and they explain that Kerr supported the policy of coercion coupled with very limited Home Rule. This does not adequately convey Kerr's attitude to Ireland in the 1919–21 period. When Lloyd George turned his attention to settling the Irish question in 1919, his motives and constraints were a world apart from those that Gladstone faced during the era of the first and second Home Rule Bills. Therefore, the fourth Home Rule Bill would develop into an entirely different beast to those bills introduced by Gladstone in 1886 and 1893, and Kerr's own approach was not always typically Gladstonian. The ending of the First World War and the peace talks that followed were an important context for the development of the 1920 Irish Bill. Throughout 1919, Kerr had been preoccupied with representing Lloyd George at the Paris Peace Conference and had drafted large sections of the Treaty of Versailles. Towards the end of 1919, Lloyd George had no option but to deal with Ireland. There had been attempts to solve the Irish problem in 1916 and 1918; there was now the added factor of time. As the 1914 Home Rule Act had been suspended for the duration of the war, it would eventually come into being with the ratification of the Peace Treaty with Turkey. The government could either repeal the act, allow it to come into force or replace it with another statute.[16] The first meeting of the 'Cabinet Committee on Ireland' took place on 14 October 1919. It was charged with the task of

13 John Turner, *Lloyd George's secretariat* (Cambridge, 1980), p. 1.   14 John Turner, 'The formation of Lloyd George's "Garden Suburb": "Fabian-like Milnerite penetration"?' *The Historical Journal*, 20 (Mar. 1977), 166–7.   15 Ibid., 174–5.   16 Nicholas Mansergh, *The unresolved question: the Anglo-Irish settlement and its undoing, 1912–72* (London, 1991), p. 122.

advising on Irish policy and the drafting of new legislation. Kerr was appointed as one of the joint secretaries to the committee and in this role he held a considerable degree of influence on Irish policy behind the scenes.

Works by Sheila Lawlor and John McColgan published in the 1980s describe the events leading up to the 1920 Government of Ireland Bill and the practical elements of the settlement in some detail.[17] Nicolas Mansergh's later work, *The unresolved question: the Anglo-Irish settlement and its undoing*, published in 1991, added significantly to the literature produced in the 1980s due to the way in which he described the making of the settlement, its aftermath and the way in which it fell apart with the suspension of Stormont in 1972.[18] Although Kerr's biographers and historians exploring his work in the secretariat have acknowledged his role in the making of the Government of Ireland Bill, historians of Anglo-Irish history have rarely done so.[19] In December 1919, Maurice Hankey noted in his diary that Kerr had been the driving force behind the proposals for the new act. He stated that 'Philip Kerr was the originator of the general scheme and has piloted it through its preliminary stages'.[20] There is no reason to doubt this, as Kerr was well versed in the numerous factors that had to be taken into consideration in the designing of the bill. Along with the element of time, the federalist agitation was another important frame of reference. Walter Long, a keen federalist, was appointed as the committee's chairman. The committee proposed

> That there should be two chambers, one for the north and another for the south of Ireland, with a common council with certain powers for the whole of Ireland. Such a scheme not to be inconsistent with a federal system of government for the United Kingdom.[21]

As a founding member of the Round Table, Kerr supported this and hoped that the deal that was put together in 1919–1920 would form part of a wider federal reform. He recognized the need to deal with Ulster separately and felt that partition of the country was a necessity.

The Ulster question was the most distinct difference between Gladstone's Home Rule bills and the 1920 settlement. The 1920 bill was designed specifically to pacify Ulster. According to James Loughlin, Gladstone's conception of the separate interests of the Ulster Protestants was inadequate.[22] He preferred to

17 Sheila Lawlor, *Britain and Ireland, 1914–23* (Dublin, 1983); John McColgan, *British policy and the Irish administration, 1920–22* (London, 1983). 18 Mansergh, *The unresolved question*. 19 The main works on Kerr are J.R.M. Butler, *Lord Lothian (Philip Kerr), 1882–1940* (London, 1960); D.P. Billington, *Lothian, Philip Kerr and the quest for world order* (Westport, CT, 2006). 20 Diary entry '29 Dec. 1919' printed in Stephen Roskill, *Hankey, man of secrets, vol. II: 1919–1931* (London, 1972), p. 137. 21 'War cabinet committee on Ireland', 15 Oct. 1919, Cabinet papers CAB27/68. 22 James Loughlin, *Gladstone, Home Rule and the Ulster question,*

leave the Ulster question open, although it would not interfere with conferring a parliament on Ireland. His position remained largely the same throughout the Home Rule debate. Loughlin attributes this to a number of factors. Firstly, the tactics of the Ulster unionists in this period meant that Gladstone never fully realized the extent of Ulster's resistance to Home Rule. In refusing to formulate any special arrangement for Ulster alone, the Ulster unionists helped to sustain Gladstone's ignorance of the strength and nature of Ulster unionism. They were convinced that they could defeat Home Rule for Ireland in its entirety. Loughlin has suggested that had they made separate proposals for Ulster, there was a good chance that their wishes would have been fulfilled.[23] Secondly, it is probable that Gladstone was influenced by the Parnellite sweep in the 1885 general election, which gave the Irish Party a psychologically important parliamentary majority of one in Ulster. Ultimately, Gladstone endorsed Parnell's view that a Home Rule parliament for all Ireland would dissolve divisions between the people.

Unlike Gladstone, Kerr fully understood the strength of Ulster Unionism. Not only was he in contact with prominent unionists, he was fully aware that Britain had been on the brink of civil war over the Ulster question in 1912–14. Loughlin notes that in the 1880s there were neither armed volunteers in the province, nor any mass agitation exploiting religious fears.[24] The situation was completely different in 1920 and Kerr explained to Horace Plunkett that

> There is war in Ireland today because the three parties to it are divided by principles which are irreconcilable, and yet which each holds with the strongest conviction. I don't see how you are to get peace in Ireland any more than you could in South Africa, until the said three parties can agree upon the fundamental basis of a settlement.[25]

The government had no choice but to make separate provision for Ulster in 1919–20. The decision to appoint Walter Long as chairman of the Committee on Ireland was in part to reassure the unionist leaders, as Long had been chairman of the Irish Unionists in the House of Commons from 1906 to 1910.[26] Kerr's own appointment may have consoled the unionists as he knew Sir Edward Carson through his Round Table connections. There were further reasons why he was well suited to the appointment. Lloyd George had shown a great deal of trust in Kerr at the Paris Peace Conference and Kerr had proved his ability as a skilled draftsman. As a result, he would personally draft most of the 1920 Irish

*1882–93* (Dublin, 1986), p. 139.  **23** Ibid., p. 140.  **24** Ibid., p. 102.  **25** Philip Kerr to Horace Plunkett, 24 Mar. 1921, Lothian papers GD40/17/80/175.  **26** Richard Murphy, 'Walter Long and the making of the Government of Ireland Act, 1919–20', *Irish Historical Studies*, 25 (May 1986), 83.

Bill. Furthermore, he had expertise in areas that had to be considered, such as the United States.

By 1919, American opinion had become an important factor in designing an Irish settlement. Irish-American agitation at the Peace Conference and extreme Irish nationalist activity in the United States meant that the United Kingdom government was under greater pressure internationally to settle the Irish question. A report by the Cabinet Committee stated that 'The impression that a small nationality is not "getting a fair show" at British hands is easily implemented'.[27] The American context was therefore an important consideration in the committee's proceedings. As a keen Americanist and someone who was committed to maintaining strong Anglo-American relations, Kerr took a particular interest in the American aspects of the problem. He kept the prime minister updated on American opinion and oversaw the British press campaign in the United States when the proposals for the Irish Bill were announced in parliament. Letters to Lloyd George from Louis Tracy at the British Bureau of Information in New York warned of Sinn Féin activity in the United States. He described a well-organized scheme by Eamonn de Valera and his associates that aimed to control American public opinion in such a way that it would sway Congress to recognize the Irish Republic. Tracy claimed that the movement was 'widespread, well organized and malignant in purpose'.[28]

Parallels can be drawn with the Fenian agitation in the United States during Gladstone's era. Just as Kerr was concerned by de Valera's 1919–21 American campaign, Charles Stewart Parnell had also made an American trip to gain support for the Land League in 1879. Further parallels can be drawn in noting that both had strong connections with the United States. De Valera was born there, while Parnell's mother, Delia Tudor Stewart, was an American. Gladstone had taken a completely different view of Irish nationalist movements in the United States and American support for them. In 1938, J.L. Hammond wrote that Gladstone was different to his fellow countrymen in his ability to see things in a greater perspective.[29] He explained that Gladstone was able to see things from another nation's point of view. As he had thought of the Italian problem in the Italian sense, he could not think of the Irish problem purely in the English sense. Gladstone believed that thousands of Irish men and women were in the United States as a result of a land system so unjust that the English government had been compelled to destroy it. He asked what right had Englishmen 'who had given a home to Mazzini and other exiles … to complain of American sympathy with Ireland or of the sacrifices made by the Irish in the United States for the Irish in Ireland?'[30]

Kerr, on the other hand, viewed the Sinn Féin campaign as traitorous and as a threat to the Empire. In September 1921, he warned the prime minister that

27 Ibid.  28 Louis Tracy to Lloyd George, 24 Feb. 1920, Lothian papers GD40/17/78/75–9.
29 J.L. Hammond, *Gladstone and the Irish nation* (London, 1938), p. 559.  30 Ibid., p. 560.

American Sinn Féin, as opposed to Irish Sinn Féin, is animated by
hatred of Great Britain far more than love of Ireland. A very large
number of people live upon this hatred, making millions of dollars
out of Irish newspapers, films and propaganda.[31]

He claimed that Irish-American camarilla had linked with 'haters' of England
abroad and 'They see or think they see a real chance of smashing the British
Empire'.[32] Kerr consoled himself that the American politicians did not take the
Irish campaigning too seriously. In response to a letter from Congress to the
prime minister, protesting against the imprisonment of Irishmen without trial,
Kerr said to Lloyd George 'everybody knows that every politician in America has
to play up to the Irish game, and that all this agitation is merely window dressing
with a view to meeting the presidential election'.[33] The situation was different
from Gladstone's era in as much as in the 1880s–90s the Irish campaign was
primarily for a measure of self-government. By 1919–21, it had developed into
a ruthless campaign for complete independence. With regards to the American
dimension, Kerr was addressing a Gladstonian theme, but he was not adopting
a typically Gladstonian position.

Kerr's attitude to Ireland between 1919 and 1921 tended to reflect that of
Lloyd George. Following the announcement by the government in December
1919 that it was to introduce the new Irish Bill, the violence in Ireland had
increased at an alarming rate. When the government auxiliary force, nicknamed
'the Black and Tans', was sent into Ireland to assist the regular army and police
force in March 1920, the situation escalated to full-scale war on account of
reports of reprisals by the British forces. Kerr was not prepared to tolerate the
threat of Sinn Féin violence. In Kerr's view British reprisals were merely an
answer to Sinn Féin's attempt to achieve their goals through murder and assassination. He claimed that this activity had paralyzed Ireland's sympathizers
across the world and would continue to do so while Sinn Féin continued in this
manner. Kerr emphasized that only when they stopped using such methods
would the British government consider negotiating with them. Until then, Kerr
stated that the British campaign to defeat Sinn Féin would only intensify.[34] Like
Lloyd George, Kerr agreed with the policy of repression with regards to what
he dismissed as the 'murder gang' in Ireland.[35] According to Frank Owen, Lloyd
George believed that the only alternative to 'official' reprisal was to surrender to
the tactics of terror and to let Sinn Féin have its Republic, which neither he nor
Kerr were prepared to do.[36] Kerr's reaction is perhaps surprising in view of his

31 Philip Kerr to Lloyd George, 14 Sept. 1921, Lloyd George papers, Parliamentary Archives
F/34/2/7. 32 Ibid. 33 Philip Kerr to Lloyd George, 8 May 1920, Lothian papers
GD40/17/1276. 34 Kerr to C.J. Phillips, 11 Nov. 1920, Lloyd George papers, F/91/7/11.
35 K.O. Morgan, *Consensus and disunity: the Lloyd George coalition government, 1918–1922*
(Oxford, 1979), p. 130; Frank Owen, *Tempestuous journey* (London, 1954), p. 567. 36 Owen,

concern over Irish activity in the United States. He was not, however, prepared to give in to intimidation on home soil.

Moderate Irish nationalists attempted to influence a solution through Kerr in 1919–21. Notable figures such as Sir Horace Plunkett and George W. Russell ('Æ') supported a dominion plan and wrote to Kerr in order to gain support. Russell believed that dominion status was more acceptable to Irish national aspirations than the measures allowed for in the Government of Ireland Bill. Economic grievances were a particular complaint. He claimed that Irish spending power had been exercised for British and not for Irish purposes and there was no provision in the Home Rule Bill that imperial expenditure would be balanced by an equivalent expenditure in Ireland. Therefore, Russell urged financial independence as a necessary factor if friendship was to replace hostility.[37] Kerr believed in the merits of the Bill as it stood, however, and supported Lloyd George's view with regard to the financial aspects. When it had been suggested at a cabinet meeting in October 1920 that the government take a more liberal attitude to finance, Lloyd George had refused. He had argued that 'The giving of customs, excise and income tax meant a great deal, and if this were done Ireland could not remain part of the United Kingdom'. He had further claimed that he was 'still a Gladstonian Home Ruler' but 'that was not the Home Rule on which he had been brought up'.[38]

Both Kerr and Lloyd George invoked Gladstone when it suited their purpose. The situation in 1919–21 was completely different from the conditions under which the first two Home Rule bills were drafted. The 1920 bill was not designed to be long lasting; rather, it anticipated eventual Irish unity. The Government of Ireland Bill was enacted on 23 December 1920, creating two parliaments in Ireland, one for the south and one for the north; a Council of Ireland would also be created in order to promote unity between the two regions. Although Kerr recognized the defects of the fourth Home Rule Bill, he believed that it was the best that could be achieved from the present government and according to the constraints that applied. He believed that

> it would at least accomplish two essential things: it would take Ulster out of the Irish question, which it had blocked for a generation and it would take Ireland out of English party controversies. He believed that there would never be another special Irish Bill.[39]

Kerr sent a memo to Lloyd George regarding the bill in March 1920 when he was in the process of arranging a comparison between the 1914 Home Rule Act

*Tempestuous journey*, p. 567.   **37** G.W. Russell to Philip Kerr, 9 Dec. 1920, Lloyd George papers F/91/7/23.   **38** D.G. Boyce, *Englishmen and Irish troubles: British public opinion and the making of Irish policy, 1918–22* (London, 1972), p. 121.   **39** Trevor Wilson (ed.), *The political diaries of C.P. Scott, 1911–1928* (London, 1970), p. 382.

and the 1920 bill. Kerr claimed that he could not find any body of opinion in either Ireland or England that preferred the 1914 act and he did not think that there would be any difficulty in establishing that the 1920 bill was a better and a more generous one than the previous three. He attributed this to the adoption of the two parliament system and to the great increase of taxation in the United Kingdom owing to the war.[40] He was aware of Irish opinion regarding the exclusion of the six Ulster counties, claiming that the nationalist press was howling in a rather meaningless way about partition. Kerr stated that 'It clearly has not yet accommodated itself to the fundamental fact that Ulster is going to have Home Rule'.[41] In Kerr's view, this was a fundamental fact and not up for negotiation and therefore the nationalist backlash was pointless. He believed that the sooner the idea was accepted, the sooner things would begin to settle down in Ireland. He argued that the best course of action was to push the bill through as fast as possible. In doing so, the policy of Sinn Féin and of Dominion Home Rule became absurd as they could only be achieved through military conquest of Ulster. Kerr held faith in the ability of moderate nationalists such as Stephen Gwynn to steer Irish politics in the right direction. He explained that in putting the bill in place it would provide Stephen Gwynn and his people with a chance of proposing their policy of 'abandoning factious agitation and violence and working the bill with the deliberate object of inducing Ulster by reason and conciliation and the use of the machinery of the Council of Ireland to agree to the re-union of Ireland'.[42]

This could be seen as naïve, with the current knowledge of the disastrous events in Ireland following partition. Yet Kerr clearly did not see the bill as a great piece of legislation or indeed a historic federal settlement. In his mind, it was a necessary means to an end. Kerr hoped that the bill had the potential to promote unity in Ireland and it was the first step in a gradual process of establishing a new form of governing the country. Dockrill and Turner have argued that Kerr should perhaps be seen as a nineteenth-century Liberal transposed to twentieth-century conditions. They claim that Kerr did not find it difficult to adapt the conservative creed of Gladstonian Liberalism to new situations. The fourth Home Rule Bill is a prime example of this. Kerr took the Gladstonian principle of Home Rule and worked with it according to the constraints of his own time. Where Gladstone set out to provide a measure of Home Rule to pacify Ireland, Kerr knew that times had changed by 1920 and the question of Ulster now had to be taken into consideration. The government was limited by time as the third Home Rule Bill would come into effect with the ratification of the Peace Treaty with Turkey following the war, and American opinion had to be considered. Kerr adapted Gladstonian Home Rule to these conditions. Kerr did

40 Philip Kerr to Lloyd George, 20 Mar. 1920, Lothian papers GD40/17/601/1.   41 Ibid.
42 Ibid.

not adopt Gladstonian positions; he was simply working on a Gladstonian theme. While working on the bill, Kerr looked back to Gladstone's era, saying 'If you had a Botha, or even a Parnell, you could settle both with Ulster and with nationalist Ireland on satisfactory terms. But you have got no such men'.[43] Moderate Irish nationalists that Kerr dealt with, such as Stephen Gwynn, did not hold as much influence over the Irish people due to the rise of Sinn Féin leaders.[44] Kerr looked back to a time when issues could be addressed within party politics.

Kerr maintained an interest in Gladstone as a figure during his life and career. In his review of Erich Eyck's biography of Gladstone in 1938, Kerr described his

> untiring industry, his tremendous oratory, his administrative ability, his moral fervour, his constantly expanding sense of popular needs, his passionate protests against injustice, the vehement part that he took in all the major events and controversies of the period,

concluding that these 'made him the outstanding and most dynamic figure of the Victorian century'.[45] Many of these qualities could be attributed to Kerr and they were certainly qualities that he aspired to, although he preferred to exercise his influence in a background role and through his writing. Kerr acknowledged how much the world had changed since Gladstone's time and blamed this in part for Gladstone having 'lost the immense significance he once had'.[46] He explained that new forces such as 'modern international anarchy' and 'science and machinery' had destroyed old securities, and as a result the 'moral values' that determined Gladstone's character and action had been overwhelmed by the new world situation. For these reasons, Kerr argued that 'the moral principle in public life' was as vital as ever. Rather than simply reflecting on Gladstone and his times, Kerr suggested that the Grand Old Man was important in looking to the future of world politics: 'I will venture the prophecy that before long he will once more become a significant prophet of values to which mankind will return if it is to be saved'.[47]

The times and the circumstances had changed beyond recognition since the age of Gladstone. The fourth Home Rule Bill that Kerr worked on incorporated elements that had not been relevant when the first two bills were introduced. There was a growing interest among the political elite for a federal system of government in Britain and therefore the federalist project that Kerr was part of

---

**43** Philip Kerr to Sir Auckland Geddes, 5 July 1920, Lothian papers GD40/17/1397.  **44** Michael Laffan has explored Sinn Féin's rise and subsequent hold on the Irish psyche in *The resurrection of Ireland: the Sinn Féin party, 1916–1923* (Cambridge, 1999).  **45** Philip Kerr, Lord Lothian, 'Review of Erich Eyck's *Gladstone*', 31 May 1938, Lothian papers GD40/17/361/296.  **46** Ibid.  **47** Ibid., GD40/17/361/298.

provided a different context for the shaping of Home Rule. The war was perhaps the most important factor in shaping the 1920 act as the third Home Rule Bill was already law and would come into being with the implementation of the Peace Treaties. Kerr's own role in the drafting of the 1920 bill was significant. Where Gladstone had drafted his bills in secret, alienating his cabinet, Kerr was more of a central figure and served as a link between ministers, departments and the prime minister. Kerr was especially useful to Lloyd George because he had an awareness of Irish support in America and therefore closely followed how the government's proposals were received in the United States. Kerr recognized that extreme nationalist agitation in Ireland and the question of Ulster had determined the nature of the bill and he acknowledged how times had changed since Gladstone's era. Gladstone was almost certainly in the background of Kerr's thought, as comments that he made demonstrate. He did not necessarily influence Kerr's attitude towards Ireland, rather it was Lloyd George who determined Kerr's views. Kerr worked with a Gladstonian theme and adapted it to the conditions of his own time; therefore the work that Kerr carried out in 1919–21 contributes to our understanding of the Home Rule story. The bill that he drafted would provide the framework for the government of Northern Ireland until 1972, and the 1920 act would not be repealed until the Good Friday Agreement of 1998. This points to the wider significance of Kerr's role and, like Gladstone before him, his enduring relevance to our understanding of Anglo-Irish history.

# From private visit to public opportunity: Gladstone's 1877 trip to Ireland

KEVIN Mc KENNA

Long before Home Rule became a preoccupation for Gladstone, he had been the architect of much reforming Irish legislation, first as chancellor of the exchequer, and later during his first term as prime minister. In the 1870s, all sections of the press in Britain and Ireland referred to him as the hewer of the upas tree of Protestant ascendancy, a view that stemmed from a famous election speech he gave at Wigan in 1868. In this speech, he described the three branches of this tree: the Church of Ireland, the land of Ireland and the education of Ireland, as 'like a noxious growth, lifting its head to heaven and darkening and poisoning the land so far as its shadow can extend; it is still there, gentlemen, and now at length the day has come when […] we hope, the axe has been laid to the root of that tree'.[1] When Gladstone became prime minister after the election, his own metaphorical axe hacked the branches of the upas tree with the disestablishment of the Irish Church and the introduction of his first land act, but his axe became blunted on the education branch with the defeat of his university bill in 1873. He continued to lead the Liberal Party until its defeat in the 1874 election, after which he decided to retire, but this retirement was half-hearted as he retained his Westminster seat. His period of semi-retirement was spent compiling theological assaults on ultramontanism as the Irish Catholic bishops had played a pivotal role in the defeat of his university bill.[2] With the benefit of hindsight, it is generally agreed that 1875 is the only complete year when his retirement appeared to be a reality and that by the end of 1876, after criticizing Disraeli's policy in the Balkans, he was once again flexing his political muscles. However, in 1877 he had not yet made it clear that he sought to return centre stage, although rumours were circulating in the press that this was his ambition.

Roy Jenkins has argued that during the summer of that year Gladstone developed, 'almost by accident, a form of semi-passive political campaigning' when he received large groups representing various northern liberal associations at Hawarden Castle.[3] These deputations, some in their thousands, were treated to exhibitions of his oratory at the castle and one group was led to the Hawarden

1 Gladstone's Wigan speech, *Times*, 24 Oct. 1868.   2 W.E. Gladstone, *The Vatican decrees in their bearing on civil allegiance: a political expostulation* (London, 1874); W.E. Gladstone, *Vaticanism: an answer to reproofs and replies* (London, 1875).   3 Roy Jenkins, *Gladstone* (London, 1995), p. 414.

77

parkland by Gladstone and his son who proceeded to fell an ash tree fifteen feet in circumference. *The Times* reported that as the strokes of the axes assailed the tree the crowd cheered, sang hymns and picked up the splinters that flew from Gladstone's axe 'and treasured them as relics'. It remarked that the world looked on eagerly for a hint that the 'half disguise' of his retirement would be laid aside arguing that 'the chips that flew beneath the vigorous strokes of Mr Gladstone's axe will long serve as proofs that the retired statesman is still strong enough for other work than that to which he chooses to restrict himself [...] Has Mr Gladstone really left public life forever?' the article questioned, implying that Gladstone was still a force to be reckoned with.[4]

Gladstone received his final deputation of northern liberals on 1 September and it is against this backdrop that he visited Ireland between 17 October and 12 November that year. Despite the fact that much of his recent career had been dedicated to Irish matters, it was his first time to set foot in the country. Focusing exclusively on the visit, this paper will expand on what has heretofore been restricted to brief overviews by his many biographers or, in the case of John Vincent's 1978 article, a footnote, albeit a three-quarter page footnote.[5] It will examine how it was transformed from a private visit to a public opportunity that represented a significant step in Gladstone's emergence from retirement.

Speculation about his intended visit to Ireland had been circulating in late autumn of 1877 and the *Nation* reported that it had evidence from a telegram that, officially, the visit was to be 'purely formal and private'. Expressing suspicion about the private nature of the visit, it argued that Gladstone had recently shown at 'Hawarden Castle, and at various other places throughout Great Britain, that private scenes are easily turned to public uses' and that the visit was politically motivated to gain support for the Liberals.[6] The rumours of the visit were confirmed on 8 October when a letter by Gladstone was published in the press stating that his visit to Ireland would be purely 'private and personal' and that he would 'decline all share in public celebrations unless in cases where he had local or special connection'.[7] *The Times* was more accepting of his declaration of privacy and downplayed any suspicion that the visit was politically motivated by describing him as 'an *emeritus* warrior ... whose career is already complete'.[8]

In a letter to Lord Granville on 10 October, Gladstone explained that his wife had expressed a desire to visit her old friend Lady Meath, whom she had not seen in many years, and that he could not refuse the request. Expressing apprehension about his visit, he stated that 'papal, Home Rule, Protestant, orange, parties, all have their quarrel with me. I hope they will let me be'. He referred to the rumours that the object of his visit was 'political and not personal' and that

---

4 *Times*, 6 Aug. 1877.  5 John Vincent, 'Gladstone and Ireland', *Proceedings of the British Academy*, 63 (1978), 208.  6 *Nation*, 6 Oct. 1877.  7 *Irish Times, Freeman's Journal*, 8 Oct. 1877.  8 *Times*, 10 Oct. 1877.

as far as making public speeches in Ireland he had not the slightest notion of what he 'could say without giving mortal offence'. However, revealing an ulterior motive, he admitted that he would try and do good among the Irish MPs, within the terms of privacy, but he did not expect much success.[9] Lord Granville in reply to his letter stated that there would be great pressure on him to make public speeches and advised him to make his own judgments whether he should or not. If he was unsure, Granville added, he could either remain silent or speak on inoffensive topics like material prosperity or the artistic development of the Irish.[10] The faction with the most cause to resent Gladstone was the conservative Protestant elite that opposed his legislation on disestablishment, the Land Act and his attempt to reform the universities. While disestablishment and the land act were supported by the majority of the Catholic population, his attempt to reform university education was less well received. Gladstone had proposed that a Catholic college be co-located with Trinity College at the University of Dublin and that these colleges, together with the Queen's colleges, form a national university. However, the Irish Catholic bishops campaigned for an exclusively Catholic university and used their influence to help defeat Gladstone's university bill. And partly as a consequence of the bishops' role in thwarting his legislation and bringing down his government, Gladstone penned attacks on ultramontanism in 1874 and 1875 and this further incensed Catholic opinion against him.[11]

The week before his arrival, many letters were written to the newspapers offering opinions as to how Gladstone ought to be treated during the visit, and two letters by Catholic priests to the *Nation*, in particular, illustrate the diversity of views that were held, even by clergymen professing the same faith. A letter by a 'Catholic priest' communicated how 'every true Irishman was rejoiced about the news that Gladstone was to visit Ireland because of the debt of gratitude that Ireland owed him'. He glossed over the pamphlet controversy, arguing that too much had been made of it and called for public bodies to present addresses in an unostentatious manner so that it would not interfere with his resolution 'to decline all share in public celebrations'.[12] However, a fellow Catholic priest was not inclined to agree with him and his letter to the *Nation* argued that 'the reception of Mr Gladstone [...] should be coolly respectful but by no means enthusiastic'. Unlike his colleague, he was unwilling to gloss over Gladstone's attacks on ultramontanism, which, he argued, were a 'vindictive' reaction to the defeat of his university bill and that he had been 'determined to punish both prelate and peasant in his pamphlet mania against the Catholic Church'.[13]

9 Gladstone to Granville, 10 Oct. 1877, Agatha Ramm (ed.), *The political correspondence of Mr Gladstone and Lord Granville, 1876–1886* (Oxford, 1962), p. 54 (henceforth *Correspondence, 1876–1886*). 10 Granville to Gladstone, 11 Oct. 1877, *Correspondence, 1876–1886*, p. 55. 11 W.E. Gladstone, *The Vatican decrees in their bearing on civil allegiance, Vaticanism: an answer to reproofs and replies*. 12 *Freeman's Journal*, 11 Oct. 1877. 13 *Freeman's Journal*, 16 Oct. 1877.

At dusk on 17 October, Gladstone arrived at Kingstown accompanied by his wife and daughter in very low-key circumstances as few people were aware that they were making the crossing that day. Illustrating the ambiguous feelings towards him in Ireland, he noted in his diary that when he arrived, a newsman called out 'You're welcome to Ireland' but that a voice in the background exclaimed 'no you're not'.[14] On the pier, William O'Brien, of the *Freeman's Journal*, the future Irish nationalist MP, managed to secure an interview and intimated that 'rumour attributed something more than a personal interest in his visit', but Gladstone replied that rumour was very attentive to him sometimes and reiterated his assertion that he would be operating in the capacity of a private citizen on his visit and not as a politician.[15] Debate continued as to the nature of his visit. The *Irish Times* considered his visit as private and personal, though it reported how there were some that believed that Gladstone was 'Tired of playing the part of the sulking Achilles' and was looking to come to the front once more.[16] The *Dublin Evening Mail*, expressing scepticism about his declaration not to make public speeches, argued that 'It is anticipated that he will speak in Ireland and only wants to be "drawn", addresses will be presented, then the spigot will be taken out of the barrel, and the flow will be abundant'. It referred to rumours that he was angling to become the Liberal leader once again and had come to Ireland to see

> whether he can secure the hearty alliance of the Irish Party in a fresh raid on Downing Street […] It is at least not impossible that this may be his calculation; and if so, an importance attaches to his visit which will cause it to be remembered. Until we have evidence, however, of his political intention in the trip, we must take it as worth exactly as he says, and respect the privacy which he desires to maintain.[17]

During his visit, Gladstone was the guest of several members of the landed aristocracy. The earl of Meath was the first to host him at his residence, Kilruddery, Co. Wicklow, where Gladstone spent the first few days exploring the locality. On Saturday, he visited Dublin city, where his first port of call was Christ Church Cathedral. This caused considerable surprise in some quarters, as he had been the architect of disestablishment, and the *Dublin Evening Mail* remarked that churchmen could not forget the injury they had suffered at Gladstone's hand. However, it argued that the church had remained strong even though Gladstone had 'cut down upas trees which he had never seen and' had torn 'up institutions whose roots underlay the whole social fabric'.[18] After

---

14 M.R.D. Foot & H.C.G. Matthew (eds), *The Gladstone diaries*, 14 vols (Oxford, 1968–94), ix, 259. 15 *Freeman's Journal*, 18 Oct. 1877. 16 *Irish Times*, 17 Oct. 1877. 17 *Dublin Evening Mail*, 19 Oct. 1877. 18 *Dublin Evening Mail*, 22 Oct. 1877.

service, he had lunch with the lord lieutenant and spent a few hours at the vice-regal lodge before returning to Kilruddery, where he spent the rest of the weekend, attending both services in Bray on Sunday. Gladstone had adhered to his policy of strict privacy for the first few days but this resolution was tested the next day, Monday, when he visited Trinity College. He was given a tour of the library and viewed the college's most prized manuscripts including the Book of Kells, and as he crossed the college campus a large group of students 'pressed hard' and persuaded him to deliver a short address.[19] He began the speech by noting how he had been compelled to depart from his resolution not to make public speeches and spoke for about five minutes eulogizing the university, its long history, the scholars of great renown that had passed through its halls and his desire to see it attract the youth of Ireland from all faiths and discharge the 'functions of a national university'.[20]

Although Gladstone had technically broken his promise not to make public speeches or declarations on Irish issues, the curtness of his speech at Trinity did not draw the wrath of the Tory press. The *Dublin Evening Mail* regarded the Trinity address as 'rather a happy illustration than a violation of the rule which he has set down for himself'. It referred to the respect that the provost and fellows had for Gladstone as a scholar and as an

> eminent public man [who] had come to see the place they were proud of. Old quarrels were forgotten and the youth of Protestant Trinity, as its adversaries delight to describe it, not only gave Mr Gladstone a hearty welcome but insisted that their welcome be acknowledged.[21]

The *Nation* was not so forgiving and was, perhaps, a little irked that a 'Protestant' institution had provided a welcoming reception for Gladstone. It argued that the 'gushing laudations of what he called their national and glorious university' were 'hardly within the spirit of his promises' not to make public speeches.[22] From Trinity College, Gladstone went to the Bank of Ireland, the former home of the Irish parliament, and nationalist publications readily capitalized on the symbolism of this. The editor of the *Freeman's Journal* recalled how the parliament had voted itself out of existence and how ironic it was that Gladstone, the 'champion of liberty', was heartily cheered 'when he entered the portals of the house where liberty was done to death'.[23] A monument to Henry Grattan had been erected on College Green in 1876 to much Home Rule rhetoric[24] and the *Freeeman's Journal*, again emphasizing the once independent

**19** Foot & Matthew (eds), *Gladstone diaries*, ix, 260. **20** *Freeman's Journal*, 23 Oct. 1877. **21** *Dublin Evening Mail*, 26 Oct. 1877. **22** *Nation*, 27 Oct. 1877. **23** *Freeman's Journal*, 23 Oct. 1877. **24** Judith Hill, 'Ideology and cultural production: nationalism and the public monument in mid-nineteenth century Ireland' in Tadhg Foley & Sean Ryder (eds), *Ideology and Ireland in the nineteenth century* (Dublin, 1998), p. 57.

Irish parliament, reported how Gladstone 'stood in College Green, close to the
Grattan statue, gazing with intense admiration at the noble architecture of our
old parliament house'.[25] Dense crowds gathered at College Green cheering
Gladstone repeatedly and for a while it was expected that he would make a
speech, but he gave no further addresses that day.

Gladstone's declaration not to give public speeches had disappointed many
people who had hoped to hear one of his renowned orations. A letter to the
editor of the *Irish Times* printed on 25 October observed how Gladstone was
wise not to speak on political issues and respected his determination 'to preserve
the private nature of his visit'; however, it pointed out that while Gladstone had
promised not to speak on political issues there was no reason why he could not
give an address on some literary subject. The contributor thought it a shame that
'the greatest English orator of our time should abide so long in our midst, and
depart from amongst us without affording the Irish people a single opportunity
of admiring and enjoying one of his public utterances upon any topic'.[26] While
Gladstone was economical with his oratorical exhibitions, all his movements
were tracked by the press so it would be difficult to claim that any part of his trip
was private. The day after his brief speech at Trinity College he climbed the
Little Sugar Loaf Mountain with a small party, and newspaper reports
commented on his vitality and defiance of old age. The *Irish Times* related that
'Although the right hon. gentleman is 68 years of age, he walked as straight as a
lath, and cleared whatever obstacles were encountered in the course of the walk
with as little trouble as the youngest of the party'.[27]

Gladstone remained as a guest at Kilruddery for a week, after which he set
out for Coolatin, the home of Lord Fitzwilliam. En route there, on Thursday 25
October, he spent some time at the early Christian site of Glendalough and
travelled through the Vale of Avoca, where 'he visited several cottie houses' and
made enquiries about 'wages, tillage and other rural matters'. Interestingly he
visited the farm of one of C.S. Parnell's tenants, where he made further
inquiries and heard how 'the people of the farm were loud in their praises of the
kindness and generosity of their young landlord'.[28] At this stage of his visit,
rumours were circulating that Dublin Corporation was planning to offer him
the freedom of the city and on Friday 26 October the *Irish Times* reported that
it had information on very good authority that Gladstone would decline the
honour unless it was passed by unanimous vote.[29] The following Monday, an
anonymous letter to the *Freeman's Journal* argued that many Irish Protestants
and conservatives had good reason to be displeased with Gladstone because of
disestablishment, the land act and his attempt to deprive them of their monopoly
of university education. Despite this, it continued, when Gladstone 'came

25 *Freeman's Journal*, 23 Oct. 1877.   26 *Irish Times*, 25 Oct. 1877.   27 *Irish Times*, 24 Oct.
1877.   28 *Freeman's Journal*, 27 Oct. 1877.   29 *Irish Times*, 26 Oct. 1877.

amongst them in Trinity College the other day, they forgot the assailant of their former ascendancy and remembered only the greatness of the man. They welcomed him and honoured him, and in doing so they honoured themselves and their country'. It expressed shame that no Catholic priests had met him in Wicklow and that no municipal council had offered him the freedom of a city, arguing further that there was a lamentable contrast between Protestant Trinity, which was capable of overlooking its differences with Gladstone, and the Catholic metropolis that harboured resentment for the offensive pamphlets he had written.[30]

Gladstone remained for the weekend of 27–8 October at Coolatin, where he spent a considerable amount of time with the under-steward of the estate, who informed him on many issues relating to Irish agriculture. On Sunday, he went to the local church and recuperated before he made his way to his next host, Lord Powerscourt, the following day. As if responding to the letter that criticized the Catholic clergy's lack of hospitality to Gladstone, he now was met by Catholic clergy at every turn. At the railway station, en route to Powerscourt, he was met by the Revd Prof. James Kavanagh, president of Carlow College, who had published a pamphlet in response to Gladstone's *Vaticanism* in 1875, pointing out weaknesses in his argument.[31] While the pamphlet was critical of Gladstone, it made reference to all the good he had done for Ireland and as Gladstone waited on the platform for his train, he conversed with Kavanagh about the 'university question and the cause of the opposition on the part of the Catholic bishops of Ireland to [his] university bill'.[32]

As the guest of Lord Powerscourt, he spoke to local farmers on agricultural matters, visited the local schools, conversed with clergymen of various denominations and even made a short address to the boys at Glencree Industrial School. Most of his interaction with rural Irish people was as a guest of the Wicklow aristocrats in whose houses he stayed. The furthest extent of his Irish travels was to Kilkenny on a day-trip from Abbeyleix where he was a guest of Lord de Vesci. Gladstone seemed to have wanted to travel more extensively in Ireland than he did but early into the visit he remarked in his diary that 'the larger parts of my programme fade from view, and my movements must be in a smaller circle'.[33] The *Freeman's Journal* praised Gladstone's visits to various places and his 'questioning people of all classes and laying up for future use valuable information'. However, it pointed out that Wicklow was not very representative of the general condition of Ireland as the land was fertile and most of the landowners were not only resident 'but excellent and kind hearted men'. Furthermore, it argued that Gladstone would not be able to satisfy his wish to gain knowledge of rural Ireland 'by traversing the demesnes and model estates which surround the

**30** *Freeman's Journal*, 29 Oct. 1877.  **31** James Kavanagh, *A reply to Mr Gladstone's Vaticanism* (Dublin, 1875).  **32** *Freeman's Journal*, 30 Oct. 1877.  **33** Foot & Matthew (eds), *Gladstone diaries*, ix, 259.

princely chateaux of the Irish Switzerland. He must turn to the north and the west and visit therein vast districts of the island which are drained by absentee landlords, and are the seats of misery, poverty and neglect'.[34]

On 31 October, after two weeks in Ireland, Gladstone informed Granville that he had spoken publicly on only two occasions and that his lips had been open for not more than five minutes. He mentioned that there was speculation that Dublin Corporation was going to offer him the freedom of the city but he did not think it would be passed unanimously so 'I will escape this which is all the better and get back with my design of privacy fully accomplished'.[35] However, this was not to be, as Dublin Corporation voted unanimously the next day to award him the freedom of the city. He received the news while visiting Lord Monck, a neighbour of Lord Powerscourt, and he replied that he would be happy to accept the honour. He spent his final day as the guest of Lord Powerscourt taking walks in the demesne and visiting places of scenic interest in the locality. Before moving to Carton near Maynooth and his next host, the duke of Leinster, on Saturday 2 November, he visited Dublin again where he called to the National Gallery, the College of Physicians and the industrial school at Artane as well as visiting the O'Connell crypt at Glasnevin, where the *Freeman's Journal* observed him inspecting the graves of 'the many celebrated men who slept in the magic O'Connell circle'.[36]

After service in Maynooth on Sunday a *déjeuner* was held at Carton where he spoke to the local rector, the Revd Robert William Whelan, and to Canon John O'Rourke,[37] the Catholic parish priest. The next day he visited the college at Maynooth; Gladstone may have been somewhat apprehensive about this visit as he had resigned from Peel's government in 1845 because of the increased endowment to the college and while his Irish Church Act was mostly welcomed by the Catholic Church as it disestablished the state religion in Ireland it had also resulted in the loss of an endowment worth £12,000 per annum to the college. Due to the absence of the president he was shown around the college by the vice-president, the Revd Dr Daniel McCarthy, who did not neglect to remind Gladstone how the college was £12,000 per annum worse off since the loss of the endowment. Furthermore, he added that there had been a 20 per cent drop in admissions, which had rendered a wing of the college vacant and the college supply of new books was dependent on private benefactors. In his diary, perhaps feeling somewhat guilty, Gladstone noted how the visit 'produced upon the whole a saddening impression: what havoc have we made of the vineyard of the Lord'.[38] He left Maynooth that evening and travelled to Dublin, where he stayed until he received the freedom of the city.

34 *Freeman's Journal*, 1 Nov. 1877. 35 Gladstone to Granville, 31 Oct. 1877, *Correspondence, 1876–1896*, p. 56. 36 *Freeman's Journal*, 3 Nov. 1877. 37 O'Rourke was the author of *The history of the Great Irish Famine of 1847* (Dublin, 1874), and *The centenary life of O'Connell* (Dublin, 1875) and he conversed with Gladstone about Irish history. 38 Foot & Matthew (eds),

Surprisingly, he stayed in Dublin as the guest of Archbishop Chenevix-Trench, one of the most vehement opponents of disestablishment. The following day, another surprise was in store as he paid a visit to Cardinal Cullen, who, according to Gladstone, 'delivered a mournful diatribe on the state of Ireland'. Over the course of their conversation Cullen informed Gladstone that a warmer reception could have been provided for him 'if it had not been for certain pamphlets which we in Ireland did not like very well'.[39] Other appointments that day included the Four Courts, St Michan's Church and Dublin Castle, as well as the model school on Marlborough Street. When he returned to the archbishop's palace that evening, he was met by a deputation of tenants from the estate of Major R.G. Sharman-Crawford, Ulster landlord and advocate of tenant rights. They presented him with an address that expressed indebtedness for the benefits that the tenant farmers of Ireland had derived from his land act. The legislation, they argued, was 'aimed at compelling bad landlords to recognize the rights that good landlords had never thought of contesting'. Furthermore, while recognizing the shortcomings of the act, they 'were aware that his bill suffered considerable mutilation on its progress through parliament, and that the act now unfortunately presents some imperfections at variance with the original design of its author'. They had further praise for Gladstone's ballot act and assured him they would send MPs to parliament to make their cause 'felt in the legislature and demand as full a measure of justice to the tenant farmers of Ireland as [he] had originally contemplated'.[40]

Crowds gathered outside City Hall to greet him as he arrived to accept the freedom of the city the following day. The certificate of freedom was presented in a bog oak casket which he accepted from the lord mayor and then he made a fifty-minute speech about issues relating to the economy, emigration and the beneficial effects of the legislation he had introduced. In his diary, he described the experience as 'treading upon eggs the whole time'.[41] Once again he expressed his continuing hope that the University of Dublin would become a truly national university and without mentioning the term Home Rule he spoke of his conviction that local government in all its 'shapes in which it is known to our history or agreeable to the spirit of our arrangements [...] is fundamental to the greatness of the country and the safety of its institutions'. Gladstone referred to the land act of 1870, noting that it had been introduced to benefit 'the occupiers of the soil [...] to give them fair play, which they never had'. He stated that he would not address the defects of the bill that day but he argued that 'something at least has been done, and something has been gained – something toward relieving the wants of those who were in penury'. He spoke at length about the success of the church act in creating 5,000 owner occupiers and he regretted to say that there

*Gladstone diaries*, ix, 264. **39** Foot & Matthew (eds), *Gladstone diaries*, ix, 265. **40** Down farmers address to Gladstone, *Freeman's Journal*, 8 Nov. 1877. **41** Foot & Matthew (eds), *Gladstone diaries*, ix, 265.

were not as many as he had hoped under the land act.[42] Gladstone described his own creed on the issue of land as one which 'attached no value to the [...] system of land laws with respect to entails and settlements'. In England, he regarded the 'relation of landlord and tenant as inseparable from [the] social state', but the situation was 'different in Ireland' and while he 'attached small importance to the acquisition of small properties in England, [he attached] great importance to it in Ireland'. Concluding his speech, Gladstone stated that he was speaking in his capacity as a private citizen, and that while he was not an Irishman and had acquired the character of an Irish citizen only recently, he argued

> there is no Irishman within these walls who more heartily and more profoundly than myself longs and prays that this country may be and may become more [...] prosperous and powerful, and free and glorious, a happy and contented part of the great united empire.[43]

Gladstone made a second speech at a lunch given in his honour in the Mansion House and while this was only half the length of his address in the City Hall, there were 'plenty more eggs' to be trodden on.[44] He eulogized Daniel O'Connell as a great Liberal who taught English Liberals 'to hope and desire that they might be found fighting shoulder to shoulder with men who profess the same opinions in Ireland'. He had much praise for the work of Irish silversmiths, remarking that Ireland had its own tradition in this craft, and he expressed the hope that Ireland would retain its distinct identity:

> I trust that Ireland, England, Wales and Scotland, while all closely associated together, will never lose, and will never seek or desire to be content to lose, their distinctive points of character. It is perfectly possible for them to remain in union, and yet to maintain all those distinctions, of which even a style in a work of art is an emblem and an instance. I believe that a dead and slavish uniformity is one of the greatest enemies of national excellence.[45]

Gladstone's speeches that day were interpreted in different ways. The *Irish Times* believed 'he had very much avoided allusion to current political topics, and confined himself almost altogether to a defence of his own policy, and the measures which were its outcome'.[46] On the other hand, the *Freeman's Journal* argued that 'all candid students of his speech will admit that we may look to

---

42 The disestablishment of the Church of Ireland resulted in the sale of church land creating 5,000 owner occupiers while under the Bright clauses of Gladstone's 1870 land act less than 1,000 were created. 43 *Freeman's Journal*, 8 Nov. 1877. 44 Foot & Matthew (eds), *Gladstone diaries*, ix, 265. 45 *Freeman's Journal*, 8 Nov. 1877. 46 *Irish Times*, 8 Nov. 1877.

some modification of the land act, at least in the direction of favouring a peasant proprietorship'.[47] The *Dublin Evening Mail* declared that Gladstone had 'emerged from the shell of his strictly private visit [to] flatter Irish councillors, and suggest ever so distant a hope that something will be made of him in time to come'.[48] There was a similar disparity of opinion in the London press. *The Times* suggested that the whole event from the offering of the freedom by unanimous vote to the speeches on the day was

> a good omen for Irish political life and Ireland as a whole … Something, perhaps, is to be ascribed to the fact that Mr Gladstone's visit was so completely disassociated from any political object; and in the actual ceremony of presentation still more may be due to the singular grace with which, while touching on nearly every subject of interest to Ireland, the speaker avoided the least approach to partisanship.[49]

The *London Standard*, however, described his speech as

> a genuine political manifesto [...] His studied panegyric on local government will deceive nobody. In the circumstances of the country in which it was delivered, and in the midst of a corporation notoriously nationalist in sentiment, it plainly means a compromise with Home Rule.[50]

It is hardly surprising that *The Times* sought to portray Gladstone's visit with a degree of innocence, as the paper's proprietor, John Walters, was a Liberal MP. However, the suspicions of ulterior motives that some publications had aired at the beginning of his visit appeared to have been confirmed. During the trip, he had doffed his cap to Irish nationalism and O'Connell in particular. He visited the Bank of Ireland, the former home of the Irish parliament, 'the magic O'Connell circle' at Glasnevin, and in his Mansion House speech he alluded to O'Connell's wish that Irish and English Liberals could work together. As H.G.C. Matthew has argued, 'Gladstone … publicly associated himself with O'Connellism at just the moment Parnell was coming to the fore in Irish politics'.[51] There is no doubt that Gladstone was, at this stage, considering all his options and, shortly after his return from Ireland, he wrote to Granville stating that if the Home Rulers had 'a real leader whom they were disposed to follow, I cannot think it would be difficult to arrange a *modus vivendi* with them'.[52]

**47** *Freeman's Journal*, 8 Nov. 1877.   **48** *Dublin Evening Mail*, 9 Nov. 1877.   **49** *Times*, 9 Nov. 1877.   **50** *London Standard*, 8 Nov. 1877.   **51** H.G.C. Matthew, 'Gladstone, O'Connellism, and Home Rule' in R.V. Comerford & Enda Delany (eds), *National questions: reflections on Daniel O'Connell and contemporary Ireland* (Dublin, 2000), p. 24.   **52** Gladstone to Granville, 20 Nov.

Gladstone remained in Ireland for a further five days but they were fairly uneventful; he attended no more public functions and did not speak in public. His only activities of a public nature were a visit to Kilkenny city on Friday and to service at St Patrick's Cathedral on Sunday, where he remarked in his diary on the great crowd, the magnificent music and the presence of the vice-regal court.[53] On the same day, Cardinal Cullen responded to Gladstone's repeated wishes to see the University of Dublin become a national university by issuing a pastoral letter that was read in all the Catholic churches of the Dublin diocese. The pastoral recommended that the faithful read Monsignor Bartholmew Woodlock's pamphlet on the Irish university question.[54] This pamphlet, which was published in the newspapers the following week, criticized the lack of university education available to Irish Catholics and dismissed the argument that Trinity College was open to them as the provost and the fellows of the college were Protestant. If the shoe were on the other foot, Woodlock argued, Gladstone, 'as a Protestant parent, […] would, without doubt, be the first to exclaim against the tyranny of handing over Protestant youth to be taught by Catholic clergymen'. Furthermore, he argued, that it was ridiculous to claim that there was religious equality when a college like Trinity was endowed from the income it derived from lands confiscated from Irish chieftains. To correct the imbalance, he called for either endowment of the Catholic University or the complete disendowment of all educational institutions including Trinity College.[55]

The success of Gladstone's visit was acknowledged by almost all sections of the press. The *Nation* held that reports in the English press about his reception in Ireland were overstated, arguing that 'excepting the hissing with which he was received on emerging from St Patrick's [Cathedral], […] he was met with respect and cordiality, but certainly not with enthusiasm as some English papers represent'.[56] However, it was not only the English press that claimed that he was met with enthusiasm, the *Dublin Evening Mail*, usually one of his staunchest critics, remarked how the visit was an entire success: 'Trinity students, peers and peasants, parish priests and town councillors had submitted helplessly to his mesmeric sway. … Even the great cardinal […] with a nice sense of hospitality deputed the publication of his fiery pastoral to the meeker Dr Bartholomew Woodlock'.[57] Gladstone's visit began as 'strictly private and personal', but by the time it finished, as the *Irish Times* observed, it had become 'public and general'.[58] In 1877, Gladstone's return to the political arena gathered momentum and his Irish visit was another step in consolidating his position. During the summer, he

1877, *Correspondence, 1876–1886*, p. 58.   **53** Foot & Matthew (eds), *Gladstone diaries*, ix, 267.
**54** From 1861, Monsignor Woodlock served as the rector of the Catholic University of Ireland until his appointment as bishop of Ardagh and Clonfert in 1879.   **55** Monsignor Woodlock's circular, *Freeman's Journal*, 12 Nov. 1877.   **56** *Nation*, 17 Nov. 1877.   **57** *Dublin Evening Mail*, 13 Nov. 1977.   **58** *Irish Times*, 12 Nov. 1877.

had hosted deputations of northern liberals and through 'an almost accidental' form of semi-passive political campaigning succeeded in impressing constituents from where he would seek election in 1879. It could also be argued that the success of his Irish visit was 'almost accidental' and that Gladstone, the passive tourist, was carried along by forces not of his design and managed to secure the Irish vote that was crucial in returning him and the Liberal Party to power in Westminster. However, two 'almost accidental' successes in such a short timeframe raise the suspicion that there was nothing accidental at all about them. It is quite possible that Gladstone had considered the potential offered by such occasions for political exploitation and capitalized on them when he spotted the opportunity. Had he come over to Ireland on an active political campaign, his reception would probably have been quite different. However, Gladstone, uncertain about how he would be received in Ireland, declared his visit to be 'private and personal' at the beginning, and this gave him the space to assess which way public opinion was blowing. Had it turned out unfavourably, he could have done his rounds of the country houses and returned to England without losing face. As it turned out, the offer of the freedom of Dublin by unanimous vote provided an unmissable opportunity for him to crown his visit in triumph and make a play for the Irish vote, so he took full advantage of it. One week after his return, Gladstone reflected on the outcome of his trip in a letter to Granville recounting an anecdote

> about an Irishman who wanted to take his pig to Kilkenny. With this view he drove the pig to Cork; for, he said, if the pig thinks I want him to go to Kilkenny, he will go to Cork for a shurety ... I think my announcement of 'strict privacy' may in like manner have promoted a prosperous publicity.[59]

Gladstone, it appears, was becoming adept in the art of passive political campaigning. He could not have hoped for a better outcome from his trip, he had made his peace, for the time being, with institutions like Maynooth and Trinity colleges, and with diverse leaders of the people such as Archbishop Chenevix-Trench and Cardinal Cullen, and laid the foundations for the next election campaign in Ireland.

59 Gladstone to Granville, 10 Oct. 1877, *Correspondence, 1876–1886*, p. 57.

# 'Irish peers are deservedly unpopular': dealing with your father's *faux pas* within the nineteenth-century family

DEVON McHUGH

> The Irish peers are deservedly unpopular. They are anti-national. They are an inferior set of men. But it is desirable if we can bring them back to nationality, to love of country, to popularity; for they are the natural heads of Irish society, and in the eighteenth century they were true Irishmen and of a higher intellectual level than now.[1]

Gladstone's words do not strike the twenty-first-century historian as surprising: his dedication to Home Rule in Ireland throughout the last two decades of his career is a keystone of his political legacy, and his attitude to the preferential existence of the ascendancy gentry and aristocracy of Ireland was born of this commitment. However, when his personal, rather than his political, record is examined, more is revealed: in 1861, his niece, Anne Elizabeth Honoria ('Nora') Gladstone (1841–1919), married Somerset Richard Lowry Corry, the fourth earl of Belmore (1835–1913). As representative peer for Ireland, and as the holder of estates in Ulster as well as a title, Belmore was exactly the sort of man about whom Gladstone was writing. Between the late 1860s and Gladstone's death in 1898, Gladstone would encounter political conflict with the Unionist, Conservative earl of Belmore repeatedly. How was this professional discord dealt with within the closely connected extended Gladstone family?

The specifics of family life and familial dynamics have been under-examined as influences in the lives of politicians, and historical work has primarily concentrated on dynastic influences (biographies on the Cecil and Londonderry clans in the nineteenth century, for example),[2] or the role of aristocratic women and political wives,[3] rather than on the family group as a whole. The family of William Ewart Gladstone has suffered similar lack of treatment. S.G. Checkland's biography of the Gladstones was comprehensive, but was primarily

---

1 William Gladstone, as quoted in D.G. Boyce, 'In the front rank of the nation: Gladstone and the Unionists of Ireland, 1868–1893' in D. Bebbington & R. Swift (eds), *Gladstone centenary essays* (Liverpool, 2000), p. 198.   2 D. Cecil, *The Cecils of Hatfield House: a portrait of an English ruling family* (London, 1973); D. Urquhart, *The ladies of Londonderry: women and political patronage* (London, 2007).   3 P. Jalland, *Women, marriage and politics, 1860–1914* (Oxford, 1986); K. Reynolds, *Aristocratic women and political society in Victorian Britain* (Oxford, 1998).

90

an explanation of the prime minister's politics as based in his relationship with his father, and failed to examine or interpret the actual relationships within the family as Gladstone's career progressed.[4] Importantly, Checkland's work was dedicated to the formative years of Gladstone's life, and does not closely examine the influences of family in the politician's life in the years after his marriage and as his children reached adulthood. While Catherine Gladstone has been the subject of biography,[5] on the whole the Gladstone children have not had this sort of attention.[6] Additionally, the role of the family group, which placed William Ewart Gladstone within an extended cousinhood of powerful, wealthy, and politically active elite families, including the Lyttletons, Cavendishes, Spencers and Talbots, among others, has been largely neglected.

The intention of this essay is to begin this examination, by looking at the connection between the Gladstone family and the family of the earls of Belmore, through the marriage of Nora Gladstone to the fourth earl of Belmore. Specifically, the essay will look at the role of informal networks of feminine correspondence as tools in perpetuating dynastic communication, even, perhaps especially, in the face of those difficulties caused by political careers. In this instance, the letters of Agnes Gladstone (1842–1931), daughter of William Ewart Gladstone, to her cousin, Lady Belmore, during the years between 1868 and 1871 will be used to examine how the larger Gladstone clan sidestepped the divisive issues of national and international politics to retain and sustain connections within the extended family.

The essay will begin by examining the union between the earl of Belmore and Nora Gladstone in 1861. The marriage can be used to illustrate some of the factors that usually influenced marriages in the second half of the nineteenth century, as well as illuminating the respective social and economic trajectories of the Gladstone and Belmore families. The discussion will then briefly turn to the career of the earl of Belmore, establishing the political and diplomatic fields in which he was operating in the 1860s and 1870s, before examining how these politics could have presented an arena of conflict within the larger Belmore-Gladstone family group. The essay will then examine more closely the letters sent to Lady Belmore during her husband's service as Governor of New South Wales from 1868 to 1871, a time when the Belmores were starting a family, but also found themselves far from their home and their own families. The letters date from what is likely to have been the first period of major political conflict in the Belmore-Gladstone family, and this conflict happened to coincide with the removal of the earl and countess from Britain. Agnes Gladstone's letters are

---

4 S.G. Checkland, *The Gladstones: a family biography, 1764–1851* (Cambridge, 1971).   5 M. Drew, *Catherine Gladstone, by her daughter* (London, 1919); G. Battiscombe, *Mrs Gladstone: the portrait of a marriage* (London, 1956).   6 P. Jalland, 'Mr Gladstone's daughters: the domestic price of Victorian politics' in B.L. Kinzer (ed.), *The Gladstonian turn of mind* (Toronto, 1985), pp 97–122; M. Bentley, 'Gladstone's heir', *English Historical Review*, 107 (Oct. 1992), 901–24.

supplemented with a lengthy correspondence from Lady Belmore's six sisters, the daughters of John Neilson Gladstone, and with letters from other young women in the family, in order to best examine the typicality of Agnes' letters to Lady Belmore, and to give a fuller picture of the family's correspondence to Honoria. These letters, many written in the wake of the disestablishment of the Church of Ireland, between the family of the Liberal politician who conceived and implemented disestablishment and the wife of a Conservative lord who strongly opposed the change, may have established a template for the ways the family could negotiate and overcome political conflict in the years to come.

In these years, the correspondence between members of the extended Gladstone family was significant, although not unusually so. The family (and in the instance of these letters, primarily the daughters of the four sons of W.E. Gladstone's father, John) stayed in contact through a circuit of letters and visits to London and to family homes across the United Kingdom at Bowden Park (Wiltshire), Fasque (Aberdeenshire), Hawarden Castle (Flintshire), Penmaer Mawr (Conwy) and Belvoir Park (Down). Yet, despite the politically active nature of these families, politics was not a frequent topic of correspondence among the women of the family, and primarily they were interested in keeping each other abreast of family issues (such as health, marriage and education), international events (such as travel, European conflict and the movement of the royals) and, largely, family and society gossip. The most illustrious members of the family, like William Gladstone, make occasional appearances: Uncle William 'has a terribly anxious time now' or 'has kept well in spite of all his work', but the subject of these letters is the family life and shared experiences of these young women, not the political and diplomatic manoeuvrings of the families as a whole.[7]

As for many elite families at this time, letters played an important role in the day-to-day maintenance of the family, both offering news for far-away friends and relatives, and acting as a demand on time, especially for women. Within the Gladstone family, the women seem to have carried on the majority of the social and familial correspondence. Based on his own meticulous record of correspondence, William Gladstone never contacted the earl of Belmore directly, and rarely wrote to his nieces and nephews, although he was involved in their lives, particularly after the death of Nora's father, John Neilson Gladstone.[8] In this instance, letter writing seems to have fallen to the younger members of the

7 Public Record Office of Northern Ireland (PRONI), Belmore papers, D/3007/I/4 (BP). Mary Gladstone to Lady Belmore, 5 Aug. 1870, Fasque; Catherine Gladstone to Lady Belmore, 29 July [no year], Hawarden Castle.  8 At the death of John Neilson Gladstone in 1862, William Gladstone assumed the guardianship of his brother's six unmarried daughters and young son, a responsibility which he shared with his two surviving brothers. Jenkins has recorded Gladstone's primary role in supporting his brother's children and in arranging the legal and financial technicalities, a pursuit to which he dedicated a stupendous amount of effort, and no little macabre enthusiasm for mourning; R. Jenkins, *Gladstone* (London, 1995), pp 231–2.

family, no less because Catherine Gladstone, though a central link between dozens of families across Britain and Ireland, was a notoriously haphazard correspondent.[9]

As scholars have recognized, letters play to a particular audience, and are therefore necessarily limited as historical sources by their bias and intentionally limited scope.[10] Nineteenth-century letters were part of a social contract of exchange and debt, and the letters written to Lady Belmore during her time in Australia were intended to help her continue to feel a connection to her home and family during a long and difficult sojourn. As such, family and society business, not politics or international news, was their central concern. Within the letters inclusions such as photographs, which were regularly sent between the cousins, of themselves and of their children, were deeply meaningful. The letters of Agnes Gladstone stress how important these keepsakes were to her, both as a reminder of the family abroad, and as a record of those changes that occurred while the family was distant, especially the growth of the children.[11]

* * *

The union between the earl of Belmore and Nora Gladstone was a sensible one in those terms that Patricia Jalland has established as being central to the aristo-cratic ethos in the late nineteenth century.[12] Nora Gladstone and the earl of Belmore had much in common in those areas that Victorian society judged to be important, including religion, social station, politics, age, health and finances. Religiously, the two families had much shared ground, and the evangelical faith of the Gladstone family, as imbued in William Gladstone and his siblings partic-ularly by their mother, was echoed in the strong, and strongly Protestant, faith of the Lowry-Corrys. Nora Gladstone, the daughter of an English member of parliament and county landowner, already had a connection to the north of Ireland through her mother: Mrs Gladstone had been Elizabeth Bateson of Belvoir Park, Co. Down, daughter of Sir Robert Bateson, first baronet (1782–1863), formerly MP for Co. Londonderry, and sister of Sir Thomas Bateson, second baronet and first Lord Deramore (1819–90), leader of the Ulster Conservatives and an early proponent of Ulster Unionism.[13] Politically, John Neilson Gladstone and the earl of Belmore shared much, not least membership of the

---

9 Battiscombe, *Mrs Gladstone*, p. 32. Battiscombe remarks early on in her biography that Catherine Glynne was originally in possession of an 'exquisite copybook hand' which in later life became largely illegible (p. 9), as is certainly the case of the single letter from Mrs Gladstone to Lady Belmore (PRONI, BP, [no date]). 10 S. Pearsall, *Atlantic families* (Oxford, 2008); L. Stanley, 'Letters as/not a genre', *Life Writing*, 2:2 (2005), 75–101. 11 PRONI, BP. Agnes Gladstone to Lady Belmore, 2 Oct. 1869, Hawarden Castle. 12 Jalland, *Women, marriage and politics*, pp 144–6. 13 A. Jackson, *The Ulster party: Irish Unionists in the House of Commons, 1884–1991* (Oxford, 1989).

Carlton Club, although it is clear that the extended Gladstone family did not always agree politically.

Questions about marital suitability were important to the Gladstones, and were widely discussed in letters among the young women of the family. The respective ages of bride and groom were significant: while Nora Gladstone and the earl of Belmore would have been considered well suited at the respective ages of 20 and 25, older husbands were spoken of with less enthusiasm among the family. Despite the widespread affection held in the family for William Dumaresq, who would marry Nora's sister Edith in 1870, his age was seen as a drawback. 'I am sorry he is so much older than she is', Mary, Nora's cousin, wrote from Fasque during their long engagement. 'He must feel she is quite a child compared with him'.[14] Dumaresq was born in 1835, the same year as Belmore, but by 1870 was 35 years of age, compared to Edith Gladstone's 19. This was not, however, the only difficulty, and the question of age may have gone unremarked without the introduction of an additional question regarding finances. The couple had met in Dumaresq's hometown of Sydney, when Edith had accompanied her sister's family to New South Wales. Accordingly, although educated as a barrister at the Inner Temple in 1861, and from a suitably august English family with Norman origins, the groom's fortune and financial records were in Australia, which caused a great deal of delay in establishing the settlement for the couple. As trustees for all five of the late John Neilson Gladstone's unmarried daughters, 'the Uncles' (Thomas, Robertson and William Gladstone), as Kate Gladstone referred to them, were extremely exact about the establishment of financial security for Edith on her wedding.[15]

The alliance of the Belmore and Gladstone families tied a lengthy record of status to a family of rising political and economic prospects, made possible by the conscious choice of John Gladstone to encourage upward mobility in his sons through education at Eton and introduction into landed society. This was largely due to the combined force of John Gladstone's enormous success as a merchant and the attraction held by William Gladstone's personality and political success. At the same time, those elite families with whom the Gladstones would become linked (the Glynnes, the Belmores) were beginning to experience a decline in their own fortunes. This is clear in the pattern of marriage within the Belmore family (which actually experienced a clear decline of social and economic status as the nineteenth century progressed), as well as in the economics of landownership in Ireland, the profits of which would begin to sharply fall in the 1880s. This is also recognized by Georgiana Battiscombe in her biography of Catherine Gladstone in reference to her own family, the Glynnes,[16] and the growing power of mercantile finance over the increasingly beleaguered economies of the landed

---

14 PRONI, BP. Mary Gladstone to Lady Belmore, 5 Aug. 1870, Fasque.  15 PRONI, BP. Kate Gladstone to Nora Belmore, 20 Aug. 1870, Bowden Park.  16 Battiscombe, *Mrs Gladstone*, p. 1.

classes would make an ever-clearer mark on the British political elite as the
nineteenth century progressed. The connection of the Gladstone family to
established members of the gentry and aristocracy like the Glynnes, and then the
Belmores, demonstrated how far they had come in the previous fifty years,
gaining in social and financial power at the same time that some aristocratic
families were beginning to struggle financially.

* * *

By the mid-1860s, the earl of Belmore appeared to have begun to reap the
rewards of his connection to William Ewart Gladstone, though not in any way
so grand as to excite charges of nepotism. In 1865, Gladstone asked Belmore to
join a new royal commission on railways, reflecting his previous experiences with
railways and agricultural management in parliament.[17] This appointment led to
advancement within the next few years, and in 1866 Belmore was given the role
of undersecretary at the home office, a position of which he would be proud his
entire life.[18]

However, despite these advancements under Gladstone's government, the
primary political mentor in the earl of Belmore's career was never his wife's
uncle, but rather his own uncle, Henry Corry (1803–73), who assumed the
position of first lord of the admiralty in the same year, and continued to act as
the major influence on Belmore's early career.[19] When Belmore decided that he
wanted a position with a greater salary on which to support his growing family,
and the opportunity to see them more regularly, it was his uncle he approached,
and his uncle who shared his dreams of being granted the position of governor
general of Canada. Unfortunately, the position was filled by the first Baron
Lisgar, who left New South Wales to take the Canadian stewardship. Belmore
was instead offered his previous position as governor, based in Sydney.

Almost immediately, Belmore was embroiled in the financial difficulties of
the province, where the debt-ridden elite contrasted sharply with his own
frugality. While the economy of the Belmores has been lauded in retrospect, at
the time, the gubernatorial couple were widely criticized by Sydney society, both
for unconcern for what the earl termed 'trivialities', and for rumours that the
£6,000 annual salary of the diplomatic position was all that kept the Belmores
from penury at home in Ireland.[20] Belmore gained recognition, however, during
the visit of the Prince of Wales in March of 1868, when the heir to the throne
was shot in the back by Henry O'Farrell, a suspected Fenian conspirator who

17 P. Marson, *Belmore: the Lowry Corrys of Castle Coole, 1646–1913* (Belfast, 2007), p. 220.
18 *Times*, 8 Apr. 1913. 19 Marson, *Belmore*, p. 221. 20 Ibid., p. 233. The *Sydney Bulletin*, on
20 Aug. 1881, accused Belmore of parsimony and of accepting the colonial position in order to
clear his landed debts: 'by diligence, thrift and the careful raising of cabbages, succeeded in
accomplishing his purpose before the usual term expired'.

was judged insane. Belmore's cool head and the comfort the couple offered the Prince during his treatment gained the favour of both the royal family and the Australian public. Furthermore, Belmore's handling of the delicate political situation in the aftermath of the shooting emphasized how seriously he took his role as diplomat. When the Orange Lodge offered a public declaration of their loyalty, he informed the organization that while he appreciated the sentiment, he was unable, as a representative of the queen, to accept any declarations that might be interpreted as political in nature.[21]

Despite his own political sympathies, Belmore recognized that the nature of his position required the suppression of his own sentiments; he may have been similarly successful in doing so to an extent within the context of his wife's extended family, and their political loyalties. During the earl's time as governor of New South Wales, Westminster passed the bill that would disestablish the Church of Ireland, a bill led by his wife's uncle. In 1870, the government then passed Gladstone's first land act, which guaranteed tenants rights in Ireland. For the Belmores, as for many northern landowners, the land act would ultimately have little effect; Ulster Right, on which the act was based, was already in effect on their lands, and no claims were brought against the earl of Belmore under the terms of the 1870 act.

The changes in land and church legislation in Ireland did, however, have a psychological effect on the earl, and may have provided a concrete reason for leaving Australia. Urged on by Lady Belmore's precarious health, he asked to be relieved of his position in June of 1871, ostensibly to resume his parliamentary career and dedicate a greater amount of time to his Irish estates. The family departed in February of the next year. According to Peter Marson, the primary reason for the curtailment of the Australian post was less Lady Belmore's health, which had recovered in the years since her miscarriage in 1869, or the progressing political situation in Ireland, but was instead her Ladyship's homesickness, which is echoed in letters from her sisters, which beg her to return to Britain.[22] Despite this, the earl's true reasons for returning to Britain in 1872 are opaque, likely influenced by factors including, but not limited to, changes in the familial, personal, political and economic factors that had brought him to accept the Australian position in 1867.

\* \* \*

The letters kept by Honoria, Lady Belmore, during her time in Australia demonstrate clearly the subjects that absorbed young women in the extended Gladstone family. The letters are overwhelmingly social, rather than political:

---

21 *Australian dictionary of national biography.*    22 Marson, *Belmore*, p. 235; PRONI, BP. See especially Kate Gladstone to Lady Belmore, 20 Apr. 1870, Bowden Park; Constance Gladstone to Lady Belmore, 23 Feb. 1871, Bowden Park.

the women of Honoria's generation were all recently married or recently debuted, and their lives were accordingly centred on subjects of visiting, engagements and marriage settlements and news about friends and royalty. It may be partly because of this clear emphasis on non-political subject matter that the correspondence flowed freely: the removal of family communication from the hands of figures like Gladstone and Belmore, who were largely preoccupied with matters of state and their careers, allowed these subjects, which became increasingly fraught as Belmore and Gladstone's politics diverged through the last years of the nineteenth century, to be sidelined by concerns that were less contentious, and more central for less politically active members of the family.

Marriage and engagements tended to be the primary subject of the letters between the Gladstone cousins during these years. The women of Lady Belmore's generation were understandably occupied primarily with the debut, engagements and young families of their relatives and friends, and news, gossip and speculation filled the pages of the correspondence of Lady Belmore while she was in Australia.

A topic of particular interest to the extended family was the marital status of the children of William and Catherine Gladstone. In 1870, Mary Gladstone, daughter of Sir Thomas of Fasque, wrote to Lady Belmore to relate the news of a recent party thrown by Catherine Gladstone for the Prince and Princess of Wales. She remarked that the Gladstone daughters, at the time aged 28, 23 and 21, were 'very flourishing', especially the eldest, Agnes. 'I wish so much that some of them would follow Edith's good example [and marry]', she wrote. 'It is really time'.[23] Scholars have since remarked on the reluctance of the Gladstone children to marry, Jalland attributing this in part to the dominant character of their famous parents.[24] Agnes Gladstone would marry within a few years of this letter, in 1873, but later revealed in a letter to her mother her own awareness of how unusual this was within her family. 'I am the only one of the seven with a separate home and life apart'.[25] As such, Agnes may have been the most conventional of the Gladstone children; she certainly was the preferred cousin among Lady Belmore and her sisters, who made this clear in the direction of their correspondence and, from time to time, simply stated the fact.[26]

This particular connection may have been partly because, like Lady Belmore, Agnes Gladstone clearly had a passion for children. This is demonstrated throughout her letters, and it is this additional subject that dominates much of her correspondence with her cousin. The subject also clearly dominated Lady Belmore's mind at the time: during the period of these letters (1868–71), Lady Belmore miscarried once and finally gave birth to her fourth child and first son,

23 PRONI, BP. Mary Gladstone to Lady Belmore, 24 Feb. 1870, Fairlawn, Tunbridge. 24 Jalland, *Marriage, women and politics*, p. 97. 25 St Deiniol's Library, Glynne-Gladstone MS 30/10. Agnes Wickham to Catherine Gladstone, 29 Sept. 1891. 26 PRONI, BP. Alice Gladstone to Lady Belmore, 17 May 1870, Bowden Park.

in 1870. Agnes' correspondence is largely concerned with the wellbeing of Lady Belmore's actual and future offspring, enquiring after the Belmore children and requesting their photographs, and giving detailed accounts of the birth, behaviour and appearance of the children of their mutual friends. Agnes Gladstone relished the company of young children, and regretted not being able to have been present during the early years of her cousin's elder children. But she also recognized the stresses young wives were under: in 1868, before the birth of the Belmore's son and heir, Armar, she wrote to Lady Belmore about the longing of her own cousin, Lucy Cavendish, for a child, and sent her hopes that Lady Belmore would soon produce a son to join her daughters.[27]

Frequent pregnancies during the years in Australia, as well as the physical and emotional trauma of a stillborn son in 1869, rendered the subject of Lady Belmore's health a supplementary, but important, aspect of these letters. Health, generally, seems to have been an important concern for the Gladstone family at large, a legacy perhaps visited upon them by their grandmother, Anne Gladstone, who cultured a community of feminine invalidism with her two daughters, and encouraged this view of femininity in her sons.[28] In fact, Lady Belmore's health may have been the only item of Jalland's Victorian marriage criteria that did not seem to measure up in the Gladstone-Belmore match of 1861: like her grandmother, and her aunts, Nora Gladstone seems to have had a record of ill health that continued throughout her marriage. However, unlike two of her sisters, Clara and Alice, Lady Belmore's health concerns did not stop her from pursuing marriage and family life.

Questions, both genuine and hypochondriacal, about the health of the entire family pervade the Gladstone letters. Lady Belmore's own health in the wake of the stillborn child in 1869 was in danger, while at the same time both her sister Alice and a selection of her cousins were struggling with myriad health concerns.[29] In 1870, Alice and Clara Gladstone sent 'very poor accounts … from Bowden', but appeared well to Mary Gladstone, who found it 'strange that they don't get right, and yet no one seems to know really whether there is much the matter'.[30] Agnes Gladstone often reported how much improved both Alice and Clara looked through these years, though they themselves continually felt the need to seek cures and changes of air for their health.[31] Whether Agnes was really reporting an incidence of sororial hypochondria, or if she was presenting the news in the most optimistic fashion possible, knowing that from afar Lady

27 PRONI, BP. Agnes Gladstone to Lady Belmore, 30 July 1868.    28 Checkland, *Gladstones*, pp 54, 189.    29 PRONI, BP. Agnes Gladstone to Lady Belmore, 17 June 1869, 11 Carlton House Terrace.    30 PRONI, BP. Annie Gladstone to Lady Belmore, 5 Aug. 1870, Fasque; Mary Gladstone to Lady Belmore, 5 Aug. 1870, Fasque.    31 PRONI, BP. See Agnes Gladstone to Lady Belmore, 9 Sept. 1868, 23 Feb. 1871. Clara and Alice's rest cures were sought in various locations across Scotland in the summer of 1868, in Bournemouth in 1869, in northern France (Caen, Boulogne) in 1870, and in St Leonards in 1871, trips that were separate from their usual upper class peregrinations between the country homes of family and friends.

Belmore would only have cause to worry if told of her sisters' poor health, is unclear. What is clear is that like the stereotypical well-born Victorian woman, the Gladstone women characterized themselves frequently as unwell.

The letters between the cousins were otherwise occupied with somewhat more public news, although information on Society, their pursuits outside the home, and national and international events was given limited space within the correspondence. Visits to and from the royal family occupied space in the letters of Agnes Gladstone, though not in the correspondence of her cousins: either Agnes shared an interest in royalty with Lady Belmore that their relatives did not feel, or the political connections of William Gladstone's status as a politician and Lord Belmore's role as a diplomat pulled these branches of the family into different social circles from their relatives. Largely, however, discussion of meetings with the Queen, Princess Alexandra and other members of the royal family were discussed in terms very similar to those used for other families: Agnes relished meeting the young princes and princesses, remarking on the excitable manners of the children of the Prince and Princess of Wales and the 'grand' looks of Princess Alice's daughters in 1868,[32] as well as discussing the wedding gifts and upcoming nuptials of Princess Louise.[33]

Discussion of the royal family also touched, from time to time, on their involvement with or sponsorship of charities run by Agnes, her mother Catherine, or their social circle. While in 1869 the Gladstone women were occupied running a convalescent hospital, which was mentioned briefly in a letter to Lady Belmore,[34] by 1871 Catherine Gladstone had involved herself in the eradication of smallpox. According to Agnes, 'the topic of the day is vaccination', and Catherine Gladstone was assisted by Lady Lothian in organizing hospital care for sufferers.[35] Agnes was aware enough of the larger philanthropic community to recognize when their own charities would suffer: during the Franco-Prussian War (1870–1), 'the enormous quantities of money that have been subscribed to all the different funds have made many home charities suffer seriously', she wrote in 1871.[36] The war was one of the few international events that made it into these letters, but Lady Belmore's correspondents recognized that she would have been less interested in being kept informed of details of the conflict than in their own lives. Similarly, politics have little place in the letters of these young women: they are primarily mentioned incidentally within the context of movements of individual family members, particularly during elections or votes at Westminster.[37]

32  PRONI, BP. Agnes Gladstone to Lady Belmore, 13 June 1868, 30 July 1868, Hawarden Castle.
33  PRONI, BP. Agnes Gladstone to Lady Belmore, 23 Feb. 1871, 11 Carlton House Terrace.
34  PRONI, BP. Agnes Gladstone to Lady Belmore, 17 June 1869, 11 Carlton House Terrace.
35  PRONI, BP. Agnes Gladstone to Lady Belmore, 23 Feb. 1871, 11 Carlton House Terrace.
36  Ibid.   37  PRONI, BP. Agnes Gladstone to Lady Belmore, 30 July 1868, Hawarden Castle, 17 June 1869, 11 Carlton House Terrace.

*  *  *

Patricia Jalland has remarked that while the intermarriage of political families usually occurred from within the same party, this was not always the case, and differences in politics prohibited neither social interaction nor marriage between families of different political persuasions. It was generally understood that, if necessary, a woman could change her political allegiances on her marriage, and in some instances, a marriage helped to smooth over pre-existing political grievances. Jalland cites a number of examples (although primarily of a slightly later date than the Gladstone-Belmore union) to illustrate the occurrence of cross-party alliances, including the Liberal Unionist-Conservative union between Victor Cavendish and Lady Evelyn Fitzmaurice, the Liberal-Conservative marriage of Archibald Peel and Lady Georgiana Russell, and, within the Liberal party, the marriage of Lucy Lyttleton, W.E. Gladstone's niece, to Lord Frederick Cavendish, which apparently improved relations between Gladstone and Lord Hartington, Cavendish's brother.[38]

In her analysis of the role of aristocratic women in mid-Victorian political society, Kim Reynolds has observed that in this period, 'action, not analysis, sufficed', a statement she uses to explain the lack of discussion within women's writing of the time about their role as wives, mothers, or women generally.[39] This observation can, however, be applied more widely to the letters of the elite in the mid-nineteenth century: subjects were only under discussion once debate about their importance was introduced. Just as very few of the women in Reynolds' study discussed their perceptions and feelings about their role as women, for the Gladstones and Belmores, the discussion of potential political conflicts within the family was unnecessary. Action, rather than discussion, was called for, and an important aspect of this action was the strengthening of family ties around political figures at loggerheads. In the 1860s and 1870s, family connections still played a major role in British politics, and the importance of these connections were recognized and accordingly preserved.

Pursuing a correspondence between Lady Belmore and her cousin, Agnes, during the years after the disestablishment of the Church of Ireland may have additionally formed a template for the upkeep of family relationships in the years to come. The disestablishment of the church was only the first of many policies forwarded by William Gladstone that were in direct conflict with the 4th earl of Belmore's own political loyalties, and the Church Act would be followed by the greater challenge of Home Rule in the 1880s. By establishing a route for direct communication between Belmore's wife and Gladstone's daughter, the family set a precedent for correspondence that could be reinstated during other times of political struggle and conflict.

The examination of this very specific scenario highlights a number of further

---

38 Jalland, *Women, marriage and politics*, pp 90–1.   39 Reynolds, *Aristocratic women*, p. 11.

questions about the interaction of family and politics during the later nineteenth century. Questions regarding the informal role of women within society and politics have begun to be explored by historians. However, the myriad influences that would have affected family and personal politics during the Home Rule debate, and the effect of divisive politics on family life in Ulster during the late nineteenth and early twentieth centuries have as yet been neglected. The personal implications of political splits within Ireland during the years of the Home Rule debate are worthy of further exploration, and will shed light on the intersecting realms of family life and politics in the nineteenth and early twentieth centuries.

# 'This Proteus of politics': the *Dublin Evening Mail* on Gladstone, 1868–98[1]

## PATRICK MAUME

### THE *EVENING MAIL*, THE PALMERSTONIAN LEGACY AND IRISH CONSERVATIVE ANTI-GLADSTONIANISM

The *Dublin Evening Mail* of the Gladstone era represented a strand of Victorian Irish Unionism relatively neglected by historians. Such liberal Unionists as Thomas MacKnight of the Belfast *Northern Whig*[2] saw themselves as upholding Liberal traditions abandoned by Gladstone and they shared the same universe of discourse as Gladstonians or even moderate Parnellites such as Barry O'Brien, who called Gladstonian Home Rule a logical extension of earlier Whig-Liberal Irish reforms supported by Liberal Unionists.[3] The *Evening Mail*, circulating among an audience of landlords and well-to-do professionals, viscerally opposed these reforms from the beginning; though it might appeal to the popular Unionism of Ulster as a resource in defending the Irish Church Establishment or opposing Home Rule, it self-consciously presented itself as the voice of an elite defending property and civilization against the ignorant and anarchic populace. Founded as a Conservative paper opposed to Catholic Emancipation, by the mid-Victorian era, the *Mail* shifted to supporting Palmerston's Whig government as defender of property and upholder of Protestantism and freedom. With the demise of Palmerston and the rise of Gladstone to the Liberal leadership, the *Mail* reverted to conservatism, after a brief flirtation with Buttite Home Rule in despair at Disraeli's ambivalent response to Gladstone's successful onslaught against the Irish Church Establishment.

This essay begins with a brief outline of the *Mail*'s history. It then outlines how between Gladstone's rise to power in 1868 and his last Home Rule crusade in the late 1880s and early 1890s, the *Mail* lambasted him as a dangerously irresponsible demagogue whose 'heroic' reforms encouraged unrest in Ireland and threatened property rights in Britain, and whose attempted appeasement of

---

1 All references are to the *Warder and Weekly Mail* (the weekly edition of the *Evening Mail*, comprising a selection of the week's news stories and editorials) unless otherwise stated. 2 Thomas MacKnight, *Ulster as it is*, 2 vols (London, 1896); Patrick Maume, 'Burke in Belfast: Thomas MacKnight, Gladstone and Liberal Unionism' in Alan O'Day & D.G. Boyce (eds), *Gladstone and Ireland: politics, religion and nationality in the Victorian age* (London, 2010). 3 Patrick Maume, 'Richard Barry O'Brien', *ODNB*.

foreign and domestic threats endangered not only the Anglo-Irish Union but the whole empire. Only a neo-Palmerstonian political realignment, with Whigs joining Conservatives to contain the anarchy unleashed by Gladstone, could allow the long-term assimilative forces of civilization to do their work.

After outlining how the *Mail* challenged Gladstone's moral professions by citing problematic aspects of his earlier career, anatomizing the theatrical techniques involved in his self-presentation to popular audiences, and subjecting him to stage-Irish ridicule to reinforce its portrayal of him as a mountebank outside the boundaries of civil discourse, the essay offers a chronological treatment of its response to Gladstone 1868–92. Over this period, the *Mail* moved from opposing Disestablishment on the basis that the state should uphold Protestantism because it was true and Catholicism was false, to arguing that the Irish policy of Gladstone's first administration was placing itself on the wrong side of the European *Kulturkampf*, to welcoming Disraeli as Palmerston's heir whose masterly inactivity in Ireland and reassertions of imperial prestige would restore normality after the downfall of Gladstonian recklessness in 1874. The *Mail*'s predictions that the internal dissensions of Butt's Home Rule League in the 1870s showed that Irish nationalism was dying and there would never be another nationalist movement on the scale of those led by O'Connell, and that after Gladstone's 1870 Land Act British legislators would never set a further precedent for interference with the rights of property, were decisively falsified by the Land War. In the early 1880s, the *Mail* accused Gladstone of connivance with Irish anarchy, demanded martial law in Ireland to save the loyalist 'garrison' from aboriginal barbarism, and repeated calls for Whigs to join the Tories. The *Mail* found solace in the firm rule of Lord Spencer (for which it gave Gladstone no credit). Having predicted as early as 1881 that Gladstone might adopt Home Rule, the *Mail* flung itself into the struggle when Gladstone's open conversion in 1885 brought the realignment it longed for. Constructive Unionism, the Parnell Split and Gladstone's failure to secure a substantial Liberal majority in 1892 gave the *Mail* cause for celebration, but in the long run its neo-Palmerstonianism evaded the social and political weaknesses of diehard Irish conservatism; studying the *Mail* serves as a reminder of how opposition to Gladstone's Irish policies tapped wider British fears about Gladstone, while its angry myopia points up the vision and courage of Gladstone's attempts to contain Irish discontent.

## THE HISTORY OF THE *EVENING MAIL*

The *Mail* was founded in 1823 as a Conservative paper opposing Catholic Emancipation. From the 1840s, the editors/proprietors were the novelist Joseph Sheridan Le Fanu (1814–73; his weekly *Warder* became the *Evening Mail*'s

weekly edition) and Dr Henry Maunsell (1806–79), a Dublin surgeon.[4] From
*c*.1860 its principal financial backer was George Tickell, Clontarf auctioneer,
furniture merchant and estate agent.[5] Maunsell's son James Poole Maunsell,
non-practising barrister and recent Trinity graduate, became editor and junior
proprietor on his father's death. He left Ireland in 1886 to edit a paper in Derby
but returned in 1888 to take over the *Daily Express* (the other Dublin ultra-Tory
paper). After Tickell's death (1892), Maunsell acquired the *Mail*.[6]

The fourth major shaper of the late Victorian *Mail* was George Ferdinand
Shaw (1821–99), a Fellow of Trinity prominent in Dublin Tory journalism.[7] In
1859, he was the first editor of the *Irish Times*. Shaw was principal *Evening Mail*
leader-writer in 1870 and still prominent at Tickell's funeral.[8] Much of the late
Victorian paper's core management and readership came of age during the Tithe
War of the 1830s (a concerted campaign in which tenants – mostly Catholic –
refused to pay tithes to the Church of Ireland; accompanied by widespread
police and popular violence, seen by conservatives as proof of the folly of
concessions to O'Connell), O'Connell's alliance with the Whig government of
Lord Melbourne (1835–41), and the Repeal campaign of the early 1840s. The
late Victorian *Mail* rarely mentions the subsequent Famine; when the Famine
dead were cited by Home Rulers, the *Mail* replied that the numbers would have
been greater without British assistance.[9] Its comments on emigration imply a
Malthusian interpretation.[10]

The paper's unashamed elitism, its aggressively provocative self-presentation
as defender of civilization (embodied in Trinity) against Celtic papist barbarians
and English Radical demagogues, probably owed much to Shaw. Where the *Irish
Times* appealed to a wider Protestant middle-class audience, the *Evening Mail*
(still more the *Warder*, circulating outside Dublin) called itself the paper of the
gentry, scorning English plebeians as well as Irish 'hordes'. It regretted the
Second Reform Act, though relieved that 'the more than questionable boon of a
£4 borough franchise' had not quite lowered the Irish franchise 'to the level of
the slums';[11] it raged against the Third Reform Act for subjecting Irish property
and intellect to 'a mud-hovel franchise'.[12]

For much of the 1850s and 1860s, the *Mail* endorsed Palmerston as
Protestant patriot, attacking the Irish Conservative Party as manipulated by
greedy lawyers and criticizing Disraeli's intrigues for Irish Catholic support.[13]
As Irish Unionists just before the First World War looked back to the Salisbury

---

4 4 Oct. 1879. Andrew O'Brien & Linde Lunny, 'Henry Maunsell', *Dictionary of Irish biography*
(Cambridge, 2009), say that Maunsell bought the *Mail* in 1858 and remained with it until 1870,
but his son's succession suggests that he retained a stake in it.   5 25 June 1892.   6 16 Jan. 1897.
7 Cathy Hayes, 'George Ferdinand Shaw', *DIB*.   8 Dermot James, *From the margins to the
centre: a history of the* Irish Times (Dublin, 2008), p. 5; 25 June 1892.   9 23 Jan. 1892.   10 10
Jan., 17 Jan. 1880.   11 20 June 1868.   12 3 Feb. 1883.   13 29 Feb. 1868. For conservative Irish
Protestant Palmerstonianism, see John Bew, *The glory of being Britons: civic Unionism in
nineteenth-century Belfast* (Dublin, 2009).

and Balfour administrations (1886–92, 1895–1905), and in the 1970s many older Ulster Unionists regarded their formative period in the Brookeborough era as 'normality' which might yet be regained, throughout the Gladstonian era the *Mail* invoked Palmerston's conservative Whig hegemony, upholding Anglican Protestantism and landlords' rights, and asserting imperial strength and European liberalism against ultramontane Catholic absolutism.

Others might argue that Fenianism and land agitation showed the instability of the Palmerstonian equilibrium; the *Mail* claimed the 1867 Fenian debacle showed the movement's inherent weakness, that market forces and emigration were resolving the land question, and that agitation and agrarian violence derived from heightened expectations stimulated by Gladstonian reforms. The solution to Ireland's problems lay in a neo-Palmerstonian alliance of Tories and conservative Whigs excluding Gladstone and ruling without reference to 'Irish Ultramontanes' and land agitators (the *Mail*'s optimism about the speed of such realignment reflected its failure to grasp how British Whigs saw Gladstone as bulwark against Radicalism).[14] The Palmerstonian legacy helps to explain why, until the Land War, the *Mail* asserted that history was on its side, that there would never be another mass nationalist movement resembling O'Connell's, that Disestablishment was the last kick of ultramontanism,[15] and that Gladstone's 1870 Land Act was futile.

## GLADSTONE AS SEEN BY THE *EVENING MAIL*

Gladstone's emergence as heir-apparent after Palmerston's death detached the *Mail* from Liberalism, though for some time it remained suspicious of Disraeli. Whatever the *Mail* may have thought of the young High Tory Gladstone, the Liberal leader attracted consistent contempt as a reckless, self-promoting demagogue – and, like other opponents, the *Mail* drew extensively on Gladstone's earlier changes of policy to support its accusations of hypocrisy. When the 1881 Land Act failed to compensate landlords for rent reductions, the *Mail* recalled Gladstone's youthful solicitude for compensating West India slave-holders such as his father.[16] When Gladstone advocated Irish Disestablishment, the *Mail* quoted his 1838 High Tory manifesto in defence of the Anglican confessional state, *The state in its relations with the church*, which said that dises-tablishing the Church of Ireland would purchase Irish Catholics' applause at the expense of their spiritual interests. Now this ever-changing 'Proteus of politics … wishes to purchase power by a sacrifice of … the "spiritual interests" of the Protestants, who for centuries have been the support of loyalty and order, and

**14** H.C.G. Mathew, *Gladstone, 1875–1898* (Oxford, 1995), pp 104–7. **15** 5 Sept. 1868. **16** 17 Feb. 1883.

the chief authors of what prosperity Ireland enjoys'.[17] Discussing the financial provisions of the first Home Rule Bill, the *Mail* recalled that Gladstone extended income tax to Ireland in 1853 and his emphasis as chancellor of the exchequer on indirect taxation weighed particularly heavily on Ireland.[18] When Gladstone provoked complaints from female Liberal activists by opposing woman suffrage in 1892, the *Mail*, itself anti-suffragist, noted that his 1866 rhetorical statement on parliamentary reform that there could be no objection to enfranchising 'fellow subjects, fellow Christians, our own flesh and blood' seemed to justify the suffragette demand.[19]

Gladstone's statement that Manchester and Clerkenwell (the killing of a Manchester policeman when Fenians rescued two imprisoned colleagues on 18 September 1867, the execution of three of the rescuers and the killing of twelve civilians, with many more injured, when Fenians trying to free two activists bombed Clerkenwell Prison in London on 13 December) helped to convince British public opinion of the necessity for Irish reform, was cited as proving that the reforms of Gladstone's first administration were driven by fear. When Irish-American dynamiters exploded bombs in London in 1883, a satirist in the *Mail* wondered

> iv the blowin up ov the wall ov Clarkinwell jail brought about sich changes in the policy ov the Prime Ministher fifteen years ago ... Are we to luk out for Home Rule, or Repale... 'Number Wan' [supposed leader of the Invincibles who assassinated the chief secretary and under-secretary in the Phoenix Park in 1882] offered a place in the ministhry ... Is Parnell to be made chief sakketary, and [JJ] O'Kelly [Parnellite MP with IRB connections] sint over to the castel ... as the nixt criminal investigathor?[20]

Writing for a select upper-class readership, the *Mail* ridiculed the techniques whereby Gladstone projected himself to popular audiences. It scornfully anatomized and parodied Gladstone's deployment of actors' and preachers' techniques and mannerisms,[21] including such symbols as the tree-felling axe (fig. 5.4), the nickname 'Grand Old Man', and easily assimilable slogans (in 1892, the *Mail* commented on the slogan 'Remember Mitchelstown' (adopted by Gladstone after police fired on demonstrators at Mitchelstown, Co. Cork, in September 1887, killing three men) (fig. 5.5) – 'In writing a high-class magazine article, Mr Gladstone dispenses with the artful aid of apt alliteration, but when addressing the Irish masses he knows its value').[22] Its review of his *Bulgarian*

17 21 Mar., 28 Mar. 1868.   18 19 June 1880.   19 Richard Shannon, *Gladstone: heroic minister, 1865–1898* (London, 1999), p. 14.   20 31 Mar. 1883.   21 Glynne Wickham, 'Gladstone, oratory and the theatre' in P.J. Jagger (ed.), *Gladstone* (London, 1998), pp 1–32.   22 16 Apr. 1892.

*horrors* pamphlet presents Gladstone as a cheap showman 'from whom his constituents have extorted this profession by an express demand for something "sensational" ... Mr Gladstone is the real stage-Minister ... The strong epithets are the roll of back-scene thunder. ... He is very careful of his words when it comes to a point – very profuse of them when he is scattering fireballs in the air to dazzle the gaping crowd with their false and fitful flash'.[23]

The vehemence of the *Mail*'s anti-Gladstonian invective conveyed its view that, like Irish nationalists, he stood outside the honour community entitled to the normal courtesies of political life. The most forthright expressions of this contempt occur in a satirical column in the *Warder* from 1875 by the loyalist cartoonist J.R. Clegg.[24] These dialect letters between Barney Burke of Glasnevin and his London friend Christy Cullen were partly exempt from journalistic decorum (they note Queen Victoria's personal hatred for Gladstone, decorously unmentioned in editorials).[25] In 1890, commenting on one of Gladstone's railway speaking tours:

> The Grand Old Man reminded me at times of Henry Irvine [*sic*], the actor, doin' 'Yougin Arm', ['The dream of Eugene Aram' by Thomas Hood] ... somehow he doesn't convince as much as he thrills you.[26]

From 1883, Clegg illustrated these letters. An early vignette on the debates over the atheist Radical MP Charles Bradlaugh, whose election to the House of Commons in 1880 was ruthlessly exploited by Conservative MPs to divide Liberals and present Gladstone as defender of atheism, blasphemy and birth control, shows 'Professor Gladstoni' [nicknamed by the Trinity College Conservative MP Edward Gibson, whose anti-Bradlaugh speeches roused the *Mail* to ecstasy][27] supervised by the Devil, playing a three-card trick with the Bible, Bradlaugh's paper the *National Reformer*, and the birth control tract *Fruits of philosophy*, which Bradlaugh disseminated (fig. 5.1).[28] Between 1886 and 1891, annual cartoon selections appeared as *Barney Burke's Diorama*.[29]

## THE STRUGGLE OVER DISESTABLISHMENT

Early in 1868, as Disraeli became prime minister, Gladstone proposed resolutions committing the Commons to Irish Disestablishment. The *Mail* denounced Gladstone as a puppet 'of the Roman Catholic episcopacy and a democratic

**23** 9 Sept. 1876. **24** Clegg obituary, *Irish Times*, 10 July 1922. **25** 25 Feb. 1882. **26** 8 Mar. 1890; for Gladstone & Irving, see Wickham, 'Gladstone, oratory and the theatre' in Jagger (ed.), *Gladstone*, pp 26–31. **27** For example, 26 June, 10 July, 7 Aug., 6 Nov. 1880; 28 Apr. 1883. **28** 19 May 1883. **29** National Library of Ireland has 1886 and 1887 editions bound as one volume; for later issues see advertisement 4 Jan. 1890.

PROF. GLADSTONI:- "No deception
here, ladies and gentlemen."

5.1

THE "RALE" STAR OF THE COLLECTION.

THIS fine paintin is self-explanatory, as Pat Hogan remarked when he appeared with a
black eye afther marryin' the Widow Mahloon.
The picther shows how matthers stood in the Spring of the year, when the ground was
bein' levelled for Home Rule.

POLKY BY THE ORKESTHER—"*Jump Jim Crow.*"

5.2

**5.1** The *Evening Mail* contrasts Gladstone's outspoken religious beliefs with his defence of
the right of the atheist and birth-control advocate Charles Bradlaugh to sit in parliament
(from the *Warder & Weekly Evening Mail*, 19 May 1883; all images (figs 5.1–5.8)
reproduced courtesy of the National Library of Ireland).

**5.2** Gladstone's 1886 Home Rule conversion (from *Barney Burke's Diorama, 1886*).

**5.3** The new 'King William' crosses the Boyne in the wrong direction to force Home Rule
on Ulster. The *Evening Mail* hoped Ulster Unionist resistance would preserve the whole
island for the Union (from *Barney Burke's Diorama, 1886*).

**5.4** Gladstone's image as axe-wielding woodman assailing the 'upas tree' of Irish
misgovernment, and the contrast between his repressing nationalist agitators in the early
1880s and supporting agitation against the post-1886 Unionist government, were frequent
*Evening Mail* targets (from *Barney Burke's Diorama, 1887*).

CROSSING THE BOYNE.

THE Battle commenced in rale earnest, and William of Hawarden put on his uniform,
mounted his charger, and crossed the Boyne. His war-steed was restive, as you may
persave, and throbble loomed on all sides. The whole civilized world watched his equesthrian
manoovers with a curious eye.

VIOLIN SOLO (Dhram Obligatto)—"*The Boyne Watther.*"

5.3

"UNEMPLOYED."

THE latther end of the year saw the Axe-Primear out of work.
There was noisy meetins of the unemployed in Thrafalgar Square, London.
Mr. Gladstone, who was very hard up, riz a little industhry at Hawarden, in the shape
of blocks of wood, from timber felled by himself, which he offered at eighteen pence the fut.
But thrade was dull, and disthress stared him in the face.
On his thravels he keen across a Notice Board, as above, and let us hope that there's
work in store for him.
If he should get the job, it will delight the hearts of the imprisoned Nashinalists, who
ought to be aisier on a Hawarden Plank Bed than on any other.

POLKY BY THE ORKESTHER—"*Yankee Doodle buck a saw.*"

5.4

BARNEY BURKE ON THINGS IN GENERAL.

THE BLACKTHORN.

CHRISTY CULLEN ON THINGS IN GENERAL.

THE FIRE ESCAPE.

5·5

5·6

**5.5** The *Evening Mail* presents Gladstone as reducing himself to the level of a stick-waving stage-Irishman by supporting resistance to law enforcement during the Plan of Campaign land agitation (from the *Warder & Weekly Evening Mail*, 7 June 1890).

**5.6** The impact of the O'Shea divorce case: Gladstone discovers Parnell surreptitiously leaving Mrs O'Shea's bedroom via the fire escape (from the *Warder & Weekly Evening Mail*, 22 November 1890).

**5.7** The struggle continues: the new Parnellite leader John Redmond challenges the 'giant' Gladstone, who crouches within his castle holding 'the axe which killed the uncrowned king' (from the *Warder & Weekly Evening Mail*, 20 February 1892).

**5.8** Anticipating the 1892 general election, the *Evening Mail* portrays nationalist Ireland as a spoilt brat rejecting Unionist economic reforms and 'crying for the Grand old moon' of Gladstonian Home Rule (from the *Warder & Weekly Evening Mail*, 27 February 1892).

BARNEY BURKE ON THINGS IN GENERAL.

"JACK THE GIANT KILLER."

CHRISTY CULLEN ON THINGS IN GENERAL.

THE SPOILT BOY.

5·7

5·8

faction of a lower type than the Chartists of 1848'.[30] The *Mail* equally distrusted Disraeli and his chief secretary, Lord Mayo, heavily involved in Disraeli's earlier attempts to secure Irish Catholic support.[31] The *Mail* protested that Disraeli's favoured policy, concurrent endowment, was worse than disendowment, since it meant subsidizing Irish churches in proportion to the size of their flocks.[32] Gladstone's resolutions won an unexpectedly large majority; the *Mail* blamed Disraeli for alienating Dissenters by temporizing with Ultramontanes.[33] The *Mail* complained that Conservative ministers opposed disestablishment as inexpedient, not because Protestantism was true and popery false.[34] Irish Protestants should choose outspoken Protestant MPs rather than Conservative loyalists.[35] The *Mail* endorsed William Johnston of Ballykilbeg's Orange-populist revolt in Belfast,[36] while hoping the newly enfranchised British 'middle and humbler classes' would 'support ... the constitution ... They cherish our Reformation traditions'.[37]

Replaying 1830s struggles, the *Mail* highlighted pronouncements by the veteran Liverpool Tory populist cleric Hugh M'Neile,[38] who had campaigned fervently against Whig concessions to Catholicism in the 1830s when Gladstone himself was a Tory, and reprinted letters in English newspapers by Revd Robert J. McGhee, who in June 1835 had denounced Maynooth at a London meeting with Gladstone on the platform.[39] The argument that attacking Church of Ireland property led inexorably to attacking Irish landlords, then to assaulting property in Britain as well as Ireland, and finally to secession, was put forward as in the 1830s.[40] The *Mail* hoped that a few Liberal dissentients heralded Whig revolt.[41] It rebuked opponents of the candidacy of Disraeli's Irish solicitor-general – a former Palmerstonian – for a Trinity parliamentary seat. 'Were Lord Palmerston now alive, would his defence of the Irish church be rejected?'[42] It hoped a strong Conservative opposition might better safeguard the Church than a weak Conservative government seeking ultramontane support.[43]

After Gladstone's election victory, the *Mail* claimed that the struggle was only beginning. It blamed Liberal gains in Ulster boroughs (Johnston and the Liberal Thomas McClure took both Belfast seats) on Lord Mayo's unwillingness to conciliate Orangeism and endorse Johnston.[44] Since Gladstone spent the

---

**30** 24 Oct. 1868.  **31** 15 Aug. 1868. Andrew Shields, *The Irish Conservative Party, 1852–1868: land, politics and religion* (Dublin, 2007); K.T. Hoppen, 'Tories, Catholics and the general election of 1859', *Historical Journal*, 13 (1970), 48–67.  **32** 4 Apr., 11 Apr., 13 June 1868.  **33** 2 May 1868.  **34** 11 Apr. 1868.  **35** 30 May, 15 Aug. 1868.  **36** 26 Sept., 10 Oct., 17 Oct. 1868.  **37** 4 July, 2 May 1868.  **38** 1 Aug. 1868; see also 22 May 1869; John Wolffe, 'Hugh Boyd McNeile', *ODNB*; Tom Kelley & Linde Lunney, 'Hugh Boyd McNeile', *DIB*.  **39** 15 Aug. 1868, 24 Oct.; 15 May 1869; J.L. Porter, *Life and Times of Henry Cooke, D.D, LL.D*, 3rd ed. (Belfast, 1875), p. 244; John Wolffe 'Robert James M'Ghee', *ODNB*.  **40** 21 Mar., 28 Mar. 1868; 2 Jan., 27 Mar. 1869; see Douglas Kanter, *The making of British Unionism, 1740–1848: politics, government and the Anglo-Irish constitutional relationship* (Dublin, 2009), pp 169–71.  **41** 22 Aug., 29 Aug. 1868.  **42** 24 Oct.; see also 12 Sept., 31 Oct., 7 Nov. 1868.  **43** 7 Nov. 1868.  **44** 28 Nov. 1868.

election campaigning in Lancashire, the loss of his seat there and other Liberal defeats in the region were attributed to a nascent Protestant reaction that would spread as Gladstone revealed specific proposals and Church campaigners enlightened British opinion.[45] In retrospect, the Conservative gains in the traditionally Liberal boroughs of London and Westminster (where John Stuart Mill was defeated by the newsagent W.H. Smith, a former Palmerstonian) are seen as the first sign of the realignment that led large sections of previously Liberal middle-class opinion towards Conservatism in the 1870s and 1880s. The *Mail* hoped that the defeat of 'Mill, the man of legislative fancies innumerable' indicated an immediate Protestant backlash that might save the Irish Church if the House of Lords forced a second election.

Minimizing the extent of Gladstone's mandate on disestablishment, the *Mail* predicted a Palmerstonian rebellion dissipating Gladstone's majority, as with the 1866 Reform Bill.[46] When Gladstone unveiled his proposals, the *Mail* protested that they surreptitiously endowed Romanism by diverting Church funds to Catholic institutions.[47] Though only a few Whig stragglers revolted, the *Mail* hoped that the committee stage might detach Scottish Liberal MPs;[48] when the Scots 'disgraced themselves by voting for Maynooth',[49] it urged the Lords to force a second general election.[50] The final debacle, when Lord Cairns [Conservative leader in the Lords, formerly MP for Belfast] and Disraeli threw over the more determined Lord Salisbury and compromised with Gladstone, was the crowning betrayal.[51]

During the Disestablishment campaign, the *Mail* noted anger against the Union by Protestants who previously believed it was unchangeable fundamental legislation and that the Irish Church, guaranteed in the Union, shared its inviolability.[52] It reported a speaker reciting Gladstone's prediction (*The state in its relations with the church*) that if the Irish Church were disestablished, Irish Protestants might not resist Repeal; it stated that, had Irish Protestants supported O'Connell, Repeal could not have been resisted.[53] Dr Maunsell considered Butt's nascent Home Rule movement but found it dominated by 'Ultramontanes'.[54]

WAGING *KULTURKAMPF*: THE *EVENING MAIL*
AND GLADSTONE'S FIRST MINISTRY

Having predicted 'a Land Bill of an extravagant description, intended more to consolidate the political interests of the priesthood than to serve the tenantry ... when the House of Commons, having completed the robbery of the Protestants

45 28 Nov. 1868.   46 14 Nov., 5 Dec. 1868.   47 13 Mar. 1868.   48 28 Nov., 27 Mar. 1868. 49 8 May 1869.   50 3 Apr., 24 Apr., 5 June, 12 June, 19 June, 10 July 1869.   51 24 July, 31 July 1868.   52 18 July 1868; 13 Mar., 5 June 1869.   53 20 Mar. 1869.   54 14 Feb., 21 Feb.1880.

of Ireland, shall find time to rob the landlords thereof'[55] and blaming Gladstone for agrarian shootings, which it compared to the 1830s Tithe War,[56] the *Mail* attacked the 1870 Land Act, suggesting that the famous rebuke to Irish landlords 'Property has duties as well as rights', uttered by the 1830s Whig administrator Thomas Drummond, now read 'Property has all duties and no rights'.[57]

During the Disestablishment debates, the *Mail* contrasted Gladstone's actions as 'Cardinal Cullen's puppet' with Ultramontane defeats in Italy, Spain[58] and Austria.[59] It subsequently argued that Disestablishment had encouraged ultramontane clerical aggression against the civil rights of the Catholic citizenry; if supposed religious equality were not to produce clerical tyranny, the state would have to uphold the rights of the laity by waging a *Kulturkampf* resembling that undertaken by Bismarck. The *Mail* presented the lawsuits following the dismissal of Fr Robert O'Keeffe as parish priest of Callan, Co. Kilkenny, for suing his bishop in a civil court,[60] and the prosecution of priests and a bishop for intimidation at the 1873 Galway by-election[61] as the opening battles of such a conflict.[62] The crowning enormity was the prospect of a Catholic university. 'The Church, not the state, would then define the conditions under which men should become, not merely theologians and priests, but physicians, lawyers, apothecaries, engineers and schoolmasters'.[63] The rejection of Gladstone's 1873 university proposals by Cullen showed the futility of accommodating 'ignoran-tine' interests.

By 1873, the *Mail* accepted Disraeli as Palmerston's heir. After Gladstone's 1873 resignation, the paper lamented Disraeli's refusal to form a Tory-Whig coalition.[64] The *Mail* was reassured by Disraeli's declaration that he would not depend on Irish Catholic MPs.[65] During the 1874 election, the *Mail* feared that Gladstone's promise to abolish income tax might win him support, and wanted Disraeli to match it.[66] The *Mail* predicted that the Conservative landslide would exclude Gladstone permanently;[67] a strong Tory government would pacify Ireland in Palmerstonian style, undisturbed by factious reforms.[68] It claimed that almost the only defender of Gladstone was the atheist and radical George Jacob Holyoake, ironically predicting that 'Mr Holyoake will occupy a high place in the next Gladstonian administration, at whatever distant date that meteoric govern-ment may flash into an eccentric existence'.[69]

The *Mail* celebrated Disraeli as upholder of empire, contrasting his expendi-ture to deter enemies and open new markets[70] with Gladstone's acquiescence in Russian expansion.[71] It thought Queen Victoria's assuming the title Empress of

55  24 Apr.; see also 6 Mar. 1869.   56  9 Jan., 13 Mar., 1 May 1869.   57  4 Jan., 18 Jan. 1873. 58  3 Oct. 1868.   59  25 July 1868.   60  4 Jan., 31 May 1873; Colin Barr, *The European culture wars in Ireland: the Callan schools affair, 1868–81* (Dublin, 2010).   61  22 Feb. 1874.   62  22 Feb. 1873.   63  8 Feb. 1873.   64  15 Mar. 1873.   65  22 Mar. 1873.   66  31 Jan. 1874.   67  7 Feb., 14 Feb. 1874.   68  28 Feb. 1874; 1 Jan., 12 Feb. 1876; 20 Jan. 1877.   69  14 Mar. 1874.   70  1 Jan. 1876.   71  20 May 1876.

India misjudged,[72] but such assertiveness was preferable to Gladstone's miserly caution.[73]

The internal squabbles of Butt's Home Rule movement and its clashes with neo-Fenians showed the incoherence and pending extinction of Irish nationalism.[74] Calls by Home Rulers and Liberals for land legislation were dismissed as demagoguery; their authors must realize parliament would never sanction such an attack on property and political economy,[75] tenant farmers should note labourers now made similar demands[76] (the *Mail* attributed an upsurge of trade union activity, sometimes violent, in Britain to Gladstone's agitations).[77]

Gladstone's 1874–5 pamphlets against papal infallibility prompted mocking satisfaction over Cullen denouncing 'his bosom friend of other days'.[78] By March 1876, however, the *Mail* suspected Gladstone's retirement was temporary. 'Ultramontanes' were trying to

> induce Mr Gladstone to give up felling trees and writing infallible pamphlets ... Let him put out the Conservatives, and he shall have the plenitude of absolution ... at the head of the allied armies of Rome and Manchester, with Major O'Gorman [obese obstructionist MP for Waterford City] for first lieutenant and Mr Butt as trumpeter ... The readiness of the Ultramontanists to accept Mr Gladstone's perilous aid – after all that he has done and written – is truly the most humiliating exhibition at once of Ultramontane cunning and weakness yet witnessed.[79]

Gladstone's Bulgarian atrocities campaign brought comparisons to the eighteenth-century Protestant demagogue Lord George Gordon and Wat Tyler (leader of the 1381 Peasants' Revolt). Gladstone should raise his concerns in parliament, not at public meetings. 'Are the Hackney operatives the judges in such a matter to which one who has felt the weight of office should refer its decision?'[80] While admitting Turkey's guilt, the *Mail* complained that Russia, by stirring up Balkan insurgency, provoked the horrors,[81] and that Gladstone presented the Russian war party as faultless[82] and used language implying holy war against Islam.[83] It noted that Disraeli's much-criticized statement that Gladstone's pamphlet was worse than the Bulgarian atrocities meant that by misleading Russia into believing that Britain would not support Turkey, Gladstone might cause European war.[84] The *Mail* noted that by having his pamphlet translated into Russian, Gladstone promoted such an impression.[85]

**72** 18 Mar. 1876.   **73** 28 Feb. 1874.   **74** 22 Apr., 8 July, 30 Sept. 1876.   **75** 15 Jan., 4 Mar., 18 Mar. 1876.   **76** 7 Oct. 1876.   **77** 11 Jan., 24 May 1873.   **78** 6 May 1876.   **79** 11 Mar. 1876. **80** 2 Sept. 1876.   **81** 9 Sept. 1876.   **82** 4 Nov. 1876; 27 Jan. 1877.   **83** 9 Sept., 16 Sept., 30 Sept. 1876.   **84** 23 Sept., 7 Oct. 1876.   **85** 21 Oct., 18 Nov. 1876; see Mathew, *Gladstone, 1875–1898*, p. 25; Shannon, *Gladstone: heroic minister*, p. 188 n.

THE IRISH 'JEHAD': THE *EVENING MAIL* ON THE
GLADSTONIAN RESPONSE TO THE LAND WAR

The *Mail* initially predicted that the Land League would soon subside.[86] By
January 1880, it acknowledged that 'social war' had broken out, but the
Conservative government would crush 'the miserable retrograde policy that
would sever Ireland from England, and entail an inheritance of barbarism on the
former country and weakness on the latter'.[87] It predicted a large Conservative
majority in the 1880 general election,[88] and was dismayed at Gladstone's
triumph. Predicting imperial surrender, legislation against property and concessions to Irish agitation, the *Mail* hoped that Gladstone might be too busy
imposing misguided reforms on Scots 'to promote the revolutionary forces that
are now demoralizing the Irish peasantry and seeking to disintegrate the empire
by setting up an "independent" Irish parliament'.[89]

The *Mail* zealously opposed Gladstone's July 1880 Compensation for
Disturbance Bill, claiming that 'a radical triumvirate' (Gladstone, Forster and
Bright) imposed it on Whig ministers. It welcomed the emergence of 'a Whig
cave' of dissident MPs during the Commons debate, hoped Whig defections
would bring a speedy election,[90] and eulogized the Lords' rejection of the bill:

> The masses are pretty well enfranchized, and they are beginning to
> use their franchises as a shortcut to the acquisition of their neigh-
> bours' property. The old functions of the Whig party have
> disappeared. They must in future be conservative.[91]

To read the *Mail* during 1881–3 is to realize how fiercely Irish landlords and
their allies reacted to Land War violence. Claims that agitators and clerics were
unrepresentative of an Irish population increasingly acquiescent in the union
were replaced by eulogies of an embattled English garrison facing a murderous
'Jehad',[92] whose existence derived from 'the patronage extended by Mr
Gladstone to such manifestations of popular feeling as the Clerkenwell and
Manchester outrages'.[93] A satiric sketch (parodying Gladstone's orchestrating
an international anti-Turkish naval demonstration to help the Montenegrins)[94]
depicted the Sultan instructing a Turkish fleet to demonstrate off Ireland to
deter 'Celtic' atrocities against 'Saxons' and demanding that 'Grand Vizier
Gladstone' deploy the English-born Valentine Baker Pasha, who as a Turkish
officer protected Armenians from massacre by Kurds.[95] Chief Secretary W.E.

---

86 4 Oct. 1879. For fuller discussion of *Evening Mail* Land War coverage, see Patrick Maume,
'The *Dublin Evening Mail* and pro-landlord conservatism in the age of Gladstone and Parnell',
*Irish Historical Studies* (pending, 2011).  87 13 Mar. 1880.  88 31 Jan. 1880.  89 10 Apr. 1880.
90 17 July 1880.  91 4 Sept. 1880.  92 9 July, 26 Nov., 10 Dec. 1881.  93 13 Nov. 1880.
94 25 Sept. 1880; Shannon, *Gladstone: heroic minister*, pp 265–8.  95 16 Oct. 1880.

Forster was accused of passivity (while nationalists denounced Forster as a tyrant).[96]

The 1881 Land Act was denounced as flouting political economy, 'which Mr Gladstone once championed so ably, but now thinks fit only for the inhabitants of Jupiter and Saturn'.[97] By enacting 'the tenant may put the landlord's indulgence up to auction', Gladstone merely allowed tenants to be rack-rented by moneylenders;[98] the act was deliberately obscure to conceal abandonment of the 'final' principles of the 1870 act.[99] The *Mail* warned that this would endanger property rights in Britain as well as in Ireland: 'if employers are not free to dismiss unsatisfactory employees, there is an end to the profitable management of business, and to this end we shall quickly come if a beginning be made with employers who happen to be landlords'.[1]

The arrest of Parnell was attributed to British public opinion;[2] however Gladstone yearned for Parnellite votes, he knew he would lose English support by temporizing with them.[3] The *Mail* claimed that Gladstone tolerated the agitation to pass his Land Bill, then could not control it.[4] With Gladstone, the Radical ministers Bright and Chamberlain were accused of blocking Forster's attempts to restore order.[5] The *Mail* recalled Palmerston's prediction that Gladstone would destroy the Liberal Party.[6] From April 1882, the *Mail* demanded military reconquest, martial law, Cromwellian dictatorship and wholesale clearances.[7]

After the Phoenix Park Murders, the *Mail* hoped that Gladstone might fall if the opposition were more aggressive.[8] The slaughter by moonlighters of a family of smallholders at Maamtrasna in Connemara (17/18 August 1882) was declared the crowning 'success' of governmental 'devotion to the cause of disorder and encouragement of the policy of murder'.

Just as the *Mail* claimed that the Land Act threatened property in Britain when urging an anti-Gladstonian realignment of Whigs with Tories, it linked the Kilmainham Treaty (the informal understanding between Parnell and Gladstone to secure the former's release from internment in May 1882) to wider imperial retreat:

> Mr Gladstone has surrendered under as disgraceful circumstances as he surrendered to Count Karolyi [apologized to the Austrian foreign minister for denouncing Austria during the 1880 election campaign][9] to Ayoub Khan [in Afghanistan], and to the Dutch Boers ... the result will soon be felt by movements in various parts of the empire.[10]

---

**96** 25 Sept., 27 Nov. 1880; 9 Apr. 1881.   **97** 16 Apr., 11 June 1881.   **98** 16 Apr. 1881.   **99** 23 Apr. 1881.   **1** 21 May 1881.   **2** 15 Oct., 22 Oct. 1881.   **3** 16 Oct. 1880.   **4** 18 Feb. 1882. **5** 4 June 1881.   **6** 31 July 1880; see Richard Shannon, *Gladstone: Peel's inheritor, 1809–1865* (London, 1982), p. 556.   **7** 8 Apr., 15 Apr. 1882.   **8** 13 May, 27 May, 1 July 1882.   **9** 15 May 1880; Shannon, *Gladstone: heroic minister*, pp 243, 249.   **10** 6 May, 13 May 1882.

Only Irish loyalist generals – Roberts' victory in Afghanistan and Wolseley defeating Arabi in Egypt[11] – preserved the empire, incidentally vindicating Disraeli's imperial policies so denounced by Gladstone.[12] Having supported evacuation of the Transvaal because Gladstone's election commitments made it inevitable,[13] the *Mail* presented Boer defeats of British troops before withdrawal as Gladstonian surrender.[14] It highlighted anti-Gladstone demonstrations by British settlers. At Grahamstown in the Eastern Cape, a transparency showed the British Lion shot by Boers and Gladstone tossed on the horns of a bull named 'John'; a Gladstone effigy was tried for treason and burned.[15]

'The Pretoria convention is as unfortunate a performance as the Kilmainham Treaty' commented the *Mail*, when Forster exposed Boer retaliation against native allies of the British. Since military expeditions were expensive, the natives were compensated – unlike 'the hunted and shot-down Irish landlords'.[16] Forster protested that failure to protect natives undermined imperial credibility, risking withdrawal from the Cape and India. The *Mail* suggested Parnellites added 'from Ireland'.[17]

The *Mail* raged that British opinion was fatally unaware of the extent to which Irish loyalists represented the first line of defence against anarchy. 'Until an English lord was butchered under the eyes of Her Majesty's representative', Gladstone allowed 'loyal and law-abiding Irishmen' to be 'mulcted of their properties, humiliated in their social standing, pursued with calumny in his parliamentary and platform utterances … flung naked and defenceless to the Irish thug'.[18] The government restricted explosives after dynamite attacks in London; the *Mail* thought Sackville Street and Trinity College might have been destroyed without triggering such firmness.[19] While the *Mail* continued to attack Gladstone after 1882, it eulogized Lord Spencer for pressurizing Gladstone into firm administration of the law.[20] Criticism of death sentences passed by packed juries under Spencer was dismissed as temporizing with murder: 'five times that number were executed [by assassins] … from the murder of Lord Mountmorres [25 September 1880] to the summer of last year [1882]'.[21]

## GLADSTONIAN HOME RULE

Reporting Gladstone's one-day visit to Dublin of 29 August 1880, the *Mail* noted that as he left Christ Church a cheering crowd cried 'the next Land Bill … Home Rule next'.[22] As early as October 1881, the *Mail* openly speculated that

11 3 June, 17 June, 29 July, 16 Sept., 11 Nov., 9 Dec. 1882.   12 12 Aug. 1882.   13 29 Jan. 1881. 14 5 Mar., 26 Mar. 1881.   15 14 May 1881.   16 17 Mar. 1883.   17 24 Mar. 1883.   18 27 Jan. 1883.   19 14 Apr. 1883.   20 30 Dec. 1882; 14 Apr., 7 July 1883.   21 27 Jan. 1883.   22 4 Sept. 1880.

Gladstone might turn Home Ruler, noting an admission by Hartington's secretary that Gladstone contemplated remodelling Irish government, and

> a significant passage in the premier's speech at the Guildhall in which he expressed his readiness to concede to Ireland the most complete system of self government ... consistent with the unimpaired supremacy of the imperial parliament. Mr Gladstone's views of what constitutes this supremacy may prove as elastic as his views about the Irish Land Question between 1870 and 1881.[23]

In 1882, Clegg satirically predicted that Biggar would be chief secretary and Davitt opposition leader when Gladstone conceded Home Rule.[24]

Gladstone's 1886 public conversion to Home Rule was called an electoral dodge inspired by eighty-five Irish votes in parliament (fig. 5.2).[25] The *Mail* mocked his resistance to the 1887 Crimes Act as complicity with moonlighters[26] and his claims that Balfour's treatment of nationalist prisoners outdid repression of Neapolitan liberals by 'King Bomba' (denounced by Gladstone in 1851) because the Neapolitans were subjected to legal formalities, noting how Gladstone overlooked this parallel when interning Land Leaguers and supporting Spencer's tribunals (figs 5.4, 5.5).[27] It mocked Gladstone's appeal to the masses against the classes as implying education and taxpaying 'militate against the voter's political sagacity and moral integrity'.[28]

Much British Gladstonian support, the *Mail* noted, reflected hostility rather than love of Ireland and was motivated by a desire to 'send home working people who compete with them'.[29] 'Spalding labourers and Durham miners ... should be shown that their own condition will not be benefited but rather impaired by turning Ireland into a Hayti; that "the Irish question" will not be got rid of but very much aggravated by Mr Gladstone's Home Rule nostrum'.[30] Even if immediate anarchy were avoided, the *Mail* argued, a Home Rule Ireland would find it had less rather than more control over its destiny; a subordinate legislature must obey British decisions it could not influence, as in the eighteenth century.[31] This, it suggested, implied that Gladstone himself was less benevolent towards Ireland than he claimed. Recalling 'the enormous tribute which Mr Gladstone fixed in 1886 as the price of the rickety constitution he proposed to confer upon us', the *Mail* concluded that 'there is not an old gentleman in Great Britain who has a keener sense of the value of a bawbee'.[32]

Political economy being a lost cause, Balfour's 'constructive Unionist' measures were defended by Gladstonian precedent:

---

23 29 Oct. 1881; see also 18 Feb. 1882.  24 4 Nov. 1882.  25 18 Jan. 1890.  26 1 Nov. 1890.  27 24 May 1890; Shannon, *Gladstone: heroic minister*, pp 431, 436, 445.  28 8 Mar., 27 Sept., 20 Dec. 1890.  29 16 Jan. 1892.  30 6 Feb. 1892.  31 9 Jan. 1892.  32 5 July 1890.

> The land legislation of Mr Gladstone [supposes] the Irish tenant is a
> weak, improvident creature who must not be held fast to his bargains
> ... but must be protected from competition and from his own land
> hunger ... so we are in favour of keeping the poor Western cottier
> alive by alms, and imperial alms in the first place, even though he be
> foolish enough to live and breed on a barren moor or rock, and trust
> to a precarious root for his sustenance.[33]

Reviving Irish share prices were attributed to firm law enforcement, echoing the
Palmerstonian era: 'Ireland in the last half-century has been one of the most
progressive countries in Europe. No one will wish to arrest this progress except
to put money in his purse with the help of a Thieves' Kitchen in College
Green'.[34] Ulster showed the economic fruits of Protestantism and loyalty. A
*Mail* cartoon represented 'Paddy' as a spoiled brat spurning Unionist remedial
legislation: 'I'd sooner have moonshine, I want the Moon! Gimme the Grand
Old Moo-oo-oon!' (fig. 5.8).[35]

These professions of constructive Unionism coexisted with continuing insistence that the Irish masses were barbarians unfit for self-government, and that
surrender in Ireland would foreshadow a wider failure of governmental
willpower, presaging wider imperial downfall. The *Mail* mocked the Irish-born
London barrister and Gladstonian MP Charles Russell (later Lord Russell of
Killowen) for complaining that Salisbury sneered at Indians. Would Russell give
*them* Home Rule?

> They are not half so contrary to civilization and enlightenment as the
> majority of the Irish popular constituencies; but still, they are utterly
> unfit for the working of a free constitution, and the first use they
> would make of their constitutional powers would be to expel the
> British and drift back into the condition of anarchy and civil war and
> ever-recurring famine in which we found them. Still more swift would
> be the return of the Irish to their tribal savagery.[36]

### THE LAST BATTLES AND THE LIMITS OF VICTORY

Throughout 1890, the *Mail* mocked Parnellite attempts to ignore the pending
case of O'Shea versus O'Shea and Parnell, suggesting that Gladstone was
revising his well-known hostility to divorce (fig. 5.6).[37] Expressing surprise after
the divorce case came to court that Gladstonian Nonconformists exempted Irish

---

33 30 Aug. 1890.   34 18 June 1892.   35 27 Feb. 1892.   36 13 Feb. 1892.   37 4 Jan., 11 Jan.,
18 Jan. 1890.

agitators from nine commandments but balked at adultery,[38] it expressed regret at Parnell's imminent political demise since his residual conservatism might have temporarily restrained 'the brigand legislators of College Green'.[39]

The *Mail* had assumed that after his divorce court humiliation Parnell would go quietly; his resistance to deposition was celebrated with satiric glee. Parnell's description of Gladstone as 'an unrivalled sophist'[40] was cited by the *Mail*, while it responded to *Freeman's Journal* denunciation of anti-Parnellites' throwing lime in Parnell's eye by recalling that the *Freeman* had justified using vitriol to resist evictions.[41] With Parnell safely dead, the *Mail* praised 'that typical landlord, Protestant and specimen of the great Anglo-Irish race'.[42] The new Parnellite leader John Redmond was portrayed as Jack the Giant Killer challenging Gladstone (fig. 5.7).[43] The *Mail* took up the Parnellite claim that Anti-Parnellites sold themselves to Gladstone for jobs.[44] It added that the Parnellites were no better, and only fought on after their chief's death to make Gladstone buy them off with a share of official appointments.[45]

The Parnell Split reinforced the Unionist message that the Irish Party did not, as Gladstone maintained, represent a definite and fixed nationality, but a confederation of pre-political self-seekers.[46] The *Mail* emphasized a more fundamental division when denying that Ireland possessed a settled national will: 'Ulster is imperialist rather than Irish, and would cut its connection with the three southern provinces tomorrow, were a parliament set up in College Green' (fig. 5.3).[47]

As the 1892 election approached, the *Evening Mail* characteristically worried that the Liberals' Newcastle Programme of social reforms heralded an alliance of British and Irish demagogues against property. The *Mail* feared the 'new Unionism' of Ben Tillett (leader of the great London dock strike of 1889). 'Mr Tillett and his friends are quite prepared to sacrifice the minority in Ireland … if only the majority will assist them … to make ducks and drakes of the wealth and commercial prosperity of England'.[48]

The *Mail* maintained that a Gladstonian majority derived from many different promises lacked a mandate for any single measure.[49] The *Mail* endorsed Salisbury's statement that Ulster Unionists would be justified in resisting such a pseudo-mandate by force of arms.[50] When the 1892 election campaign opened, the *Mail* predicted a narrow Liberal majority, dependent on Irish votes, too weak to force Home Rule on the Lords;[51] and so it proved.

The defeat of the second Home Rule Bill in 1893, the political demise of Gladstone, and the Unionist landslide at the 1895 general election seemed to

38 29 Nov., 6 Dec. 1890.  39 22 Nov. 1890.  40 13 Dec. 1890.  41 20 Dec. 1890.  42 30 Jan. 1892.  43 20 Feb. 1892.  44 27 Dec. 1890, 16 Jan., 23 Jan. 1892.  45 2 Jan. 1892.  46 11 June 1892.  47 27 Jan. 1883.  48 14 May 1892.  49 21 May 1892.  50 21 May 1892.  51 4 June, 2 July 1892.

banish the Home Rule threat. Contemplating Gladstone in retirement in January 1897, the *Mail* remarked magnanimously

> He would be a churlish journalist or politician who would refuse to the birthday celebrations at Hawarden the homage of a human sympathy. The spectacle ... is certainly one which even the bitterest opponents of Mr Gladstone may look upon with pleasure.[52]

\* \* \*

The realignment of 1886 seemed to vindicate hopes for a neo-Palmerstonian alliance in defence of property and empire; but for the *Evening Mail* and its constituency this would prove a hollow victory. Before 1886, many Whigs had gone further with Gladstone than the *Mail* had thought possible in tactical concessions to the growing forces of radicalism; in the long run, the new British Unionist alliance would treat Irish landlordism as provoking rather than repelling anarchy; as a liability to be written off on acceptable terms rather than, as the *Mail* proclaimed, an indispensable bulwark of empire.

The *Mail* was not universally obtuse. Its very hatred of Gladstone made it quicker than many of his liberal Unionist admirers to perceive that in the early 1880s he was already enunciating principles that logically implied Home Rule; the conversion which seemed to Thomas MacKnight a cataclysmic lapse into insanity and abandonment of all claim to moral consistency was no more than the *Mail* expected from the author of both *The state in its relations with the church* and the Disestablishment Act. The *Mail* was often shrewd in its irreverent satirical dissections of Gladstone's techniques of popular persuasion, his self-dramatization through the techniques of theatre and pulpit, the elements of political calculation in his assertions of high moral purpose. Its aggressive breaches of verbal decorum, like those of the populist nationalist journals that it denounced, helped to mobilize its followers by demonizing Gladstone and the nationalists as outside the pale of civility; but its British allies were hardly more reliable, and though it might invoke populist Ulster Unionism when resisting Disestablishment or Home Rule, in the end this too would prove a separate phenomenon from the diehard elitism of the *Evening Mail*.

The *Mail* had shared with the most radical Irish separatists the belief that an aristocratic parliament would never undercut Irish landlordism and set a precedent for interference with property elsewhere in Britain.[53] Gladstone's 1881 Land Act, passed amid the *Mail*'s denunciations, falsified such predictions and

52 2 Jan. 1897.  53 Paul Bew, *Land and the national question* (Dublin, 1979); for an example of such resistance in Britain, see Séamus Ó Síocháin, 'Sir Henry Maine and the survival of the fittest' in Séamus Ó Síocháin (ed.), *Social thought on Ireland in the nineteenth century* (Dublin, 2009), pp 67–96.

defused the immediate threat of Irish agrarian revolution. The *Mail* serves as a useful reminder of the shock inflicted on Irish elites and British opinion by the agrarian violence of the Land War, but that shock led it to overestimate the revolutionary potential of 1880s Ireland. Its Malthusian critique of agrarian radicalism, like its assessment of Irish nationalism as a threat to empire, may have been borne out in the long term, but both rested to a considerable extent on a view of the Irish populace as simply an elemental pre-political mob. The Irish nationalist population were both more politically aware, and more susceptible to co-option for Gladstonian and parliamentary nationalist purposes, than the *Mail*'s worldview could accommodate; Gladstone perceived this, with whatever limitations.

The *Mail* was correct in noting that much British support for Home Rule derived from the desire to get rid of the troublesome Irish rather than the desire for national reconciliation invoked by Gladstonian rhetoric; its points about the limits of Gladstonian sympathy for Ireland and the self-deception and expediency in Gladstone's own analysis are often well made. The *Mail* was not entirely intransigent; it was capable of moving from explicit political Protestantism to a more muted form of conservatism after 1868, and of tactically muting its adherence to strict political economy in the interests of Balfourian constructive Unionism, but its neo-Palmerstonian ideal was ultimately incompatible with the extended franchise. The savagery of the *Mail*'s response to the upheavals of the early 1880s showed that, with the undercutting of Palmerston-era hopes for speedy assimilation,[54] in the last resort it offered only repression irrespective of cost.

Whatever the limits of Gladstonian populist moralism, with its projection of sentimental unity to secure a popular mandate for vaguely defined principles while leaving their working out in detail to a Peelite-style heroic minister, it tried to accommodate Irish majority concerns and recognized the need to harness rather than defy pressures from below. The rhetoric of national reconciliation ultimately proved more effective than the invective of *Mail* editorials and the dialect sneers of J.R. Clegg. Gladstonian Liberalism and constructive Unionism helped lay the foundations for post-independence Irish society, with its achievements and faults; if it was not an Irish Haiti, this was no thanks to the *Dublin Evening Mail*.

---

**54** See K.T. Hoppen, 'Gladstone, Salisbury and the end of Irish assimilationism', above, pp 45–63.

# The *Irish Times*, southern Protestants and the memory of Gladstone, 1898–1938[1]

## EUGENIO BIAGINI

The announcement of the death of the great orator and statesman was received in Dublin with feelings of the deepest regret by men of all shades of political thought.[2]

> Wondrous magician! Dying thou canst claim
> Tribute from all. In every mouth thy name,
> And spoken softly. In thy dying hour
> Thou hast constrained what in thy day of pow'r
> Was still denied thee – homage from us all.[3]

### THE MEMORY OF GLADSTONE

In his contribution to the *Gladstone centenary essays*, D. George Boyce explored the relationship between the Victorian statesman and the Unionists of Ireland, focusing on southern Protestants during the period 1868–93. Boyce argued that, far from ignoring Irish Protestants, as some scholars had previously maintained, Gladstone operated on the assumption that Home Rule would reinstate them 'in the front rank of the nation', to a position similar to the one that they had occupied between 1782 and 1798: he hoped that parliamentary devolution would complete the process initiated by Church disestablishment and land reform, in freeing them from 'a position which is false, and leav[ing] them in a position which is true, sound and normal'.[4] Although it was quite clear that the overwhelming majority of Irish Protestants opposed Home Rule, the Liberal leader believed that one day they would come to see the wisdom of his strategy and renew their allegiance to the Irish nation, of which they had always been an

1 I am grateful to Dr Ian D'Alton for his perceptive and helpful comments on a previous draft of the present paper, and to all the participants in the 2009 Hawarden conference on 'Gladstone and Ireland' for their questions and criticism. 2 'Reference by the Lord Mayor of Dublin', *Irish Times* (henceforth *IT*), 20 May 1898, p. 5. 3 'W.E. Gladstone' signed by 'M.G.B.', *IT*, 20 May 1898. 4 Cited in D.G. Boyce, 'In the front rank of the nation: Gladstone and the Unionists of Ireland, 1868–1893' in D. Bebbington & R. Swift (eds), *Gladstone centenary essays* (Liverpool, 2000), p. 186.

integral part: they (and especially the gentry and professional elite) would then be able to play the role which was historically their own; that is, that of leaders of the Irish people. Boyce concluded that, by the end of the century, Gladstone's strategy backfired. The southern Protestants, 'the people who Gladstone hoped would stand between the "Orangemen" and the "law haters"[,] not only failed to do so, but opposed Irish self-government and in the end were politically ruined'.[5]

In the present essay, I pick up the story where Boyce left it, covering the period from Gladstone's death in 1898 to 1938, when the identity of independent Ireland was firmly established, with de Valera's constitution defining Éire/Ireland as a republic in everything but name. I shall argue that throughout this period Irish Protestants continued to be very interested in Gladstone. This reflected a wider awareness of the fact that, as Ian D'Alton has recently put it,

> [a]t the end of the day, it was Gladstone who [had] set the agenda ...
> that sent all parties on their particular road towards self-
> determination – Liberals towards an imperial self-government
> solution, Nationalists towards independence, British Unionists
> towards local government reform, southern Irish Unionists towards a
> necessary accommodation, Northern Unionists towards the laager.[6]

Between 1898 and 1906, southern Protestants remembered the GOM as a great statesman 'perverted' by his own success, and a profoundly dividing figure who was 'to some ... the embodiment of all that is noblest in thought and action. To many ... the impersonation of all that makes for political disintegration and dishonesty'.[7] Later, during 1910–14, he became the symbol of the Union crisis, which he had allegedly encouraged by courting the nationalists in the last phase of his career. But from 1919, when southern Unionists realized that they had lost the battle, the Liberal leader began to be reassessed from a more benign perspective. Eventually, by 1938, Gladstone had become a sort of Cassandra, a prophet whose word had gone unheeded, although he had pointed the way to a constitutional strategy which – for the Protestant minority – might have been much better than the one with which they were forced to come to terms under Collins, Cosgrave and de Valera. Thus, while Boyce is right in maintaining that in 1895 the GOM was both defeated and rejected by Irish Unionists, I shall argue that over the following forty years his memory continued to haunt the southern Protestant imagination, his historical and political significance being periodically revisited and reassessed. My essay explores the way in which this happened. In

---

5 Ibid., p. 198. For one example of the older assumption about Gladstone simply ignoring the Protestants, see C. Cruise O'Brien, *States of Ireland* (St Albans, Herts, 1972), p. 130.   6 In a private communication with the author.   7 *Irish Ecclesiastical Gazette*, 27 May 1898, p. 407.

so doing, it tries to fill in a gap in the 'history and memory' scholarship, which hitherto has ignored the great Victorian.[8]

As Conor Cruise O'Brien has written, in the late nineteenth century Gladstone 'obtained a popularity in Ireland ... unequalled by any Irishman ... except O'Connell and Parnell'.[9] Of course, his reputation fluctuated with the policies that the Liberal leader adopted between 1868 and 1894: Disestablishment in 1869 was excoriated in Church of Ireland circles, although it pleased some Dissenters. His 1875 attack on the Vatican Decrees appalled Protestant Liberal MPs – who were desperate to retain cross-community support – but was long celebrated as his finest hour by less ecumenically minded Evangelicals.[10] Nevertheless, from 1874

> Gladstone began steadily to decline in the estimation of the [Irish] classes who had theretofore set him on high, while Disraeli ... gradually acquired over them an ascendancy and an influence such as no English minister had ever before enjoyed.[11]

From 1886, such 'classes' regarded the Liberal leader as a bugbear insofar as he had become the chief enemy of Unionism. By the same token, between then and 1891 he was a Catholic nationalist hero, although he retained some Protestant support as well, particularly through the Irish Home Rule Association.[12] The Parnell Split – in which Gladstone was directly involved – was a major blow to his standing in nationalist circles, but the GOM remained a towering presence in Irish politics until the end of his life. Indeed, in 1895–6 he experienced a short revival when he was celebrated as the Christian champion speaking up on behalf of the persecuted Armenians, his fearless advocacy of their rights appealing to a cross-denominational constituency in Ireland.[13] This resulted in the establishment of the inter-confessional Armenian Relief Fund in Dublin, in October 1896.[14]

Of course, given the extent to which Ireland was divided not only over Home Rule, but also between reciprocally hostile nationalist factions (such as the Parnellites, Dillonites and followers of Tim Healy), Gladstone's image continued to be highly contentious. Within months of his death, the Parnellites

---

8 Gladstone does not even receive an index entry in I. McBride (ed.), *History and memory in modern Ireland* (Cambridge, 2001).   9 Cruise O'Brien, *States of Ireland*, p. 67.   10 Boyce, 'In the front rank of the nation', p. 185.   11 'Men and the world', *IT*, 10 Oct. 1903.   12 Boyce, 'In the front rank of the nation', p. 190. See J. Loughlin, 'The Irish Protestant Home Rule Association and nationalist politics, 1886–93', *Irish Historical Studies*, 24 (1985); J.R.B. McMinn, *Against the tide: a calendar of the papers of the Reverend J.M. Armour, Irish Presbyterian minister and Home Ruler, 1869–1914* (Belfast, 1985); M. Hay, *Bulmer Hobson and the nationalist movement in twentieth-century Ireland* (Manchester, 2009), pp 1, 9, 251–2.   13 'Sympathy for the Armenians: enthusiastic meeting in Dublin', *Freeman's Journal*, 25 Sept. 1895.   14 'Irish Armenian Relief Fund', *Freeman's Journal*, 22 Sept. 1896.

and Unionists on the Dublin Corporation cooperated to stop a Dillonite proposal to honour the GOM's memory with a statue in the city.[15] The monument was not erected, and instead eventually went to rest at Hawarden. This was the beginning of the tendency for both nationalists and Unionists to belittle or even 'erase' his memory from Irish history. I shall focus on the *Irish Times*, one of the national institutions which – together with the churches and Trinity College Dublin (TCD) – contributed most to the shaping of the minority's cultural outlook.[16]

The great Dublin daily newspaper was founded in 1859 – a year that saw the onset of a number of cultural revolutions sparked off by the publication of works such as Charles Darwin's *Origin of species* and John S. Mill's *On liberty*. Despite the conservatism of the paper's founder, Lawrence E. Knox, and its first two editors – the TCD graduates George F. Shaw and the Revd George B. Wheeler – the *Irish Times* shared some of the unconventional and provocative spirit of the age. For example, from the start it supported some radical causes, such as land reform and the extension of the parliamentary franchise to working men. If it is true that it also championed the established Church of Ireland (a quintessentially conservative cause), it did so in the conviction that the Episcopalian elite were the harbingers of Irish 'progress'. The latter was the newspaper's battle cry. Its first editorial appealed to a 'critical and discerning constituency', who

> desire to see measures discussed with reference to their essential merits rather than to their party bearings. Warmly interested in whatever concerns the real progress of Ireland, whether moral or material, in the elevation of the standard of life among the labouring classes, in the general diffusion of education, in the security of property and of the fruits of the poor man's industry, they view with more than indifference all attempts to favour any one class or creed at the expense of the just rights of the others.[17]

There is no reason to doubt that Knox genuinely meant to reject sectionalism and was concerned to foster the country's 'real progress', which he perceived through the eyes of the business and professional class. They had interests that could best be served by the country's full integration within the British Empire as a system of global financial and commercial governance. Accordingly, the newspaper disparaged nationalism as a parochial and narrow-minded creed:

15 See the report of the relevant meeting of the City Council in *IT*, 9 Aug. 1898 and the essay by Paula Murphy below, pp 200–4.   16 M. O'Brien, *The* Irish Times*: a history* (Dublin, 2008), devotes no attention to the subject of the present paper (Gladstone is only occasionally referred to in connection to his Irish policies, pp 25–30).   17 *IT,* 27 Mar. 1859, cited in O'Brien, *The* Irish Times, p. 17.

instead, it was Unionist because it was 'patriotic'. In this sense the *Irish Times* expressed a pre-romantic vision of patriotism, which had nothing to do with Thomas Davis' exaltation of language, culture and history, but was best defined, in George Berkeley's words, as 'the love of the common good'.

Despite their opposition to separatism, editors were sufficiently tolerant to put up with the occasional nationalist, such as William O'Donovan (who, though a Fenian, was the newspaper's Paris correspondent for many years). Moreover, in 1873 the *Irish Times* adopted an open-minded attitude to the proposals put forward by the Protestant barrister and MP Isaac Butt during the first Home Rule conference. It was only when the nationalists developed subversive tactics, especially under Charles S. Parnell, that the Dublin daily concluded that there could be no compromise with what the editor decried as 'cold-blooded agrarian Jacobinism'.[18]

Having introduced some of the themes and sources, the rest of the present essay will explore our subject, focusing first on the period before 1914 and then on the years between 1919 and 1938.

### FROM FASCINATION TO FEAR, 1898–1914

Let us first consider how Gladstone's memory developed between the statesman's death and the passing of the third Home Rule Bill, a period during which it inspired first fascination, and then, again, as in 1886, fear. In the second half of the 1890s, the *Irish Times* adopted a more relaxed attitude to the GOM, because at that time Home Rule had ceased to be a political threat: Parnell was both discredited and dead and Gladstone was defeated and politically finished. By 1898, he was also seriously ill, eventually passing away on 19 May.

By then, the GOM's image had already moved from the realm of political controversy to that of 'history',[19] although it still retained the freshness and appeal of someone who was identified with the century's economic and fiscal progress. For one columnist,

> [h]is motives were the best. Every such chief among thinkers when most sure of his course at the best is fallible … It shows the honesty of the popular mind and conscience that the remembrance of his will ever be kindly despite all errors and contentions.[20]

A few months later, another article – presumably by a different editorialist – was more critical, but no less reverential:

---

18 'What Home Rule means', *IT*, 2 Jan. 1886.  19 See, for example, 'A historic Gladstone memento', *IT*, 5 Jan. 1898, about the presentation of a lamp 'which [had] been used on two public occasions by Mr Gladstone for the purpose of reading his notes', described by the *Irish Times* as 'a presentation of historic and unique interest'.  20 Leading article, *IT*, 20 May 1898.

> [t]here can be no doubt that Mr Gladstone has some claim upon the
> favourable consideration of the Irish people ... we may set to his
> credit the share which he took in the reformation of the iniquitous
> system of land tenure which wracked our peasantry with a thousand
> miseries. If he trampled popular rights under foot with the most
> ruthless Coercion Acts, and with the aid of such agents as 'Buckshot'
> Forster, we may recall his acceptance of the principle of Home Rule,
> and his success in obtaining its acceptance by the House of Commons.
> On the other hand, before we declare that the balance of the account
> is largely in his favour as regards Ireland, we must discriminate as to
> the quality and motive of the action for which credit is accorded to
> him.[21]

Not only had his motives been questionable, but also his Home Rule Bill had
been unsatisfactory. Here the *Irish Times* adopted the extraordinary step of
decrying the late Liberal leader's proposal, not because it was a threat to the
Union, but because it did not go *far enough*, arguing that '[i]t was a scheme
Irishmen would have accepted in the hope of making it the beginning towards
an end more real and sufficient'.[22] On balance, Gladstone was to be remembered
as 'an eminent senator and genius in whose career on the whole Ireland finds
much to admire', although 'a substantial portion of the Irish community' could
not consider many of his policies 'with approval or speak of [them] without
protest', while '[a] section of the Irish political party ... look[s] upon a certain act
and sudden turn of his conduct towards them as a treachery'.[23]

The contrasting associations evoked by Gladstone's memory contributed to
the deceased statesman's enduring newsworthiness in Ireland. In fact, he
received greater attention and more generous tributes in the pages of the leading
Dublin Unionist daily, than in those of its London counterpart, *The Times*.[24]
Throughout 1898 and 1899, the *Irish Times* published anecdotes and stories
about him. Readers were treated to free 'souvenir portraits' of the man who was
now described as 'the life-long friend of Ireland'.[25] Irish Protestants disliked the
defunct statesman's policies, but they seemed to admire Gladstone 'the man'.[26]
This was the line encouraged by the great Dublin daily, and more than once it
said so explicitly: for example, in August 1898, decrying the polemics which
accompanied the proposed erection of his monument in Dublin, the editors

---

21 *IT*, 8 Aug. 1898.  22 Leading article, *IT*, 11 Aug. 1898.  23 Leading article, *IT*, 8 Aug.
1898.  24 But see the long and generous obituary in *The Times*, 20 May 1898.  25 'Gladstone,
the life-long friend of Ireland', advertisement by the United Kingdom Tea Company: *IT*, 4 June
1898.  26 See, for one example, 'Mr Gladstone's dodge foiled', *IT*, 19 Aug. 1899, p. 5, about the
late statesman's attempt to dodge a detective providing his escort at night. For further examples,
see 'What was Mr Gladstone's religion?', *IT*, 22 Aug. 1899, and an untitled 'little story, illustrative of Mr Gladstone's courtesy', *IT*, 30 Aug. 1899, which was republished as 'Mr Gladstone and
the old lady's basket', *IT*, 2 Sept. 1899.

expressed their eagerness 'to acknowledge his intellect and humanity, his earnestness and unselfishness'.[27]

The shift in editorial emphasis from Gladstone's policies to 'the man' took place during the first six months of 1898 – as the GOM was going through the final stage of his physical decline and approaching his demise. From January until early June, the *Irish Times* covered in detail first his health problems and the development of his last illness, and then his 'saintly' death and the public response which it generated both in the United Kingdom and abroad. On 20 May, the leading article announcing that he had finally passed away contained an unqualified eulogy:

> At the moment when the sorrow for his death is universal, when the grief will find expression in all lands, there is no duty upon us to offer more than respectful tribute to the memory and sincere admiration for the singular genius and abundant service to his country for years numbering so many and eventful, of William Ewart Gladstone. ... His life was a national boast and has closed in honour. It is for all true men a solemn delight and lesson that the last hours of such a master in thought and in experience were a testimony to the common faith, simple, confident and clear.

The article went on to praise a life

> everywhere marked by moral courage, hope in the better future, trust in the people's honesty, contempt for prejudice, sympathy with the downtrodden, belief in the history of right, a hasty chivalry occasionally, some may have thought, but at any rate a crusader's vigour in the championship of freedom.[28]

It is important to note that the enthusiasm of this tribute went well beyond the convention of the time. For example, the editor's response to Parnell's death in 1891 had not been generous at all.[29] Even the long obituary of Lord Salisbury in 1903, although full of respect and gratitude, contained nothing like the praise lavished on his great rival in 1898: instead, it rather half-heartedly concluded that '[p]ossibly the future biographer may accord Lord Salisbury greater eminence as a critic than as a constructive statesman'.[30] The contrast between such a comparatively muted obituary and the extravagant commendation reserved for Gladstone is all the more striking since both statesmen had been known to be fervent churchmen. Yet, in death, the Christian faith of the Liberal

27 Leading article, *IT*, 8 Aug. 1898.   28 Leading article, *IT*, 20 May 1898.   29 Leading article, *IT*, 8 Oct. 1891.   30 Leading article, *IT*, 24 Aug. 1903, and obituary ibid.

leader received greater prominence than that of the Unionist chief, and furthermore, an accolade which was theologically very Protestant, as illustrated by the
following anonymous poem, also published on May 20:

> Peace! While the wearied spirit takes its flight,
> Behold! 'at evening time it shall be light'.
> And now to Death's dark valley thou art led,
> But all around thee God's own light is shed;
> And in that radiance scales fall from our eyes,
> And we look up, and see with glad surprise
> Nought but the soul of earnest, strong intent,
> The lofty genius willing to be spent
> For God and man. And now we bow the head
> Silenced in the presence of the mighty dead.[31]

This poem emphasized Gladstone's Christian humanitarianism as his ultimate
legacy and eternal monument. Such themes were further stressed two years
later, in the obituaries for Catherine Gladstone and, as we shall see, were to
become more frequently associated with the GOM's memory in the 1930s.[32]

Similar tones were used also by the official organ of the Church of Ireland.
Reviewing the career and historical significance of the late Liberal leader, the
*Irish Ecclesiastical Gazette* deplored Disestablishment, land reform and Home
Rule, but praised Gladstone's 'splendid example of heroic fortitude [during his
illness, as] a triumphant display of Christian hope and faith', and concluded by
praising him as 'the greatest Englishman of the century. Scholar, patriot, orator,
Christian, he united in his person a host of attainments, any one of which was in
itself a guarantee of fame. His last resting place will fitly be the fame in which
the nation enshrines the memory of its greatest'.[33]

In a less elegiac mode, some of the most robust Irish nonconformist
Unionists celebrated his campaigns for church disestablishment and social
reform. The best example is provided by T.W. Russell, the maverick MP for
South Tyrone. In a speech in 1900, he identified Gladstone as the champion of
the Presbyterian tenants: he said that, with his drastic 1881 Land Act, the GOM

---

31 M.G.B., 'W.E. Gladstone', *IT*, 20 May 1898.   32 When, in 1900, Catherine Gladstone
passed away, the newspaper's commentary was again dominated by the same Christian themes:
'The widow of the great statesman died as she lived, in peace and perfect charity ... regretted by
men and women of many nationalities, who respected her name and who unfeignedly admired
her qualities. Mrs Gladstone never sought honour for herself. She gave her life to her husband.
Not even in romance have the men and women of the time read of a more perfect marriage of
true minds', *IT*, 15 June 1900.   33 *Irish Ecclesiastical Gazette*, 27 May 1898, p. 407. This assessment paralleled that expressed by Temple, the archbishop of Canterbury, who combined what
*The Times* described as 'a highly coloured eulogy' of the dead statesman's Christian virtues with
a bitter condemnation of his 'most serious' political mistakes: *The Times*, 23 May 1898.

'went to the heart of things', because he recognized that talk which entailed equating Irish landlords with English ones 'was utter nonsense'.[34] About the legacy of his ecclesiastical policies, Russell was equally upbeat. He conceded 'that passion still prevailed on the Irish Church question, and those who were disestablished and partly disendowed could never think other than that Mr Gladstone did aught but wrong in that great act. They believed that they were robbed'. But he concluded that the act was a great blessing in disguise for Irish Protestantism:

> what do we see today in this country? A self-governed Church, and one of the freest in the world; its pastors doing God's work amongst the people, and doing it with the good will of everyone. On the Irish Church question, Mr Gladstone's policy was sound, and that Church is now doing a great work for Christianity and humanity in the country.[35]

Likewise, he reviewed favourably both the 1870 Land Act and the University Education Bill of 1873, on which the first Gladstone government resigned following the defeat of the proposal in the Commons. Although official Anglican attitudes to Disestablishment were notoriously bitter, remembering it 'as an act not of liberation, but of spoliation and humiliation',[36] to an extent Russell's gung-ho approach was consistent with the feelings expressed in other contemporary commentaries published in the *Irish Times*. Several of them combined admiration for the deceased statesman's unrivalled powers and achievements with a predominantly negative assessment of his policies.

Such mixed feelings and memories are further exemplified by the newspaper's response to the biographies and political studies of Gladstone and the Gladstonian Liberal party, published between 1898 and 1903. They included works by Lionel Tollemache, W.E.H. Lecky, Moisei Ostrogorski and John Morley. The *Irish Times* reviewed them all, starting from as early as July 1898, with a long editorial on the articles and essays that had been published in the immediate aftermath of Gladstone's death. The Liberal leader was described as 'one who, undoubtedly, whether for their good or ill, was one of the makers of his times'. The *Irish Times* argued that, like William Pitt and Robert Peel,

> MR GLADSTONE had his years of unpopularity. Time was when he was distrusted and disbelieved in. Time was when he became the accred-

---

34 'The Kingstown Literary and Dramatic Society', speech by T.W. Russell, MP, *IT*, 29 Nov. 1900. As late as 1911, when he reverted to his earlier allegiance and served as a Liberal MP (having broken his links with the Unionists in 1906), Russell argued that the 1881 Act was 'Mr Gladstone's best title ... to the gratitude of the Irish people' ('Eighty Club Visit – Mr Russell's ideal', *IT*, 18 Sept. 1911). 35 *IT*, 29 Nov. 1900. 36 M. Tanner, *Ireland's holy wars: the struggle for a nation's soul, 1500–2000* (New Haven, CT, & London, 2003), p. 226.

ited mouthpiece of often reactionary opinion, when none other of his political compeers could compare with him in the weaving of subtle distinctions and complicated reasonings, which … sometimes bewildered rather than convinced his hearers. And finally, a time came when he became the ideal idol of the democracy, and was endued by the common imagination with possession of a political second-sight which he never had, and the imputation of which to him represented the source of not a few political lapses and the temptation to commit many blunders.[37]

These themes also dominated a review of Tollemache's *Every-day conversation of Mr Gladstone*. Although the book focused on the statesman's private life, particularly his scholarly interests, the reviewer did not pass up the opportunity to comment on how the peculiarities of his character explained his political trajectory:

> No man ever had greater powers of self-persuasion than Mr Gladstone, and this is the key to most of his acts and words. Once he convinced himself, and the process had often the excusatory merit of being slow, nothing could move him from his conclusion. His Homeric hallucinations led him as a literary critic astray, just as in political matters his imperious judgment egregiously deceived him.[38]

As a consequence of these personality flaws, '[i]n his later years, "the Demagogue in his nature steadily grew"'.[39] In a similar spirit, in 1903, the anonymous reviewer of Moisei Ostrogorski's *Democracy and the organization of political parties* emphasized that 'the secret of Mr Gladstone's power over the masses was … that of the hypnotist. He did not enlighten their judgment; he satisfied rather their thirst for strong sensations', and his 'great meetings' were 'political orgies'.[40]

Morley's monumental three-volume biography, also published in 1903, received a special treatment. From as early as 1898, when it was first announced that the family had asked him to write Gladstone's official life, the *Irish Times* had followed the progress of the project, providing its readers with regular updates on Morley's research and writing. When the work was eventually published, the Dublin daily reviewed it in two long articles on 9 and 12 October. The reviewer complained that the biography was too long and dealt too exclusively with the political side of its subject, neglecting 'Gladstone, the Man, in his

---

**37** Leading article, *IT*, 4 July 1898.  **38** 'Books of the day. *The every-day conversation of Mr Gladstone*', *IT*, 6 June 1898.  **39** 'Mr Lecky on Mr Gladstone', *IT*, 11 Jan. 1899. This was W.E.H. Lecky, *Map of life, conduct and character* (London, 1899).  **40** 'Books and their writers', *IT*, 25 Feb. 1903.

domestic circle' – an interest which, as we have seen, had already been expressed by earlier commentaries and obituaries. The writer tried to use evidence from Morley's overwhelmingly positive account to shed light on what he regarded as the statesman's weaknesses. For example, of the GOM's approach to parliamentary debates the reviewer said that Morley contradicted himself, claiming on the one hand that 'Mr Gladstone conquered the House ... because he plainly believed every word he said', and on the other, that his overriding concern was to win an argument, whether he was right or wrong. 'Is not this tantamount to saying "The question at issue does not matter; the great thing to secure is the division, or the Treasury Bench[?]"'[41] His review of the third and last volume was simply an extended summary of its contents, with many long quotations from the primary sources to which Morley had had exclusive access, but without any real attempt at assessing his argument and interpretation.[42]

The period 1904–10 saw a decline in the number of references to Gladstone. However, interest revived in 1910–11, during the debates in preparation for the third Home Rule Bill. Some of the stereotypes of the 1880s were then repeated: for example, as we might expect from a Unionist paper, Gladstone was primarily remembered as the man who bore the greatest responsibility for the threatened 'disruption' of the empire and his memory was frequently associated with that of Parnell.[43] His ability to reshape Anglo-Irish relations and secure legislation was explained by saying that he possessed '[the] power of hypnotizing the House of Commons'.[44] Moreover, his name was now predictably a byword for the whole constitutional philosophy behind Home Rule, and especially for its alleged flaws.[45] However, he was also cited as an authority against the arrogance of the pope, especially with reference to the marriage laws and the *ne temere* decree.[46] Furthermore, his pronouncements on private matters – and the high esteem in which he had held Dr Salmon, provost of Trinity College Dublin – were reported and commented upon as if they were opinions deserving the greatest public consideration.[47]

Having surveyed how the build-up to the third Home Rule Bill affected

**41** 'Mr Morley's "Life of Gladstone"', *IT*, 9 Oct. 1903. **42** *IT*, 12 Oct. 1903: perhaps overwhelmed by the weight of the new evidence, the reviewer did not try to offer any assessment whatsoever of either Gladstone's achievements and motives or of the way Morley presented his subject. **43** Major G.B. O'Connor, 'Irish Unionism' (letter to the editor), *IT*, 29 Dec. 1910; see also the report of a meeting of the 'Irish Unionist Alliance', *IT*, 15 Apr. 1911. **44** 'South County Dublin – Unionist Registration Association', *IT*, 10 June 1911. **45** 'Home Rule – a suggestion. Letter from Dr Edward Thompson', *IT*, 18 Apr. 1911; 'Ulster and a separate parliament', letter by an 'Ex-official', *IT*, 28 Sept. 1911. **46** Letter by 'Presbyterian', 'The marriage laws', *IT*, 27 Dec. 1910: 'Mr Gladstone described the state of fact created by the highest authorities of the Roman Church as "horrible and revolting in itself, and dangerous to the morals of society, the structure of the family and the place of life" ... The decree *Ne Temere* has added new force to these words'. **47** See Lord Ashbourne's letter, *IT*, 17 June 1911, and the comment by J.G. Swift McNeill, 'Provost Salmon and Mr Gladstone', *IT*, 19 June 1911.

Gladstone's image, in the last section we shall focus on how his memory was further transformed by the experiences of civil war and independence.

'WHAT FOOLS WE WERE': THE CHANGE OF HEART, 1919–38

'What fools we were ... not to have accepted Gladstone's Home Rule Bill. The empire now would not have had the Irish Free State giving us so much trouble and pulling us to pieces'.[48] This is the view reportedly expressed by King George V to his prime minister, Ramsay MacDonald, during a private conversation in 1930. Replace 'the empire' with 'the Irish Protestants' and you have a fairly accurate summary of the views expressed by or echoed in the *Irish Times* in the inter-war period.

The u-turn about the comparative advantages of Home Rule and the union took some time to complete. Patrick Buckland has argued that, although there was a weakening of Unionist sentiment in the south during the First World War, it was not until 1920–1 that demoralization and political defeat caused southern Protestants to revise their opinion both of the original Home Rule scheme and of the more radical proposal that the country should be given dominion status.[49] However, from as early as the 1890s, a series of episodes – ranging from flirtations with William O'Brien, to involvement in the devolution scheme, the Irish Councils Bill and the Buckingham Palace Conference – had provided some indication that a section of southern Protestantism was coming to accept that Home Rule, in one form or other, was inevitable. Indeed, Buckland himself has accepted that even *before* 1914 some sections of the southern Unionist movement, such as the 'Midletonites', had started to soften their strategy and attitudes to nationalism.[50] To begin with, they now showed a new propensity for regarding the argument – much exploited by Gladstone in 1886 – that the passing of the 1800 Act of Union 'was assisted by methods whose morality, to put it mildly, was somewhat dubious'.[51] More importantly, they were now prepared to accept nationalism as a genuine and worthwhile aspiration that the upper classes ought to endorse, rather than resist and despise – an attitude that, again, was similar to what Gladstone had often advocated. As Lord Powerscourt put it, nationalism

> *cannot and should not* be squashed. Owing to this neglect by the upper
> classes of seeing the necessity of catering for this, it has fallen into the
> hands of unprincipled organizers ... If Irish national sentiment

**48** Cited in H.C.G. Matthew, *Gladstone, 1875–1898* (Oxford, 1995), p. 184.  **49** P. Buckland, *Irish Unionism 1: the Anglo-Irish and the new Ireland, 1885 to 1922* (Dublin, 1972), pp 39, 83–4, 194ff.  **50** Buckland, *Irish Unionism*, pp 84, 218–19.  **51** G. Hanlon, letter to *IT*, 8 Apr. 1918, cited in Buckland, *Irish Unionism*, p. 84.

became respectable ... it would be a great power for good in our country.[52]

Buckland has concluded that by 1918, 'some southern Unionists could foresee a new peaceful Ireland, governed by an Irish parliament which would be dominated by a centre constitutional party comprising moderate nationalists and Unionists *from [both] the north and the south of Ireland*'.[53]

This, including the emphasis on the importance of avoiding partition, was again what Gladstone had in vain urged in 1886. As the *Church of Ireland Gazette* commented in 1916, 'Home Rule without Ulster would have been thoroughly bad. Home Rule with Ulster would have been less bad'.[54] In May 1917, three eminent Church of Ireland bishops – Plunket, Berry and Gregg – signed a petition against partition, stating that

> Nationalist Ireland desires and, if Home Rule for any part of Ireland is to come, southern Unionists desire with it, to maintain the unity of Ireland on the basis of Home Rule for all Ireland. The only common ground between them, on which the two churches [Protestant and Roman Catholic] meet in this manifesto, is allegiance to an idea of an Ireland 'one and undivided'.[55]

At the time, this petition caused considerable uproar among Ulster Protestants, although at least some of them saw perfectly well the point made by their southern co-religionists. In fact, as early as 1908, Lord Atkinson – formerly the MP for North Derry – had argued that he had no fear of religious discrimination for he believed that 'the strength of the Protestant minority in an independent Ireland was in itself sufficient guarantee against majority repression'.[56] However, Atkinson remained a bitter enemy of Home Rule because he disliked the idea of mixing devolution with a continuing connection with the United Kingdom, believing that under such an arrangement, in case of a minority rebellion, London would always back the Catholic majority. At the time, Atkinson claimed that full separation and an Irish republic would have been preferable to Home Rule.[57]

Whether Atkinson meant what he said or was merely boasting, most northerners opted for both partition and (Ulster) Home Rule. Under the

---

52 Memorandum by the 8th Viscount Powerscourt on 'Reasons for present rebellion, n.d., British Library, Add. MS 52782, fos 50–1, cited in Buckland, *Irish Unionism*, p. 87. Emphasis in the text. For similar and even more radical views, see Lord Oranmore in the House of Lords, May 1920, cited in Buckland, *Irish Unionism*, p. 217. 53 Buckland, *Irish Unionism*, p. 88. My emphasis. 54 Cited in M. Tanner, *Ireland's holy wars*, p. 284. 55 Cited in G. Seaver, *John Allen Fitzgerald Gregg Archbishop* (Leighton Buzzard, Beds, 1963), p. 88. 56 A. Jackson, *The Ulster party: Irish Unionists in the House of Commons, 1884–1911* (Oxford, 1989), p. 122. 57 Ibid.

circumstances, southern Protestants had to look for allies elsewhere, and if the choice lay between Sinn Féin and the Irish National Party, they far preferred the latter: Marcus Tanner has argued that by 1918 they 'were ... much fonder of Redmond than most Catholics'.[58] His involvement in the war effort and his brother's heroic death in action (1917) were evidence of his loyalty and reliability. Unionist leaders who had fought in the war felt further encouraged by the brave behaviour of the nationalist soldiers: thus Major Bryan Cooper from Sligo, recollecting his service with the 10th Division, commented in his memoirs that

> The bond of common service proved so strong and enduring that Catholic and Protestant, Unionist and Nationalist, lived and fought and died side by side like brothers. Little was spoken concerning the points on which we differed and once we had tacitly agreed to let the past be buried we found thousands of points on which we agreed.[59]

If the danger of partition helped southern Protestants to reassess Home Rule, did it also affect the way they remembered Gladstone? There is some evidence that it did. For example, in March 1919, 139 Irish army officers petitioned the government against partition, demanding referral of the Irish question to the Versailles peace conference. The signatories included Catholics such as Gen. Sir William Hickie, but also members of established Protestant families, such as J.J. Bruen from Carlow and others serving in Protestant regiments such as the Royal Inniskilling Fusiliers. They alluded to the first Home Rule Bill as a fruit of 'the democratic evolution of British institutions ... in reliance upon the pledges of Liberal statesmanship, inspired and expressed by Gladstone'.[60] So, now the defunct Liberal leader was no longer regarded as a self-deluded sophist led 'astray' by political 'hallucinations' (as Lecky and others had claimed), but as a visionary ahead of his time. The document was also interesting because it adopted and implicitly endorsed the 'Gladstonian' account of Irish nationality: it referred to Grattan's Parliament as the founding myth of modern Ireland, invoked the passing of Home Rule in 1914 as the culmination of a process of national awakening and argued that there existed an inclusive Irish sense of national identity that ought not to be sacrificed to Ulster separatism.[61]

At this stage, southern Unionist impatience with the Northern anti-Home Rule position found repeated, if not frequent, expression in both letters and

---

58 Tanner, *Ireland's holy wars*, p. 284.  59 B. Cooper, *The Tenth (Irish) division at Gallipoli* (London, 1918), p. 253.  60 'Ireland and the Peace Conference – petition to the king – signed by Irish officers', *IT*, 10 Mar. 1919, p. 5.  61 The London *Times* commented dryly that, although a non-partitioned Home Rule Ireland may now have become the wish of some southern officers, the officers of the Ulster Division went to war exactly for the opposite reason, i.e. to preserve the Union *or* separate the north from a self-governing south, see leading article, *The Times*, 17 Mar. 1919.

leading articles in the *Irish Times*.[62] The Liberal ideal of devolution was now rehabilitated and indeed celebrated. Thus, in December 1921, a leading article endorsing the Treaty quoted Gladstone's speech on the second reading of the Home Rule Bill, to the effect that Ireland was offered both a 'great day of hope' and that 'cup' of liberty, which in the past England had 'ruthlessly dashed ... to the ground'.[63] A year later, on ratification of the Treaty, the newspaper contrasted the euphoria that had saluted 'the triumphs of Mr Gladstone and of Mr Asquith' in the past, with the sober attitude that then accompanied the proclamation of the Irish Free State to which the editors offered their undivided support and loyalty: 'Freedom comes to us at the last, not blithe or smiling, but with a countenance severe and even tragic. Therefore, we greet her cordially, indeed, and hopefully, but without exultation'.[64] The article conveyed the impression that, had 'freedom' come in 1886 or 1914 without bloodshed or destruction of property, the *Irish Times* would have greeted it 'with exultation'. This was obviously far from the truth, but sounded like the view expressed at the time by W.B. Yeats – himself a more genuine Protestant nationalist than the *Irish Times* editor – who felt that, '[i]f Ireland had attained Home Rule under Gladstone', the transformation 'would have been pleasanter'.[65]

If such views did not yet amount to a full change of heart, the transformation was completed over the following fifteen years. In this respect, the *Irish Times*' welcome to J.L. Hammond's *Gladstone and the Irish nation* – published in 1938 – was particularly significant. Hammond and his wife Barbara had long been highly regarded in Ireland, especially in Fianna Fáil circles, partly because their work on the labourers and the industrial revolution, which was required reading among history students at University College Dublin, was perceived as an indictment of industrial and urban lifestyle and a celebration of the values of the traditional rural community.[66] Hammond's Gladstone book was advertised in the newspaper for two months before it was finally reviewed.[67] The actual review was flattering: the book was described as 'brilliant', 'wholly delightful and splendidly exact', the work of an author who stood out '[a]mong [the] English historical scholars of the day' for his 'extensive' knowledge of the sources, only comparable to Sidney Webb.[68] The anonymous reviewer further praised Hammond's personal political opinions and record:

62 Thus a correspondent observed in 1922 that the Irish Unionist Alliance operated as if they were still living in 'the dear old times of Salisbury and Gladstone' (letter by 'A southern Unionist', 'The Irish Unionist outlook', *IT*, 26 May 1920).  63 Leading article, 'The nation's voice', *IT*, 28 Dec. 1921.  64 Leading article, 'The Free State', *IT*, 4 Dec. 1922.  65 R. Foster, *W.B. Yeats: a life*, 2 vols (Oxford, 2003), i, 265.  66 However, it does not seem that this Fianna Fáil rural piety was shared by the reviewer of *Gladstone and the Irish Nation*, who compared Hammond to Sidney Webb, a defender of urban values and industrialism, and claimed that the two of them were the greatest modern historians.  67 *IT*, 29 Oct. 1938. For Hammond's attitude to, and continuing political interest in, Ireland, see G.K. Peatling, 'New liberalism, J.L. Hammond and the Irish problem, 1897–1949', *Historical Research*, 73 (2000), 48–65.  68 'The

he has been one of the most steadfast advocates of Irish liberty for at
least a generation ... As one of the brilliant band which assisted Scott
to make the *Manchester Guardian* respected in Ireland ... [he] must be
saluted by the present generation.[69]

As for the new light the book cast on the events, the reviewer said that
Hammond had set the record straight on many counts: 'he has no trouble in
demolishing the notion that Gladstone adopted the policy of Home Rule in 1885
because of his desire for office. Nor is there any difficulty in disproving the
charge of hypocrisy and dishonour in the Gladstonian dealings with Parnell',
including the divorce crisis. It was a tragedy, however, that the two did not
understand each other better, a problem compounded by Parnell's apparent
contempt for parliament, which Gladstone venerated. The GOM had 'a
"European mind", which envisaged the Irish problem imaginatively rather than
intellectually', though 'from those colleagues who were unversed in European
humanism he was estranged'. These included – besides Parnell – Joseph
Chamberlain and Lord Hartington. The details and prospects of success of his
Home Rule strategy were not discussed, but the reviewer conveyed the impression that the fatal flaw was not the policy. Instead, it was Gladstone's insensitive
handling of philistine but strategically important colleagues, and concluded:

> [w]hat is demonstrated beyond question is Gladstone's essential
> consistency and continuity of policy. His Irish policy was sincere ...
> In this great book is the portrait of 'a great Christian gentleman'
> whose magnanimity is unapproached in modern history.[70]

Thus, in the aftermath of the passing of de Valera's constitution and on the
eve of the Second World War, Gladstone's stock was higher than it had ever
been: although the leading Protestant newspaper did not quite come round to the
view expressed by King George V to MacDonald in 1930, and cited at the beginning of the present section, it came very close to it.

Even granting that some southern Protestants had started to change their
mind about the merits of both Home Rule and Gladstone before 1918, the
unqualified approval and enthusiasm with which Hammond's work was
welcomed twenty years later is striking. By contrast, in 1912, a book that
proposed a similar historical interpretation had been summarily dismissed by the
newspaper's reviewer, who did not find anything positive in it:

> *Gladstone and Ireland* is a study by an old Liberal in the person of
> Lord Eversley, who, as Mr Shaw-Lefebvre, was postmaster general in

mind of Gladstone: Ireland as a mirror', *IT*, 5 Dec. 1938.  **69** Ibid.  **70** Ibid.

1885–95 [*sic*], of the methods adopted by an old Liberal to bring Ireland to reason. In other words, it describes the manner in which Gladstone, with disastrous results to the Liberal Party, attempted to settle the Home Rule question.[71]

CONCLUSION

How can we account for such a change? Part of the explanation must be that in the 1930s, at least some southern Irish Protestants looked back to 1886 nostalgically as a missed opportunity, the last chance to avoid the wars of 1919–23, which resulted in over one third of their number emigrating to the United Kingdom or British dominions in America and Australasia. For those who opted to remain in the Free State, the challenges were numerous and affected not only their national identity, but also basic questions of toleration and survival: they were now a dwindling dissenting minority within a country defined primarily by Catholic, Gaelic and increasingly autarkic imperatives.

However, I would like to suggest that behind this change of heart there was also a rediscovery of Protestant patriotism and liberalism (with a small 'l'). Gladstone's rehabilitation was part of a wider political reappraisal of the identity of southern Irish Protestants. For example, from 1930 at least, Thomas Davis, the Protestant founder of Young Ireland, was celebrated in Dublin Presbyterian circles as 'an original thinker, rousing talker, vigorous writer, and a great stimulus to other men', a 'sower of many seeds, some of which had borne luxuriant crops, and others had as yet scarcely germinated'.[72] And in 1934 we find the Revd Ernest Bateman – then Church of Ireland vicar of Booterstown – taking pride in the opportunities and freedom that Disestablishment and independence had provided for the Church of Ireland:

> There was never a time since the Reformation since [*sic*] Protestantism had such a chance. When it was the Established Church, looked upon as an alien and enemy organization, the church of the wealthy land-owning classes, the church of a political party, its spiritual influence was of the smallest and as long as that state of affairs continued it could not have been otherwise. Now that it has been bereft of all outside support and is the Church of a section of the Irish people who have proved themselves ready to throw in their lot with their fellow countrymen, now that it has lost all the prestige that social and political power could give it, it has at last an opportunity to

71 'Gladstone and Ireland', *IT*, 27 Jan. 1912.   72 B.C. Waller, during a lecture delivered in the Recreation Hall of the Rathgar Presbyterian Church, Dublin; the lecture was chaired by the Revd J.J. Macaulay: 'Thomas Davis', *IT*, 13 Nov. 1930.

prove the value of the spiritual truth which is its life. The worldly prospects of Protestants in this country may have deteriorated but they have never had such an opportunity of showing themselves a spiritual [force (?)].[73]

Among the intellectuals, a similar sense both of freedom and defiance was perhaps most famously exemplified by Hubert Butler, the 'Protestant republican'.[74] Within the *Irish Times* staff, a key proponent of a similar strategy was Robert M. Smyllie, who served as its chief editor from 1934 to 1954. Under his leadership, the Dublin daily became 'the only forum available at the time where free discussion of ethics and religion could take place'.[75] The paper's strategy depended on avoiding a direct confrontation with 'the powers that be' and disclaiming any permanent alliance with parties and factions: thus, having discarded 'West Britonism', the *Irish Times* espoused W.T. Cosgrave and Fine Gael only for as long as the issues of the day warranted such a strategy. In the aftermath of the 1937 election and the passing of the new constitution, it admitted that de Valera was a more genuine democrat than his critics (including the *Irish Times* itself) had claimed. Significantly, during the Spanish Civil War, the newspaper championed the legitimacy and rights of the democratically elected Republican government and criticized Britain for its equivocal attitude to Franco's fascist movement – taking a position that was not only independent of 'West Briton' loyalism, but that was also at the time explicitly associated with the Gladstone heritage.[76] This helped the paper to establish its national and liberal reputation, one that was further consolidated by its stance during the Second World War. Then it supported de Valera's policy of neutrality as the strategy most suitable for Irish national interests, but insisted on the freedom of the press (against wartime censorship), which it used to champion the cause of the allies and denounce the crimes of Nazi-fascism. It again echoed the Gladstonian politics of humanitarianism, which in the 1930s had found its most vocal Irish advocate in Hubert Butler.

It is not clear to what extent southern Protestant opinion, more widely understood, shared this view between 1933 and 1945. However, it is significant that in 1938 the *Sixteenth annual report of the United Council of Christian Churches and Communions in Ireland for 1937–38* endorsed a series of liberal-humanitarian

73 E.M. Bateman, 'The baptismal vow' (1934), Church of Ireland Representative Church Body Library, 235. The notes end abruptly with 'a spiritual ...', the last page of the sermon having been lost. The final word in square brackets is an educated guess at what the next word of the sentence might have been.  74 R.F. Foster, *Luck and the Irish* (London, 2008), p. 100.  75 O'Brien, *The* Irish Times, p. 82.  76 Cf. 'Mr Ridley and the government', *IT*, 4 Apr. 1938, in which a Labour MP, claiming that the pro-Franco policy of the British government was 'a denial of every decency in international life', argued that '[i]n face of foreign intervention against the legitimate government of Spain ... a Gladstone would have thundered in a way that would have reverberated round the world'.

principles, in reaction to the Nazi persecution of the Jews. The report declared, among other things, that '[a]nti-semitism and all other forms of race discrimination are contrary to the Christian revelation. Every form of national egotism which results in the oppression of minorities is a sin against God'.[77] This document further insisted that

> The Church must claim that it has a message for human life in this world, as well as in the next. It must refuse the offer of safety at the cost of silence in the face of the injustices, the cruelty and the tyrannies of this life. It must not only seek to promote social justice in its own state but show sympathetic interest in the Christians and non-Christians who in other lands are victims of cruelty and oppression.[78]

The delegates then endorsed the formation of a World Council of the Churches, which they described as a sort of ecclesiastical equivalent to the Society of Nations. No mention of Gladstone was made in these documents, but the aims of this body and its whole philosophy were certainly consistent with the spirit of the GOM's ecumenism and internationalism, as analyzed by Matthew and others.[79]

In the post-war years, such Christian humanitarianism continued to be voiced by both old and new generations of churchmen and Dissenters, partly encouraged by the opening up of the Republic to the project of European integration, and, especially, by what Roy Foster has described as the Catholics becoming protestants, more secular and humanist, less dogmatic and confessional.[80] By the 1960s, leading *Irish Times* figures such as Lionel Fleming and Douglas Gageby were speaking and writing openly of their 'Protestant nationalism' – one which, in the case of another leading Church member, Martin Mansergh, was often explicitly linked to the GOM's political legacy.[81]

Did such a 'conversion' come too late for any practical purpose? In terms of the Home Rule debate, obviously yes. However, in terms of the identity of the Protestants in the Republic it had important effects because it contributed to what Tanner has described as the 'slow but steady reconciliation between southern Protestants and Irish nationalism'.[82] By the mid-1990s, *The Church of*

77 *Sixteenth annual report of [sic] United Council of Christian churches and communions in Ireland for 1937–38*, pages not numbered, in the proceedings of the 1938 Methodist Conference, Methodist Conference Blue Book, 1938–41, Public Record Office Northern Ireland, CR6/3A/1/13.  78 Ibid.  79 H.C.G. Matthew, 'Gladstone, Vaticanism and the question of the East' in D. Baker (ed.), *Religious motivation: biographical and sociological problems for the church historian*, Oxford (Ecclesiastical History Society), 1978, pp 417–41; D. Bebbington, *The mind of Gladstone: religion, Homer and politics* (Oxford, 2004); E.F. Biagini, *British democracy and Irish nationalism, 1876–1906* (Cambridge, 2007), ch. II.  80 Foster, *Luck and the Irish*, p. 64.  81 Kevin Rafter, *Martin Mansergh: a biography* (Dublin, 2002), pp 109, 132.  82 M. Tanner, *Ireland's holy wars*, p. 322.

*Ireland Gazette* boasted that 'the southern community feels itself to be moving with new confidence, well integrated into a rapidly developing society', and wondered 'why the Northern Church had been unable to divest itself of what looks like uncomfortable and anachronistic sectarian baggage'.[83] At the beginning of the twenty-first century, as Heather Crawford has recently argued, there remain underlying tensions at the level of integration and national identity, but the southern Irish Protestant community has started to reverse its historical decline, both demographically and in terms of self-confidence.[84] Indeed, in 2008 Roy Foster noted that, while Orangeism and Unionism had quietly disappeared from most of the Republic, 'by some computations, [Protestant] influence [had] actually increased disproportionately between 1926 and 1991'.[85] Of course, this concerns primarily public attitudes and a change in the popular value system.[86] In this sense, it was not what Gladstone had envisaged when he said that Ireland's self-government would bring about the re-establishment of the Protestants 'in the front rank of the nation'. But it was at least a vindication of his faith in the compatibility of pluralism and Christianity: for, as a leading southern Irish Protestant has recently observed, '[the] retreat from absolutes need not be seen as defeat or rejection'.[87]

83 In 1996: cited in Foster, *Luck and the Irish*, p. 59.   84 H. Crawford, *Outside the glow: Protestants and Irishness in independent Ireland* (Dublin, 2010); M. Macourt, *Counting the people of God? The census of population and the Church of Ireland* (Dublin, 2008), p. 111.   85 Foster, *Luck and the Irish*, p. 60.   86 See M. Gaffney, 'All change: how Ireland turned its back on dogma', *IT*, 18 Sept. 2010.   87 M. Mansergh, 'Future tense?', *Church of Ireland Gazette*, 2 Apr. 2010, p. 9.

# A careful Hellenism and a reckless Roman-ness: the Gladstone–Disraeli rivalry in the context of classics

## QUENTIN BROUGHALL

### INTRODUCTION

One of the most famous quotations in Benjamin Disraeli's fiction occurs in his novel, *Contarini Fleming* (1832), where the eponymous hero is advised by his father to '[R]ead no history: nothing but biography, for that is life without theory'.[1] Whatever the truth of such a statement, the biographies of William Gladstone and Benjamin Disraeli show plainly how their lengthy rivalry evolved to provide ample material to the historian on the age in which they lived – its principles, its passions and its progress. However, as Paul Smith has claimed in relation to Disraelian scholarship, 'while research will continue to extend our grasp of the detail and context of [Disraeli's] career, advance in understanding will come primarily by more sensitive reflection on what has, for the most part, been long familiar'.[2] Much the same could be said of Gladstone scholarship. So, with regard to new directions in studying their famous rivalry, context is everything.

Since their long political contest revolved around far more than the mundane questions of the day – effectively two clearly conflicting visions of Britain's future – it is crucial to interrogate what both men reflected upon in the formation of their opinions. Although works such as *The mind of Gladstone* and *The self-fashioning of Disraeli* exemplify a trend towards such study, certain aspects of their personal opinions and pursuits remain more studied than others.[3] I believe one under-represented feature to be Gladstone and Disraeli's relationship with the classics, which, considering the fascinating work already completed regarding the influence of Gladstone's Homeric scholarship on his life and career, makes a brief study of a classical connection within their rivalry a ripe subject for consideration and commentary now.

---

1 B. Disraeli, *Contarini Fleming* (New York, 1832), i, ch. 23, p. 101.   2 P. Smith, *Disraeli: a brief life* (Cambridge, 1996), p. 4.   3 D. Bebbington, *The mind of Gladstone: religion, Homer and politics* (Oxford, 2004), and C. Richmond & P. Smith (eds), *The self-fashioning of Disraeli, 1818–1851* (Cambridge, 1999), offer two of the best studies regarding the personalities and private pursuits of both men.

'OVERGROWN SCHOOLBOYS'

In the nineteenth century, elite education in Britain was marked by an emphasis on classical learning seldom seen either before or since.[4] According to Lord Chesterfield, writing in the mid-eighteenth century, the reason for this concentration was simple: 'Classical knowledge [...] is absolutely necessary for everybody; because everybody has agreed to think and to call it so'.[5] Gladstone and Disraeli both received their formative schooling in a culture and a society that automatically and unthinkingly continued this tradition – though importantly in very different types of institution; the former being famously an Old Etonian, while the latter attended the virtually unknown Higham Hill in Walthamstow. It was this divergence in their education that was to influence critically their lifelong relationship to classics; Gladstone taking a formal, traditional route that saw the study of Greek and Latin stressed as the mainstay of a gentleman's schooling, while Disraeli experienced a slightly more unorthodox, indeed, perhaps, more recognizably modern education that – by the standards of the day – downgraded classics to a somewhat more equal rank with other subjects.

Beginning his education at Revd William Rawson's preparatory school near his family home at Seaforth House, Gladstone then followed the example of his elder brother, Thomas, and started at Eton College in September 1821, aged 11. Here, he excelled instantly as a juvenile scholar, possessing an innate and intense gift for classical language. It was also in the school that he enjoyed his first successes in the world, finding himself 'sent up' to the infamous headmaster, Dr Keate, three times in his Eton career for various academic accomplishments. He was elected to the Literati Society (the debating club later to become 'Pop') in October 1825 and, exactly a year later, became captain of the fifth form. Soon after, in February 1827, Gladstone was promoted to the elite sixth form and also admitted to 'Play', a special class of advanced sixth formers taken by Keate himself. He capped these juvenile achievements by launching and editing the famous *Eton Miscellany*, though he never gained the much-coveted position of captain of the Oppidans.[6]

At Eton, Gladstone endured 'the pagan polish'[7] of a very mechanical classical education, revolving mainly around Latin grammar, translation and composition, with some Greek, French and mathematics thrown in for good measure.

---

**4** One of the best starting points to explore the influence of classics on Victorian society is C.A. Stray's *Classics transformed: schools, universities and society in England, 1830–1960* (Oxford, 1998), though this subject represents a rich and burgeoning area within the study of classical reception. **5** Lord Chesterfield, *Letters to his son, 1746–1771*: letter xl, 27 May 1748, O. Leigh (ed.) (Teddington, 2007), p. 77.  **6** *The Eton miscellany* (London, 1827) was published in two volumes and edited by Gladstone and his school colleague, George Selwyn, under the joint pseudonym 'Bartholomew Bouverie'.  **7** R. Shannon, *Gladstone, 1809–1865* (London, 1982), p. 6.

This represented the dominant educational thinking of the time, and, in 1826, while still a pupil, he criticized Eton's classical curriculum for being 'a great deal too exclusively attended to'.[8] Towards the end of his life, Gladstone even pronounced such an educational system to have been 'without merit', though he qualified this by admitting that

> in point it was admirable. I mean [in] its rigid, inflexible and relentless accuracy [...] it has been my habit to say that at Eton in my day a boy might if he chose learn something, or might if he chose learn nothing, but that one thing he could not do, and that was to learn anything inaccurately.

As it happened, Gladstone chose to learn quite a lot and almost all of it very accurately, classical learning acting as 'a kind of release'[9] for him from the numerous religious doubts and difficulties that seemed to vex him throughout his life. On his last day at Eton, Gladstone lamented in his diary that 'the happiest period of my life is now past [...] But oh! if anything mortal is sweet, my Eton years [...] have been so!'[10] – a remark demonstrating how bound to his schooling he felt at the time and, indeed, remained always.

Continuing on to Christ Church, Oxford, in October 1828, Gladstone would have found the education provided by 'the House', as the college was known colloquially, to be remarkably similar to that which he had already obtained at Eton, being almost entirely classical, offset only by some mathematics and theology. Here, he laid further foundations for his parliamentary career becoming both founder of the short-lived Essay Club (the Oxford version of the Cambridge 'Apostles') and president of the Oxford Union, while also achieving the unusual merit of a double first in both classics and mathematics. The educational continuity between Eton and Christ Church would have greatly assisted Gladstone's achievements at university, since his final exams interrogated him on Homer, Herodotus, Aristophanes, Plato, Thucydides, Virgil and Persius – most of these schoolboy staples of the period.[11] However, in spite of these successes, Gladstone later complained that his Eton and Oxford education had left him 'wretchedly deficient in the knowledge of modern [...] literature and history'.[12] Conversely, this was not a complaint that Benjamin Disraeli could make about his superficially inferior schooling.

Benjamin Disraeli began his education by attending two separate London preparatory schools, Miss Roper's school in Islington and Reverend John

8 Quoted in S.G. Checkland, *The Gladstones: a family biography, 1764–1851* (Cambridge, 1971), p. 211.  9 Checkland, *The Gladstones*, pp 205–6.  10 H.C.G. Matthew, *Gladstone, 1809–98* (Oxford, 1995), p. 9; 2 Dec. 1827, Foot & Matthew (eds), *The Gladstone diaries*, 14 vols (Oxford, 1968–94), i, 151.  11 17 Nov. 1831, ibid., p. 393.  12 Quoted in C. Richmond, 'Disraeli's education' in Richmond & Smith (eds), *The self-fashioning of Disraeli, 1818–1851*, p. 17.

Potticany's school at Blackheath. Although he was supposed to have attended Winchester College like his brothers, Disraeli was sent instead, from around the ages of 13 to 15, to Higham Hill, the small but unorthodox school of Revd Eli Cogan, a Unitarian minister. Here, he imbibed a curriculum that appears to have emphasized the study of English alongside modern history, literature and philosophy, buttressed by the customary contemporary fare of classics. This type of education consequently set him apart from his public-school peers, who received an almost wholly classical education, only imperfectly balanced by school sports and debates, while his seemingly lonely, introspective childhood was little compensated by the alternative schooling he received. However, not only did this appear to drive home Disraeli's own individualism and unconventionality, it also seems to have provided him with a far more sound, practical education than the purely classical, utterly conventional one that individuals like Gladstone received. In fact, in his final complete novel, *Endymion* (1881), Disraeli criticized such men for being merely 'overgrown schoolboys' who had read

> very little more than some Latin writers, some Greek plays and some treatises of Aristotle. These with a due course of Bampton lectures and some dipping into the *Quarterly Review* ... [apparently] qualified a man ... not only for being a member of parliament, but [for] becoming a candidate for the responsibility of statesmanship.[13]

In one autobiographical note, Disraeli seems to disagree with any untraditional portrayal of his former school, Higham Hill, remarking that 'nothing was thought of there but the two dead languages' and providing a relatively complete summary of the classical authors and texts he studied.[14] However, Disraeli was a notoriously unreliable narrator of his own biography, suggesting in the very same passage that he 'remained there four years' when it is clear that he must be conflating his time at Higham Hill with that spent at Potticany's school. As his early biographer, William F. Monypenny suggests

> The accounts which Disraeli gives of his early years, in such fragments of autobiography, letters, notes and conversations as have come down to us, are not easy to harmonize. Mr Potticany's school he nowhere mentions, and in later years the memory of Higham Hill seems to have absorbed many of the recollections both of what preceded and what followed in his education.[15]

---

13 B. Disraeli, *Endymion* (London, 1881), p. 10.  **14** Quoted in W.F. Monypenny & G.E. Buckle, *The life of Benjamin Disraeli*, 6 vols (London, 1910), i, 24–5.  **15** Ibid., p. 25.

One should be careful, therefore, in taking the mercurial Disraeli's word in such accounts, since the above assertion was possibly one of his common offhand remarks. Indeed, since his statement seems to run so counter to the more varied education that other accounts suggest that he received at Higham Hill, one wonders if Disraeli is, perhaps, not simply attempting to suggest parity with his public school peers who complained of Disraeli's 'un-English education'[16] by emphasizing the strength of his classical education.

Encapsulating succinctly the impact of his formal and informal education, Disraeli was probably closer to the truth of its unorthodoxy in the following remark:

> Born in a library, and trained from early childhood by learned men who did not share the passions and prejudices of our political and social life, I had imbibed on some subjects conclusions different from those which generally prevail.[17]

Similarly, his *Times* obituary suggested that 'In place of being educated, he very much educated himself, although it may be questioned whether what must have been a loss to many did not in the end prove a gain to him'.[18] In regard to his lack of university education, *The Times* noted that, 'although an outsider, he learnt more about [it] than most men do in full residence'.[19] Yet, in spite of the advantages that his more unconventional education offered, Disraeli seems to have always felt keenly the early conclusion of his formal schooling, his lack of a university education and his consequent deficiency in the matter of classics. He admitted that, not only had he not been in the first class of classical scholars at Higham Hill, but he was 'not even eminent in the second';[20] while his headmaster claimed not to have liked Disraeli because he could never get him 'to understand the subjunctive'.[21] This was something that Disraeli attempted to remedy by sequestering himself in his father Isaac's extensive library throughout 1820 and most of 1821, devoting his time to grasping the classical learning he felt he may have missed out on at Cogan's school.

In a notebook recording his progress at that time, Disraeli mentions having read an array of mostly Latin, but some Greek, authors, including Livy, Terence, Virgil, Tibullus and Lucretius, with Homer, Demosthenes, Euripides, Sophocles and Lucian somewhat balancing out his classical reading. It seems unlikely that he spent the twelve hours of diligent, daily study that he has his autobiographical protagonist, Vivian Grey, perform, but it is clear from his diary that, during this time, he became a passable Latin scholar, though he never fully gained a true grounding in Greek. Disraeli struggled evidently with Greek, since

16 Ibid., p. 24.   17 Quoted in Richmond, 'Disraeli's education', p. 25.   18 *The Times*, 20 Apr. 1881.   19 Ibid., 21 Apr. 1881.   20 Quoted in Monypenny & Buckle, i, 25.   21 Quoted in C. Hibbert, *Disraeli: a personal history* (London, 2004), p. 9.

he terms the study of Greek metres 'a dry, but necessary, study'[22] and he has to keep 'a hateful lexicon at [his] side' in order 'to wade through [the] beauties' of Demosthenes.[23] A typical example of his efforts makes this clear: 'Friday. Again at the Greek metres[,] bewildered! lost! miserable work, indeed'; though, by Monday, he writes: 'Greek metres [–] a ray of light' and, by the following Wednesday, that he had met with 'tolerable success'.[24] This 'heroic attempt' to make himself master of classical language and literature met with similarly satisfactory results, but, as Monypenny suggests, 'the Disraeli that we know would not have been himself if he had received the stamp that a public school education places upon intellect and character'.[25] His unorthodox schooling – which ended at the age of seventeen, when his father apprenticed him to a firm of solicitors – therefore induced Disraeli to develop an undoubted appreciation of antiquity, though one conditioned effectively to regard its study as only equivalent to any other subject.

Thus, from the outset, Gladstone's and Disraeli's lifelong relationship with classical culture was influenced by an early association with the subject via their divergent educations. While Gladstone's formative years were shaped by a constant and cloistered interaction with formal classical education, Disraeli balanced a more casual interest with his much broader academic and literary pursuits – consequently gaining an undeserved reputation for possessing, like Shakespeare, 'small Latin and less Greek'. Yet, in spite of their separate and dissimilar contacts with classics, both men remained active in their interest in the cultures of ancient Greece and Rome – as men of letters and as politicians. This is evident, not just from their political speeches, but also from their other writings – Gladstone's amateur Homeric studies and Disraeli's novels, in particular. Consequently, these writings reveal much about their personal attitude to classical culture and its wider reception in their own society, which their political leadership would so influence.

MEN OF LETTERS

Since classical analysis had been his business throughout his formative years at Eton and Oxford, it was natural that Gladstone would turn to antiquity for the rest of his life, both publicly and privately – though always in a very characteristically committed and systematic fashion. For instance, throughout the 1830s, in parallel to his burgeoning career as a junior cabinet minister and in preparation for the publication of his first book, *The state in its relations with the church* (1838), Gladstone embarked upon an extended personal study of Aristotle and Plato. In particular, he focused on Aristotle's *Politics* during 1834–5 and may

22 Monypenny & Buckle, i, 28.   23 Ibid., p. 29.   24 Ibid., p. 28.   25 Ibid., p. 26.

even have employed its practicality to temper Plato's more utopian, impossible visions in the formation of his own early political views. Yet, when these views matured and politics became even more his business in the 1840s and 1850s, classics became his pleasure – the world of Homer providing Gladstone with a psychological refuge from the often turbulent storms of British politics.

Over the next forty-five years, Gladstone wrote five books and an extensive series of articles on Homer – one of the former consisting of over 1,700 pages – altogether representing what Frank Turner has called 'the single most extensive body of Victorian Homeric commentary'.[26] Significantly, though, he only turned to the systematic study of Homer in periods when he was out of office and installed in his 'Temple of Peace', his study at Hawarden Castle; chiefly, in 1846, when he was out of parliament and freshly retired from the colonial office, continuing with another bout of amateur study in the late 1850s, following the fall of the Aberdeen coalition. This second writing campaign culminated in his most significant contribution to classics and to literature, his three-volume work, *Studies on Homer and the Homeric age* (1858), which, in spite of its detailed (if idiosyncratic) scholarship, was received in a rather hostile fashion by mainstream academia. For instance, the poet, Alfred Tennyson, thought Gladstone's opinions on Homer 'hobby-horsical', while, perhaps more authoritatively, the Oxford don and classicist, Benjamin Jowett, pronounced them 'mere nonsense'.[27] Yet, apart, perhaps, from his controversial approach to ancient Greek religion, Gladstone did try to make his methodologies in the work as meticulous and as reliable as he could – something solidly characteristic of his typically stout resolve and dedication in every other part of his life.

However, in spite of this being merely a private passion, Gladstone's classical studies appear to have been grounded solidly in contemporary affairs and his personal attitudes towards events. Gladstone considered the works of Homer to be far more than ancient poetry; to contain also, a 'world of religion and ethics, of civil policy, of history and ethnology, of manners and arts'[28] – a world that 'stands between Paradise and the vices of later heathenism'.[29] Gladstone seems to have firmly believed that Homeric Greece and Victorian England bore a deep affinity to each other as societies, suggesting that '[Homer] is the very picture before our own eyes in our own time and country, where visible traces of the old patriarchal mould still coexist … with political liberties of more recent fashion, because they retain their hold on the general affections'.[30] According to David Bebbington, 'Gladstone's Homeric scholarship was bound up with the evolution of his most fundamental convictions',[31] providing what Gladstone himself

---

26 F.M. Turner, *The Greek heritage in Victorian Britain* (New Haven, CT, 1981), p. 160.
27 Quoted in R. Aldous, *The lion and the unicorn: Gladstone v. Disraeli* (London, 2006), pp 97–8.
28 R. Jenkyns, *The Victorians and ancient Greece* (Oxford, 1980), p. 201.   29 Quoted in D.W. Bebbington, *The mind of Gladstone: religion, Homer and politics*, p. 148.   30 Quoted in Jenkyns, *The Victorians and ancient Greece*, p. 201.   31 Ibid., p. 143.

termed 'an admirable school of polity'.[32] Although Gladstone may have turned to classics in his leisure moments, he took his Hellenic studies extremely seriously and often intertwined them with his political opinions. For instance, as an opponent of the 1857 Divorce Bill, he wrote contemporaneously in his *Studies on Homer* that divorce was unknown to the ancient Greeks. Though this domestication of antiquity appears to counter Gladstone's characteristic meticulousness, this was more a trait of Victorian culture and less to do with his own personal attitude to classical culture, which always remained careful, reverent and fastidious.

This was not a stance that one could associate entirely with Benjamin Disraeli's more cavalier political use of classical allusion, which often employed references out of context and occasionally even bordered on the frivolous – something anathema to the scrupulous Gladstone. Yet, as Paul Smith has commented, 'in standing none of [Disraeli's] nonsense, you catch very little of his drift';[33] perhaps, indicating that we should indulge and acknowledge these foibles if we are to understand fully his character and opinions – which, according to Richard Faber, were 'not so much deep as complex'.[34] Although the famous illustrations of Disraeli's more trivial inclination towards classics date from his later political career, this approach first manifested itself in his early, autobiographical novels – in particular, *Vivian Grey* (1826) and *Contarini Fleming* (1832). One must be careful in utilizing Disraeli's early novels as autobiographical sources, as Monypenny remarked in his warning that '[n]either *Vivian Grey* nor *Contarini Fleming* can be used without discrimination as an authority for biographical details'.[35] However, although Disraeli was writing fiction, there is a definite level of autobiographical input that must be appreciated and integrated into any studies of his early life. As J.A. Froude suggested in his biography of Disraeli,

> Neither *Vivian Grey* nor *Contarini Fleming* can be trusted literally for autobiographical details; but Disraeli has identified himself with Contarini in assigning to him many of his own personal experiences, and Vivian has been always acknowledged as a portrait sketched from a looking-glass.[36]

It is in such a sceptical, yet receptive, light that I regard these sources in this study.[37] Both were closely autobiographical works and led up to a watershed in Disraeli's life in the 1830s, when he put aside his fictional alter-egos and claimed that '… I wish to act what I write', turning seriously from literature to politics.

32 Ibid., p. 201. 33 Smith, *Disraeli*, p. 7. 34 Ibid. 35 Monypenny & Buckle, i, 34. 36 J.A. Froude, *Lord Beaconsfield* (London, 1890), p. 15. 37 For a useful examination of the relationship between Disraeli's fiction and politics, see M. Flavin, *Benjamin Disraeli: the novel as political discourse* (Eastbourne, East Sussex, 2005).

*Vivian Grey*, Disraeli claimed, in particular, portrayed his 'ideal ambition' and stood as 'a secret history of [his] feelings',[38] which makes it a crucial indicator of his youthful opinions – including those on classics.

Disraeli ventriloquized his opinions of classical education via the mouth of his autobiographical protagonist, Vivian Grey, when he had him suggest that, although he possesses sub-par classical knowledge, 'in talents and various accomplishments' he remains 'immeasurably the superior'[39] of the classical students at school. According to Grey, 'distinction in such points [was] ten thousand times more admired by the multitude, than the most profound knowledge of Greek metres, or the most accurate acquaintance with the value of Roman coins'.[40] Thus, although Grey admits that 'all the wit and wisdom of the world are concentrated in some fifty antique volumes',[41] he still complains that classics is, ultimately, something 'forced and false'[42] beside everything genuine – merely an 'error'[43] into which schoolboys fall. This appears to be Disraeli outlining clearly a youthful estimation of classical culture that would go on to form the basis of his lifelong relationship to its terms and tenets.

Unlike Gladstone's regular formal and informal recourse to classical culture, Disraeli seems to have ranked other cultural parallels and paradigms either genuinely equal to, or even higher than, those associated with ancient Greece and Rome. He expressed this clearly in his 1833–4 poem, *Revolutionary epick*, when he wondered: 'Is the revolution of France a less important event than the siege of Troy? Is Achilles a less interesting character than Napoleon?'[44] – thereby drawing ancient and modern together in a comparison almost equating both. When Disraeli toured the Mediterranean and Near East in 1830–1, he described Spain and Turkey as the highlights of the trip – significantly, not Italy or Greece. The autobiographical work inspired by his Grand Tour, *Contarini Fleming*, includes a revelatory passage of reverie while Fleming stands among the ruins of the Roman Forum, ruminating on the rise and fall of the ancient empires:

> Where are the spoils of Egypt and Carthage? Where the golden tribute of Iberia? Where the long Gallic trophies? Where are the rich armour and massy cups of Macedon? Where are the pictures and statues of Corinth? Where are the libraries of Athens? Where is the broken bow of Parthia? Where are the elephants of Pontus, and the gorgeous diadems of the Asian kings? And where is Rome? All nations rose and flourished only to swell her splendour, and now I stand amid her ruins.[45]

38 Quoted in Aldous, *The lion and the unicorn*, p. 19.  39 B. Disraeli, *Vivian Grey* (Leipzig, 1826), p. 7.  40 Ibid.  41 Ibid., p. 19.  42 Ibid., p. 7.  43 Ibid., p. 19.  44 Quoted in Hibbert, *Disraeli*, p. 73.  45 *Contarini Fleming*, VII, ch. 1, p. 169.

This expulsion of antiquity to historical oblivion suggests a certain unwillingness on Disraeli's part to see the classical world as anything more than a historical phase like any other, yet one providing a wealth of references and allusions ripe for possible exploitation – or even outright corruption.

These writings – both fiction and non-fiction – provided Gladstone and Disraeli effectively with a looking-glass in which to polish and to preen their personal opinions – including those on classics – before attempting to transfer and to employ these beliefs and ideals in political reality. Another crucial contrast between their attitudes becomes apparent when one explores how they related their interest in classics to politics. For Gladstone, classical study became a means of relaxation, a respite from the strains of parliamentary politics, though when he did choose to employ classical allusions he did so in a naturally informed manner, reflecting his traditional education. He did this, for example, in imperial debates when he compared the British Empire with the ancient Athenian one, and did so in a clearly worked out parallel that reflected the veracity of each ancient and modern comparative – not, as was often the case with Disraeli, merely exploiting the past to uphold the present.

MEN OF POLITICS

William Gladstone and Benjamin Disraeli both enjoyed long parliamentary careers, in which they utilized their knowledge of classical history and literature in various parliamentary speeches and public addresses via references and allusions almost too numerous to calculate. However, taking account of the large amount already written about their political rivalry, a small number of key examples can illustrate their broader awareness and employment of classics to augment political arguments or to gain advantage over each other. Indeed, it might be worthwhile if future historians of the Gladstone/Disraeli rivalry interacted more closely with the possible influence of these often overlooked portions of both men's lives and careers. For instance, Gladstone's lifelong Hellenism and associated antipathy to Roman history and literature may well have influenced his political aversion and opposition to Roman Catholicism. So, too, Disraeli's later predilection for bombastic imperialism and dramatic political *coups de théâtre* appears to have a clear relation to his early and continued preference for ancient Rome over ancient Greece and for Latin over Hellenic literature. A few examples should suffice to demonstrate the ways in which Gladstone and Disraeli both turned to their classical backgrounds and interests over the course of their long political careers – one in a broadly Greek sense, one in a decidedly Roman one.

Gladstone and Disraeli both entered the House of Commons in the 1830s. In every other respect they had little in common. Their parliamentary behaviour was quite divergent, not least with regard to the manner in which they deployed classical references. While there is a certain continuity to the classical allusions that Gladstone drew upon in manifold parliamentary opinions and pronouncements throughout his career, Disraeli demonstrated a far more capricious and cosmetic approach. For instance, where Gladstone maintained a suspicion of any Romanized vision of the British Empire from at least *c*.1850 – as informed by his knowledge of the failure of the ancient Athenian imperial project – Disraeli seems to have called upon an assorted stock of classical paradigms and parallels throughout his career, only turning explicitly to ancient Rome in later years because of its utility in supporting his brand of British imperialism. In an important parliamentary speech, Gladstone opposed Lord Palmerston's 1850 rhetorical *civis Romanus sum* justification of a more aggressive British foreign policy – which looked ahead to similar Disraelian appropriations – going on to present instead, throughout the 1850s, a far more Hellenized model of British overseas rule. This he based on a familial Greek model of mother-city and colonies, declaring in 1855 that, in imperial terms, the English had much to learn from ancient Greece, since 'no country known to us appears so fully to have realized or to have given such remarkable effect to that idea [of colonization]'.[46] Nor was this simply a throwaway remark in a provincial address; being merely one aspect of a long, valid and detailed thesis outlining his personal vision of British imperialism and how it might avoid excess, aggressiveness, acquisitiveness, corruption and ultimate destruction.

The continuity and purpose of Gladstone's classical parallels are in stark contrast to Disraeli's, which, from his first day on the floor of the commons, seemed to reveal a far freer, even frivolous, approach to their deployment. For instance, in Disraeli's first parliamentary speech on 7 December 1837, he became slightly flustered after a boorish reception and resorted to some obscure classical comparisons, speaking of the 'new' and 'old loves' of 'the noble Tityrus of the treasury bench and the learned Daphne of Liskeard', while referring ungrammatically to 'the *amanlium iro* [sic] [that] had resulted [...] in the *amoris ingratiae*'.[47] Again, during his maiden speech as chancellor of the exchequer in 1852, he employed a Homeric phrase for 'winged words', '*epea pteroenta*', in spite of his own youthful shortcomings in the language. In both of these instances, Disraeli was climbing a little further up the 'greasy pole' of British politics and the significance of each occasion to him is indicated by his recourse to a classical reference to gild his speech with artificial proof that he was a gentleman of taste and learning – not out of a genuinely innate cultural parallel, as it was for Gladstone. Nevertheless, throughout his career, the majority of his remarks on

46 'Our colonies', a speech delivered to the Members of the Mechanics' Institute at Chester, 12 Nov. 1855; available in M. Carter & B. Harlow (eds), *Imperialism and orientalism: a documentary sourcebook* (Oxford, 1999), pp 363–78.  **47** *The Times*, 8 Dec. 1837. It is possible that this may be a misheard or misprinted version of his proper phrase; this is not clear from *Hansard*.

antiquity demonstrate the basic interest in, and respect for, classical literature
that came inherently with being the son of a renowned bibliophile. However, in
a society in which classics was venerated as a touchstone of culture and status,
classical allusion appears to have been merely a valuable cosmetic addition to
Disraeli's political arguments, helping him to banish any inferiority complex by
emphasizing parity with his more classically educated peers – and one that, as
demonstrated above, often fell short of his expectations.

In 1858, the Hellenist in Gladstone met with a golden opportunity: a chance
to become lord high commissioner extraordinary for the Ionian Islands and to
visit the lands already known to him from his beloved Homer.[48] This gave him a
unique occasion to bind both his personal and his political interests, being sent
out ostensibly to report on local sentiment regarding continued British protection versus the islands' prospective merger with Greece. However, Gladstone
also utilized his brief period in office – from November 1858 to February 1859
– as an extended and immersive classical experience, visiting sites and absorbing
himself in the local culture. Interestingly, some individuals – mostly Peelites –
saw the entire escapade as a plot engineered by Disraeli and the colonial secretary, Edward Bulwer-Lytton, to remove Gladstone from the political scene; by
taking the post, he would have to give up his seat in the Commons and might
very well fail to regain a seat in a by-election. There seems no evidence to
support this theory, but it is likely that Disraeli was pleased to see Gladstone
removed temporarily from the parliamentary scene via the exploitation of his
well-known and sometimes-maligned Hellenism.

Disraeli exposed his own, far more Roman, inclinations through his articulation of a number of specific gestures and phrases during his second term as
prime minister, 1874–80; perhaps, also detecting in classical culture – and
ancient Rome in particular – a legitimating western precedent to undercut
popular perceptions of his socially problematic Semitic origins. Most notably,
his seemingly offhand decision to pass the 1876 Royal Titles Act that named the
queen 'Empress of India' encouraged a very explicit imperial parallel with the
taxonomy of ancient Rome. This was a theatrical gesture designed both to flatter
Queen Victoria and to encourage an explicit imperial parallel that dignified his
more aggressive foreign policy decisions with recourse to a Roman allusion.
Indeed, this design also represents evidence of a clear relationship between
Disraeli's fiction and his political career, with this particular whim traceable to
his novel, *Tancred* (1847), where the adventurer, Fakredeen, suggests that the
'Queen of the English' should 'transfer the seat of her empire from London to
Delhi'.[49] Yet, the single phrase that resounds with Disraeli's clearest Roman

48 For a valuable account of the political relevance of his mission, see 'Gladstone and the
Greeks: the extraordinary mission to the Ionian Islands, 1858–1859' in R. Holland & D.
Markides, *The British and the Hellenes: struggles for mastery in the eastern Mediterranean,
1850–1960* (Oxford, 2006), pp 13–45.   49 B. Disraeli, *Tancred* (Leipzig, 1847), i, 296.

allusion lies at the heart of his famous 1879 '*imperium et libertas*' speech. This speech drew on Palmerston's notorious *civis Romanus sum* defence of British foreign policy, while justifying Disraeli's own interventionist, imperialist foreign policy. In this, he observed, using what appears to be a half-remembered, half-garbled classical phrase:

> One of the greatest of Romans, when asked what were his politics, replied, *Imperium et Libertas*. That would not make a bad programme for a British ministry. It is one from which Her Majesty's advisors do not shrink.[50]

Having always opposed such idle appropriations as adornments for political arguments, Gladstone instantly retorted that this meant merely, 'Liberty for ourselves [and] empire over the rest of mankind'.[51] As one can see, therefore, Disraeli expressed his classical interests in his political career just as Gladstone did – though in a different way, basing his interaction more in flourish than in fact.

So, while Gladstone was led by his classical interests, clearly Disraeli led his, exploiting the exclusive cultural value that Victorians such as Gladstone put on classics and flourishing it for political gain as a hallmark of his status. Gladstone truly saw in antiquity – and ancient Greece in particular – a way of life that offered a model for contemporary behaviour; Disraeli, on the other hand, seems to have perceived in the ancient world merely a variorum resource of cultural references and resonances to be thumbed through and exploited at will. This was also something that reflected their respective concentration on domestic reform and foreign policy, with Gladstone's micro-management of domestic parliamentary bills bearing little relation to the dramatic cut-and-thrust of Disraeli's overseas schemes and imperial gestures. Consequently, one can see that between the staid Gladstone and the dandified Disraeli lay a much wider cultural gulf that spoke of the growing differences between those who supported a Hellenized 'Little England' and a more Romanized vision of global British expansion. While for Gladstone, classical learning was always something formally ingrained and integrated from youth, for Disraeli it was something merely to be picked up and put down according to circumstance – a useful tool perhaps, but never a constant companion.

---

50 A speech given at the Guildhall, London, 9 Nov. 1879. Quoted in Monypenny & Buckle, vi, 495. See N. Vance, *The Victorians and ancient Rome* (Oxford, 1997), p. 231. See Vance, pp 231–2, for a fuller discussion of the derivation of this phrase.   51 W.E. Gladstone, *Political speeches in Scotland, November and December 1879* (London, 1879), p. 128.

CONCLUSION

By exploring the relationship of Greek and Roman culture to the lives and opinions of William Gladstone and Benjamin Disraeli, we gain a fresh perspective on the oft-told tale of a legendary rivalry evident even from the divergent nicknames associated with both men – the 'Grand Old Man' and 'Dizzy', respectively. As Disraeli suggests in another of his novels,

> If the history of England be ever written by one who has the knowledge and the courage, ... the world would be more astonished than when reading the Roman annals by Niebuhr. Generally speaking, all the great events have been distorted, most of the important causes concealed, some of the principal characters never appear, and all who figure are so misunderstood and misrepresented, that the result is a complete mystification.[52]

Although this essay sketches out merely a general relationship, it may be hoped that further contextual studies might attempt to right any remaining semblance of this wrong and help to demystify the events, causes and characters of one of British history's great rivalries.

The importance of a classical education in the nineteenth century makes any study of the connection between the formative years of the Victorians and its wider socio-cultural influence significant to historians. Like many individuals of their class and generation, Gladstone and Disraeli remained in lifelong thrall to classics, a cultural touchstone that defined how Victorians saw both themselves and their world, inexorably conditioned by both their upbringing and education. However, their divergent approaches to the subject were rooted in these formative years; Gladstone's Evangelical background providing him with an early diligence and moral bearing that was reinforced by the substantial classical education he received at Eton and Oxford, while Disraeli's irreverent and capricious approach to the intersection of culture and politics can be seen to have grown from his contrastingly unorthodox upbringing.

In summation, classics provided another theatre of conflict for Gladstone and Disraeli's rivalry, suggesting yet another set of cultural poles in ancient Greece and Rome for them to inhabit and to exploit for both personal and political one-upmanship. For instance, Sir Stafford Northcote once reported of Disraeli that 'the chief considered everything Gladstone had written on Homer was wrong',[53] while Gladstone later upbraided his opponent for having his personal secretary, Monty Corry, raised to the peerage, complaining that 'there has been nothing

---

52 B. Disraeli, *Sybil, or the two nations* (New York, 1845), vol. i, bk. i, ch. 2, pp 32–3.  53 Quoted in Hibbert, *Disraeli*, p. 354.

like it since Caligula created his horse a consul'.[54] These criticisms mark a fresh view of their rivalry, another offshoot of dissent, another point of variance between these men, occurring via the mutual disagreement their stances on antiquity took. Thus, between Gladstone and Disraeli lay a far wider cultural gulf separating a careful, moral Hellenism and a more open, reckless Roman-ness in a rivalry that continues to be valuable in exposing new perspectives on the history of the Victorian age.[55]

**54** Quoted in Aldous, *The lion and the unicorn*, p. 310.   **55** I would like to thank my supervisor, Professor David Scourfield, for reading and offering constructive comments on previous versions of this essay; his continued guidance and support have proved invaluable to me. I must also acknowledge the encouragement of Professor R.V. Comerford, which has proved key to my postgraduate career. I am also grateful to have been supported in my research as an IRCHSS Government of Ireland Postgraduate Scholar, 2009–11.

# The religious dimension in Gladstone's Home Rule analysis[1]

## JOHN-PAUL McCARTHY

This essay explores the way in which Gladstone's constitutional sensitivities were shaped by his religious personality. The most tantalizing aspect of the Home Rule historiography is the argument that Gladstone's Irish analysis in general was a product of his religious personality; that is to say that his Irish analysis was but a single star in a broader constellation. Some have only dealt with this in a glancing way,[2] while others like Parry gave it more thought and have argued, for example, that Gladstone's concern about the calcification of Irish Catholic culture into an ultramontane mould after 1870 played an important part in the evolving analysis. A domestic legislative assembly would, he hoped, provide the Irish poor with an alternative focus for their loyalties and as such would diminish the influence of the priesthood, the chill winds of a putative Erastian[3] parliament being his punishment of choice for the clerics who ruined his plans for reforming the University of Dublin in 1873.[4] And here, of course, in his ambition to remake popular Catholic culture in Paul Cullen's Ireland through a policy of constitutional equalization,[5] he was playing for very big stakes indeed, far bigger than anything Peel or Russell had hoped for.[6]

While the deduction of temporal or specifically constitutional principles from a religious template is a notoriously fraught enterprise,[7] there is a strong case for

---

1 This essay was inspired by my last lunch date with John Wyon Burrow, a wonderful teacher who passed away in 2009. 2 D.W. Bebbington, *William Ewart Gladstone: faith and politics in Victorian Britain* (Grand Rapids, MI, 1993), pp 222–3. 3 'Erastian' was a term of abuse used to denote profane clerical subordination to the temporal power. See, generally, D. MacCulloch, 'Richard Hooker's reputation', *English Historical Review*, 117 (2002), 804. 4 J.P. Parry, *Democracy and religion: Gladstone and the Liberal Party, 1867–75* (Cambridge, 1986), p. 177. See Henry Manning's reaction in J. Morley, *The life of William Ewart Gladstone*, 3 vols (London, 1903), iii, 325. 5 On the equality dimension to the 1886 analysis, see A. Jackson, *Home Rule: an Irish history, 1800–2000* (New York, 2004), p. 82. 6 Gladstone's ambitious belief in 1886 that 'structure' can influence 'character' – the basic insight of the entire Home Rule analysis – makes sense when set against a recurring strain within the counter-revolutionary conservative tradition in post-revolutionary Europe, a tradition that saw government primarily in terms of its capacity for inculcating moral restraint, Gladstone's own tradition since the 1830s, broadly speaking. C. Schmitt, *Political theology: four chapters on the concept of sovereignty* (Chicago, 1985), pp 55–6; M.W. McConnell, 'Establishment and toleration in Edmund Burke's "Constitution of Freedom"', *Supreme Court Review*, 275 (1996), 393–462. 7 F. Fernández-Arnesto, *Millennium: a history of the last thousand years* (London, 1996), p. 423 (arguing that deductions of this kind

going even further than Parry or Bebbington when assessing the coherence of Gladstone's Home Rule analysis, as argued below. After all, Gladstone was emphatic in his insistence that *every* aspect of his political career was ultimately shaped by his complex religious faith. He never tired for example of reminding his sons in particular that there simply was no distinction between the temporal and the spiritual, and the idea of a 'political' world conceived *in vacuo* was literally incomprehensible to a man of his sensitivities. 'Practically to us', he wrote as a young man, 'the world in this sense has ceased to exist'.[8] Above all else, Christianity was a total account of the human predicament, its prescriptions both a beacon to follow by men who were in earnest, and a hope to attain in this world.[9] Some of the psalms in particular awoke these restless chimes in his personality, and reinforced his sensitivity to those numberless afflictions which at times led him to wonder whether heaven had given life to man in mercy or in wrath.[10] There is no compelling reason in short why his mature Irish analysis should remain isolated from these themes. When we take these important religious sensitivities into account during the 1880s, we can see that there is an extraordinary similarity between the Home Rule analysis and Gladstone's understanding of how the concept of sovereignty had developed over the course of the history of the British state in its relations with the established church since the sixteenth century.

Gladstone's important paper from 1850 called *Remarks on the royal supremacy*[11] provided the crucial conceptual ballast for the later Home Rule analysis. This paper is not, however, to be read as a literal anticipation of the 1886 analysis, since it emerged from a specific doctrinal controversy in the 1850s between the crown-in-parliament, the church courts and the warring factions

are difficult because it is so hard to define the 'religious mind' in any way coherently). This scepticism is echoed in the Victorian context in E.R. Norman, *Church and society in England, 1770–1970: a historical study* (Oxford, 1976), p. 10. See B. Hilton, *The age of atonement: the influence of evangelicalism on social and economic thought, 1785–1865* (Oxford, 1988); S.A. Skinner, *Tractarians and the 'Condition of England': the social and political thought of the Oxford Movement* (Oxford, 2004). **8** D.C. Lathbury, *Correspondence on church and religion of William Ewart Gladstone*, 2 vols (London, 1910), ii, 430. 'The world and the flesh'. **9** That Gladstone's Christianity was meant to facilitate action and to save souls in real time, as distinct from some nebulous afterlife, is apparent in the writings canvassed by Hilton. B. Hilton 'Gladstone's theological politics' in M. Bentley & J. Stevenson (eds), *High and low politics in modern Britain: ten studies* (Oxford, 1983), pp 30–1. See Newman's insistence 'In truth, the Church was framed for the express purpose of interfering, or (as irreligious men will say) meddling with the world'. J.H. Newman, *The Arians of the fourth century, their doctrine, temper and conduct, chiefly as exhibited in the councils of the church between AD325 & AD381* (Oxford, 1831), pp 276–8. **10** He recurred frequently to the biblical image of man as pilgrim battling for souls in the benighted city. 'Walk about Sion, and go round about her: and tell the towers thereof: mark well her bulwarks, consider her palaces: that ye may tell them that come after'. KJV, Ps xlviii. 11, 12. Quoted in 'The parts and the whole', Lathbury, *Correspondence on church and religion*, ii, 449. **11** W.E. Gladstone, *Remarks on the royal supremacy, as it is defined by reason, history and the constitution: a letter to the lord bishop of London* (London, 1850).

within the established church. This paper needs to be read more generally so as to appreciate the manner in which Gladstone formulated key constitutional questions. His analysis of the royal supremacy is of crucial importance in assessing the analytical pedigree of Home Rule policy for three reasons. Firstly, this paper is the most extensive and dense historical meditation attempted in his career on the concept of sovereignty and the Westminster parliament's plenary powers. Sovereignty was of course at the heart of the argument in 1886 and the Home Rule analysis closely mirrored several of the key arguments advanced in this earlier paper. The 1850 paper is actually far more comprehensive and informed than those papers Gladstone wrote specifically on the looming Irish problem after 1880. This should not surprise us, considering the competing pressures on Gladstone's time and energies after 1880 as well as the myriad burdens of the Victorian premiership. The 1850 paper dealt with similar constitutional issues, but in a more comprehensive and thus revealing way.

Secondly, we must attend closely to this paper in the Home Rule context because this was Gladstone's most intense analysis of the British constitutional equipoise and the foundational principles that animated the 'ancient constitution'. These were the materials out of which the later Home Rule scheme was constructed. Home Rule was always primarily a British problem, in that it put unprecedented pressure on existing constitutional practice within the UK and thereby stretched several constitutional pieties to breaking point.[12] The 1850 paper gives a vivid insight into Gladstone's unique perspective on these constitutional pieties, and this focus helps us to see several crucial assonances between the Irish analysis in 1886 and the British constitutional tradition that served as the template for all of Gladstone's major calculations. This is simply to recognize an important analytical reality, namely the fact that Gladstone interpreted Ireland the only way he knew how, as a British prime minister. It could hardly be otherwise in fact.[13] Indeed, he told the historian Lord Acton in a remarkable letter at a crucial state in his tactical calculations towards the end of 1885 that there was no need for any analytical convulsions at this point on his behalf, since all the heavy conceptual lifting had been done years before. He was content to

12 Gladstone had written with evident derision on many occasions about the archaic quality of sundry Whiggish constitutional fictions, be it absolute parliamentary supremacy, the fiction of separation of powers, reserve executive authority of the crown or the benign impact of 1688–9. For Gladstone's criticisms on these matters see Morley, *Life*, ii, 251, 295, 363, 424, 450, 466, 652; A. Tollemache, *Gladstone's Boswell: late Victorian conversations* (Sussex, NY, 1984), p. 193 (arguing that there was little to celebrate as regards the British constitution before the Grey ministry since the constitution of 1830 was 'irredeemable'). 13 This emphasis on the way in which certain core intellectual assumptions structure even seemingly unrelated arguments follows Hilton, *Atonement*, pp 3–36; J. Huizinga, 'The task of cultural history' in J. Huizinga, *Men and ideas: history, the Middle Ages and the Renaissance* (New York, NY, 1959), pp 17–76; L.O. Mink, 'Change and causality in the history of ideas' in L.O. Mink, *Historical understanding* (Cornell, 1987), p. 221.

allow settled principles to evolve at this point. 'The truth is', Gladstone wrote, 'I have more or less of opinions and ideas. In these ideas and opinions there is, I think, little that I have not more or less conveyed in public declarations; in principle nothing'.[14] His thinking here was in many ways an example of the paradoxical characterization of the 'historical mind' insisted on by a later gener-ation of philosophers, namely the kind of mind that thinks forward so to speak, but understands backwards, that is to say, a mind that determines a future course of action by looking for the essentials of a given scenario,[15] and which then seeks to recast these in familiar categories.[16]

The third reason for carefully parsing the 1850 paper is because it dealt with the precise conceptual issue Gladstone was confronted with in specifically Irish garb after 1885. His *Remarks on the royal supremacy* dealt formally of course with the tensions that followed an Erastian veto of a church court on a matter of Anglican doctrine. This is to interpret this remarkable source at an overly specific level, however. It discussed the Gorham judgment at a formal level, but its sweep was much broader than the details of a mere doctrinal fracas between evangelicals and law lords. This paper was essentially an essay in British consti-tutional history, one designed to answer several major constitutional and political questions that were raw in the 1850s but which would recur again in more dramatic Irish terms in the 1880s. The *Remarks* and the Home Rule analysis looked at precisely the same set of conceptual problems; was the crown-in-parliament an *à priori* concept, or could the constitutional limitations it implied be interpreted in a more flexible, more imaginative light? Did this concept in fact have to be interpreted historically rather than just legally, and if so, did this suggest that the historic supremacy of the unitary parliament was actually less than the sum of its austere parts? Were the aggressive champions of absolutist

---

14 Morley, *Life*, iii, 172. 15 This cast of mind is best exemplified in a series of essays Gladstone wrote for his children in the late 1840s – essentially a series of mini prayer books – which emphasized the need to see larger patterns in the quotidian crush. 'To see the parts alone is trifling; and to see the whole alone is vague, and is like the memory of a pleasant song that has passed away, or like the beholding of a man's self in the glass, after which he goes, and forgets what manner of man he was'. 'The parts and the whole', MS from 31 Aug. 1847 in Lathbury, *Correspondence*, ii, 449–50. This yearning for wholeness mirrored the later Tractarian depiction of God as 'the Pattern Man'. D.W. Bebbington, *The mind of Gladstone: religion, Homer and politics* (Oxford, 2004), pp 67–8. See W.E. Gladstone, *Ecce homo* (London, 1868), p. 154. On 'wholeness' as the *sine qua non* of the religious intellect, see M. Oakeshott, 'Introduction to *Leviathan*' in M. Oakeshott, *Leviathan* (Oxford, 1946 ed.), p. 4. 16 F.M. Turner, '*The mind of Gladstone: religion, Homer and politics* by David Bebbington', *English Historical Review*, 122 (2007), 212. To the extent that the canonical classical curriculum taught at Oxbridge for centuries was designed to give pupils a series of basic categories through which to filter the trials of life, Christ Church reinforced this formidable tendency to reason through analogy in Gladstone. The importance of religion *qua* analogy – perhaps its key function – is emphasized over the Christian *longue durée* in M. Carruthers, *The craft of thought: mediation, rhetoric and the making of images, 400–1200* (Cambridge, 1998), pp 7–24. D. MacCulloch, *A history of Christianity: the first three thousand years* (London, 2009), pp 31, 309, 412–13, 596.

concepts of sovereignty, be they Henry VIII, Hobbes or Dicey, fundamentally mistaken in their analysis? Were there in fact what might be called constitutional spheres of influence within the 'ancient constitution' itself, that is to say, distinct areas beyond the actual reach of the formal supremacy ideal as enshrined in the crown-in-parliament idiom? (Gladstone's answer here was emphatically in the affirmative, since he argued that the church retained its historic doctrinal competences even though it was formally annexed to the crown after the Reformation).[17]

The conceptual insights of the *Remarks* intersected with Gladstone's constitutional analysis in 1886 in three crucial respects; the understanding of the doctrine of unitary sovereignty (whether in its parliamentary or in its royal contexts), the critical attitude towards absolutist definitions of constitutional concepts in the British constitutional tradition, and finally the distinctive treatment of the doctrine of constitutional equality in the context of an historically unitary kingdom. Gladstone's distinct analysis of these crucial ideas was precisely the same in 1886 as it was in 1850, and this suggests that his Irish analysis was nourished by his peculiar constitutional sensitivities that had been formally worked out in an earlier 'British' debate and that he was now applying to the most pressing constitutional conundrum of the century.

## CONCEPT OF UNITARY SOVEREIGNTY CRITICIZED IN HOME RULE AND *REMARKS*

Gladstone's Home Rule analysis can be understood as an attempt to give the Irish *some* essentially unreviewable powers in certain contexts, while preserving Westminster's exclusive historic competences in other contexts. He admitted that some of the new Irish competences would be essentially unreviewable since the very act of constitutional differentiation endowed the infant assembly with 'moral powers of influences … which we do not and *cannot* limit'.[18] In short, Gladstone wanted to give the Irish *de facto* sovereign powers in the administration of the criminal justice system, while excluding them from any formal role in the formulation of imperial policy that would remain a jealously guarded Westminster competence. While he did not use this precise language for obvious reasons, it is clear that he was trying to divide the atom of sovereignty, so to

---

17 See W.E. Gladstone, *The state in its relations with the church* (London, 1838), p. 118 (henceforth *SRC*); 'Factors in the English reformation' (n.d.), 'The three Anglican settlements' (25 Jan. 1883), 'Fragment on Queen Elizabeth' (n.d.), 'Fragment on the restoration settlement' (n.d.) in Lathbury, ii, 348–588. See, generally, H.C.G. Matthew, 'Gladstone, Vaticanism and the question of the east' in D. Baker (ed.), *Studies in church history: religion, motivation, biographical and sociological problems for the church historian*, 15 (Oxford, 1978), 420ff.   18 *Hansard* 3:305, 592 (10 May 1886). On these ambiguities, see V. Bogdanor, *Devolution in the United Kingdom* (Oxford, 2001), pp 29, 37, 42–3.

speak, in the Home Rule analysis, by dividing various competences between the infant Irish assembly on the one hand and Westminster on the other. For every one of his citations to Dicey in 1886, one can find a matching reference to the new-found 'equality' the Irish would enjoy if his bill was passed.[19] So far as the sovereignty issue was concerned, he was walking a tightrope in the Home Rule analysis. This imaginative approach to the sovereignty problem was the central pivot of the earlier *Remarks*. Here he distinguished between *kinds* of sovereign power wielded by the crown-in-parliament since the Elizabethan settlement in the late sixteenth century, namely 'corrective jurisdiction', which the crown exercised only as a last resort, a sort of reserve power, and 'directive jurisdiction' which the church possessed in matters of internal doctrine. This was the way he squared the sovereignty circle here and showed that the church could be legally subordinate in an institutional sense, yet actually free in the doctrinal sense. He argued that while *corrective* jurisdiction was secured in legal language to the temporal power, there was no distinct provision whatever made with respect to *directive* jurisdiction, that is to say, the ordinary authority by which the functions of the Church are discharged.[20]

Even though this analysis formally pertains to the foundational statutes of the Elizabethan settlement, it shows Gladstone's unusually subtle constitutional perceptions in play.

CRITICAL OF *À PRIORI* CONSTITUTIONAL
CONCEPTS IN 1886 AND IN *REMARKS*

The *Remarks* can also be read as a learned repudiation of the *à priori* tradition within the British constitutional debate. Arguments from sovereignty, he wrote in his most sustained meditation on the issue in 1850, need to 'be determined according to times and circumstances carefully considered, and not by hasty inferences from abstract principles'.[21] His religious instincts made him deeply suspicious of the Hobbesian tradition within British constitutional thought, since absolutist theories about either parliamentary sovereignty or the divine right of kings sustained the baleful Erastian legacy that did so much damage in Gladstone's reading of British history. The anti-Hobbesian note was sounded as early as 1841 in the form of references to the works of John Bramhall, Church of Ireland archbishop of Armagh after the Restoration and Hobbes' most bitter critic from the 1650s.[22] Even in diplomatic matters, he cautioned colleagues,

19 *Hansard* 3:304, 1541 (13 Apr. 1886); *Hansard* 3:305, 591 (10 May 1886); *Hansard* 3:305, 600–1 (10 May 1886). 20 Gladstone, *Royal supremacy*, p. 11. 21 Ibid., p. 23. 22 See the citations to Bramhall's *Vindication* in *SRC*, ii, 115. Gladstone did not use him directly against Hobbes here, rather as part of his argument about the historical continuities embodied in the Church of England's canons, but his enthusiasm is suggestive. On Bramhall's epistemological critique of

arguing that sovereignty – in this instance, that of the Egyptian sultan – was not a 'test or formula', but a 'general spirit'.[23] Anglicanism bred a series of nuanced constitutional theories since the seventeenth century, theories which emphasized the need for flexibility in legal thought so as to avoid the divisions that followed absolutist policies.[24] The paradox here was similar to that which lay at the heart of the Home Rule analysis, in that Westminster would retain ultimate 'corrective' sovereignty over imperial matters, whereas the infant Irish assembly would possess *de facto* 'directive' sovereignty over the criminal justice system especially. In short, in the Home Rule analysis and in the Elizabethan settlement, Westminster's obvious pre-eminence did not imply outright superiority, and the prerogatives of the junior party, whether the church or a putative infant assembly, however real in certain areas, were not sufficient to insist on total separation from the metropolis. Gladstone sought always to balance competing constitutional demands, rather than decide these kinds of questions according to a rigid, deductive, *à priori* rule. He defined his approach succinctly in 1850 as one that involved balancing conflicting principles rather than favouring one outright at the expense of its competitor.

> How to adjust the claims of these two authorities [church and state in this context] upon the same ground and in the same subject matter, each claiming universal command, though in respects primarily distinct, was a problem, not indeed impossible of solution, but yet the most difficult, as history bears witness, that has ever been presented to man in his social relations.[25]

He emphasized the need to assess competing constitutional claims in an historical context. While the lawyers can argue with some legitimacy about the formal, unlimited supremacy of the crown-in-parliament, ecclesiastical historians offered a more nuanced and more satisfying analysis of the subtle interplay of constitutional currents in modern British history. Recommending the 'firmer and safer' methodology offered by 'the traditions of English history', Gladstone

---

Hobbes' account of the passions – not dissimilar in fact to Gladstone's criticism of sensationalism in his Butler books, see Q. Skinner, *Hobbes and republican liberty* (Cambridge, 2008), pp 25–34. **23** M.R.D. Foot & H.C.G. Matthew (eds), *The Gladstone diaries: with cabinet minutes and prime ministerial correspondence*, 14 vols (Oxford, 1968–94), xi, 2 July 1883. On this interpretative tradition see Schmitt, *Political theology*, p. 16 ('Of all the juristic concepts the concept of sovereignty is the one most governed by actual interests'). **24** On the powerful anti-Hobbesian rationale inherent in Anglican High Church theology, see H.J. Berman, *Law and revolution: the impact of the Protestant Reformations on the western legal tradition*, 2 vols (Cambridge, 2004), ii, 239, 260. This anti-Erastian emphasis in Gladstone's brand of Tractarian and High Church historical polemic is discussed in P.B. Nockles, 'Anglicanism "represented" or "misrepresented"? The Oxford movement, evangelicalism and history: the controversial use of the Caroline divines in the Victorian Church of England' in S. Gilley (ed.), *Victorian churches and churchmen: essays presented to Vincent Allen McClelland* (Suffolk, 2005), p. 314. **25** Gladstone, *Royal supremacy*, p. 24.

argued that the problem of sovereignty or jurisdiction can only be assessed according to 'the actual development of our constitution',[26] a process that acknowledged the actual limitations on the crown-in-parliament idiom, and which pointed to a sort of unofficial constitutional cohabitation between church and state since the Reformation. In short, by assessing the sovereignty issue historically rather than deductively, Gladstone was able to show that the formal absolute supremacy of the crown-in-parliament was considerably constrained in practice by various historical factors. To this extent, he showed the analytical inadequacy of the absolutist, zero-sum tradition within this constitutional argument. His target in 1850 was the Hobbesian tradition. But his critique of this historical tradition applied with even more force to Dicey in 1886. Gladstone's use of Burkean arguments in the Home Rule analysis reiterated the reservations about zero-sum analysis adumbrated in 1850. He invoked Burke's first great speech at Bristol by name in one debate to make the case for liberal, voluntary concessions as a way of conciliating disaffected subordinates.[27] The other main prong in Burke's argument in this source was his contention that the metropolitan power should not insist on its literal constitutional rights in a dispute with a subordinate.[28] He asserted the bankruptcy of *à priori* legal reasoning in this text, just as he would do in his flexible, quasi-mysterious inter-pretation of the 'ancient constitution' idiom in his major speech on the pacification of the colonies in 1775,[29] also quoted by Gladstone in 1886. These strictures were precise echoes of the historical analytical methodology sketched in the extensive discussion of the crown-in-parliament in the *Remarks*. Burke merely confirmed what Gladstone had been saying for decades.

## FUNCTIONAL EQUALITY COMPATIBLE WITH FORMAL SUBORDINATION IN 1886 AND IN *REMARKS*

Gladstone argued in great detail in the Commons in 1886 that the infant Irish assembly would enjoy 'practical' independence in its local affairs. He explained that this was required by the dictates of equality within a reworked United Kingdom. He would not concede in public what he essentially conceded in private and by implication in the minutiae of the draft bill, namely the fact that the legislative differentiation required by the equality emphasis had an obvious

---

**26** Ibid., p. 37.   **27** *Hansard* 3:306, 1237 (7 June 1886).   **28** E. Burke, 'Letter to the sheriffs of Bristol on the affairs of America' (1777) in W. King & F. Laurence (eds), *The works of Edmund Burke*, 8 vols (London, 1792–1827), ii, 13 ('… legislators ought to do what lawyers cannot …' 'When any community is subordinately connected with another, the great danger of the connexion is the extreme pride and self-complacency of the superior …').   **29** E. Burke, 'Notes on conciliation with the colonies' (1775), King (ed.), ii, 56 ('All government, indeed every human benefit and enjoyment, every virtue, and every prudent act, is founded on compromise and barter. We balance inconveniences'). Invoked in Apr. 1886: *Hansard* 3:304, 1544–5 (13 Apr. 1886).

impact on the operation of the unitary parliamentary supremacy ideal.[30] In the end, he was forced to argue a paradox which contained two irreconcilable claims; firstly, the claim that Irish 'equality' was possible within the confines of the traditional parliamentary supremacy concept, and secondly, the contrary claim that the actual operation of the Westminster supremacy would be sufficiently modified or diluted so as to allow for a cultural revolution in Irish Catholic consciousness.[31]

This precarious conceptual balancing act was, of course, the central pivot of the entire Home Rule analysis, which purported to reconcile the following mutually exclusive concepts in a single sweeping bill: differentiation of legislative functions; vindication of Westminster's historical constitutional supremacy;[32] equalization between constituent nations of the kingdom; administrative delegation of strictly defined competences to a 'statutory parliament'; inauguration of a formal federalization process within the United Kingdom. There is, of course, an obvious way to account for these tensions. One might simply argue that Gladstone was hopelessly confused in his thinking, or just classify the entire process as an example of prime ministerial pragmatism at its most unedifying. While there were several confusions at the heart of his entire performance – especially on the matter of the exclusion of the Irish from Westminster[33] – the Home Rule analysis was far more analytically sophisticated than the pragmatic interpretation allowed. The paradoxical constitutional insights and sensitivities that sustained the Home Rule performance were not confined to the Irish analysis. The distinctive attempt to reconcile 'equality' with 'supremacy' was the Ariadne's thread at the heart of the *Remarks on the royal supremacy* in 1850, as the related attempt to reconcile the church's spiritual independence with the political state was the main concern of Gladstone's own spiritual life.

This analytical similarity is too precise here to be ignored, since Gladstone made almost exactly the same argument in 1850 as he did in 1886, that is to say, he tried to show in 1850 and again during the Home Rule debate that Westminster's formal supremacy could be construed in a sufficiently flexible manner so as to guarantee formally subordinate powers the requisite degree of

---

**30** §37 of the draft Home Rule bill conceded this point. A.W. Hutton & H.J. Cohen (eds), *The speeches of the rt. hon. William Ewart Gladstone* (London, 1902), p. 331. **31** Freeman saw the paradox most vividly, arguing that while the 1886 analysis formally limited the Irish assembly by denying it any voice in colonial affairs, and by extracting a financial penalty in the imperial contribution, the very process of constitutional differentiation it inaugurated meant that 'the practical empire of Great Britain over Ireland was to come to an end'. Freeman, 'Prospects for Home Rule', p. 327. See T.J. Dunne, 'La trahison des clercs: British intellectuals and the first Home Rule crisis', *Irish Historical Studies*, 23 (Nov. 1982), 134–73. **32** See his memorandum to the queen here, 'Memorandum by Mr Gladstone', part II, n. 5, viz., 'what is asked is a statutory parliament, deriving all its authority from the imperial parliament'. *Letters of Queen Victoria*, p. 87; Hutton & Cohen (eds), *Speeches*, p. 331. **33** Bogdanor, *Devolution*, p. 28.

breathing space so as to fulfil their own specific mandates in the kingdom. In this unusual account of the church–state relationship, the state, as represented by the political supremacy, was formally supreme,[34] but also actually in a kind of moral and historical partnership with the church. The church had formally surrendered her powers to the crown after the Reformation, but she was more than a mere administrative appendage here. Her unique history ensured that she could be simultaneously subordinate to the crown-in-parliament and function as an equal partner. She was a subordinate in law, but an equal in history. Gladstone's sense that the doctrine of sovereignty or 'jurisdiction', as he called it here, could be divided or manipulated or apportioned into a directive component and a corrective component allowed him to reconcile seemingly antagonistic concepts such as 'equality' and 'supremacy'.

This synthesis is achieved by the rejection of zero-sum definitions of constitutional terms in favour of a more imaginative historical interrogation of the actual operation of a symbiotic relationship. In short, he preferred Burke's mysterious constitutional approach to the mathematical certainties of Hobbes and Dicey. He tried the precise same analytical sleight of hand in the Home Rule analysis when he acted as if his [British] audience did not really have to choose between a meaningful grant of equality for the Irish on the one hand, and their historic regard for the unitary sovereignty ideal on the other. Mr Burke's method promised all things to all men in this regard. Gladstone's 1850 concept of an 'alliance between two jurisdictions'[35] looks very much like an ecclesiastical version of his later 'union of hearts'. Gladstone's paradoxical assertion in 1886 that imperial security could be reconciled with a spectacular act of constitutional innovation in the Anglo–Irish relationship, itself a positively Trinitarian act of conjury to less nimble minds, was simply a hibernicized version of his lifelong Anglican historical sensitivities. These sensitivities viewed the English parliament as occupying a grey area, hovering somewhere between the scriptural role of nursing mother,[36] and the wicked step-sister, that is to say, as something less than outright master, but more than mere companion of rival institutions in the kingdom. Church and state in his mind ideally cooperated through what he significantly termed 'an alliance of jurisdictions'.[37] His 'statutory parliament'

---

**34** See *Royal supremacy*, pp 11ff, for his unusual analysis of 1 Eliz. cap. 1 (Apr. 1559), given in H. Gee et al. (eds), *Documents illustrative of English church history* (New York, 1896), pp 442–58. Decreeing that such 'jurisdictions, privileges, superiorities and pre-eminences, spiritual and ecclesiastical, as by any spiritual or ecclesiastical power or authority have heretofore been … exercised … shall forever, by authority of this present parliament, be united and annexed to the imperial crown of this realm'. Unlike more mainstream interpreters, Gladstone read this provision non-literally however. See the blunt Erastianism of Tindale and his heirs in W. Tindale, *The obedience of a Christian man* (Antwerp, 1528), p. 39 ('God hath made the king in every realm judge over all, and over him is there no judge'). **35** *Royal supremacy*, p. 43, point 6. **36** KJV, Isa. 49:23. 'And kings shall be thy nursing fathers, and their queens thy nursing mothers: they shall bow down to thee with their face toward the earth, and lick up the dust of thy feet'. **37** Gladstone, plan implied a similar alliance of overlapping jurisdictions in that the Irish assembly had to be weak enough to be dissolved if it proved itself delinquent, yet must also be simultaneously strong enough to accomplish the enormous task Gladstone assigned it – namely affecting a revolutionary change in the Irish national character.

Gladstone's tendency towards paradox has tended to obscure the analytical core of his mature constitutional assessment. He insisted on distinctions few others could see. He was ridiculed for claiming that the Reformation church was not necessarily an Erastian one, and for arguing that spiritual independence for the church Catholic was not sufficient grounds for promoting 'incorporation', organic union or outright theocracy.[38] He argued all his life for a balanced relationship, in short, a kind of harmonious Newtonian solar system in which parliament and church were preserved as distinct spheres, each with its own mass and pull, maintained in their proper orbit by the gravitational force of a shared doctrinal heritage. Anglicans in the catholic tradition such as Gladstone lived daily with the fear that the state might assert itself too aggressively and undermine their church's ancient spiritual jurisdiction or what he termed its 'virtual sovereignty'.[39] To the extent that they deliberately developed a highly nuanced account of parliament's sovereignty and to the extent that they saw the church-state relationship as dynamic and historical, rather than fixed and theoretical, they had little time for absolute accounts of the crown's jurisdiction and parliament's plenary powers.[40] The paradoxical accent of his Home Rule gambit in 1886 makes perfect sense in this Anglican context. To appreciate these obvious similarities, a simple thought experiment seems appropriate. In his essay on the historical development of the doctrine of the royal supremacy since Cranmer's time, Gladstone summarized his balanced model of sovereignty thus:

> the power of the church to make laws was retained [in the sixteenth century], but subjected to the consent of the crown: the administration of Church law was placed under the guardianship of the crown, in a confidence not disappointed through the succession of many generations that her own bishops, divines and canonists would be the persons appointed to discharge her judicial functions.[41]

*Royal supremacy*, p. 43. **38** Emphasized in J. Keble, 'Article V: Gladstone – the state in its relations with the church', *British Critic, Quarterly Theological Review and Ecclesiastical Record*, 26 (Oct. 1839), 360. **39** Gladstone, 'The three Anglican settlements' in Lathbury, ii, 353. See S.A. Skinner, 'Keble, the Tractarians and the establishment' in K. Blair, *John Keble in context* (London, 2004), p. 37. **40** Acton's enthusiasm for federalized, or otherwise emphatically decentralized, polities has a specifically religious rationale in that he saw it as way to recreate the medieval Catholic church's greatest legacy, namely the preservation of a realm beyond the reach of a single sovereign. J.W. Burrow, *Whigs and liberals: continuity and change in English political thought* (Oxford, 1988), p. 133. **41** Gladstone, *Royal supremacy*, p. 50.

If one replaced the word, 'Church' in the above paragraph with the phrase 'Irish assembly', then it would match the core of the Home Rule analysis almost perfectly. The Irish could make laws for their internal affairs, while the crown acted as sentinel from afar. The ideal was cooperation through constitutional differentiation, rather than domination or confrontation. In a similar vein, consider his retort to Dicey when he argued that the delegation or devolution or transfer of enumerated powers to another assembly in the realm actually invigorated the metropolitan parliament's claim to pre-eminence since only an older, stronger power can call a subordinate into existence. This paradox is similar to one he offered in discussing Convocation in the sixteenth century in 1850. Its manipulation by the temporal sphere then actually served to demonstrate its importance and dynamism. 'It was under more controul; but its inherent and independent power was even thereby more directly recognized'.[42] In this unusual Anglican idiom, the desire to control discredited the would-be controller. And as the Elizabethan compromise in church doctrine showed, at least in Gladstone's theory, the opposite also held true. When the state allowed the church to settle its own doctrinal controversies without impediment, this very generosity on the state's part redounded to its favour as it solidified the church's historic regard for the crown's broadly supervisory function. In giving power away, the state really confirmed its own pre-eminence. The Home Rule paradox spoke to a similar problem.

---

42 Ibid., p. 30.

# Gladstone and imperialism

BERNARD PORTER

Academic historians are usually the last people to want to draw lessons from, or even parallels with, history. They leave that to politicians, who generally get it wrong. In recent years, however, it has been difficult to avoid being reminded of certain incidents in British imperial history by events in Iraq and Afghanistan after September 2001. Iraq and Afghanistan were both sites of British imperial activity in the past, one involving Gladstone (marginally); but it was not either of these episodes that sprang to the minds of British imperial historians when Bush and Blair together invaded Iraq in March 2003. The invasion of Iraq prompted memories of Gladstone's decision to bombard and then invade Egypt in July 1882. The resemblances seemed uncanny: a 'failed state', an assertive Islam, suspected economic motives (Haliburton, the Egyptian 'bondholders'), Christian religiosity on the western side, diplomatic problems with France, and – most strikingly, perhaps – the denial on the western side that this *was* 'imperialism', rather than a mission to simply rescue the 'people' of the country from a tyrant, and then withdraw immediately, leaving the government in local hands. Almost the only substantial difference was that Egypt in 1882 didn't even have *imaginary* 'weapons of mass destruction'. Later of course the parallels came to look even closer, as Bush and Blair became enmired in Iraq, and then in a new *jihad*, just as Gladstone had been in Egypt and the Sudan after 1882. Even before then, however, we British historians, casting aside our normal reticence over 'historical lessons', were shouting across the Atlantic at Bush, Rumsfeld and the others to at least take a look at this nineteenth-century British precedent – rather than the Second World War 'liberation of Paris' which so captivated Rumsfeld – before risking similar danger in Iraq. The parallel occurred to many. I remember looking up 'Bush + Gladstone + Egypt + Iraq' on Google at the time, and getting hundreds of results (when I repeated the same search more recently, the score was 31,900).[1] If there was ever a case for 'learning from', or at least being 'warned by', history, it must be this. If only Bush and Blair had known more British imperial history, the disaster of the Iraq invasion might have been avoided. Gladstone could be excused, perhaps. He had no such precedents available to him. But to make the same mistake twice … that was more than just carelessness.

All that is just by way of introduction. I shall not be pursuing these present-

---

1 This and the other searches recorded below were made on 10 Mar. 2010.

day parallels any further in this article, except occasionally marginally – though it is tempting to do so. The only point I want to pursue is the suggestion that 'perhaps' Gladstone could be 'excused' over Egypt because, unlike his successors, he had no historical precedents to guide him; which I do not in fact believe is so. Whether or not it was his historical reading that guided him, or his own long political experience, including a brief spell as colonial secretary, he was acutely aware of the dangers of invading Egypt; as this remarkable passage, written four years before the invasion, shows. It is worth quoting at length here, so astonishingly prescient did it turn out to be.

> Our first site in Egypt, be it by larceny or be it by emption, will be the almost certain egg of a North African Empire, that will grow and grow until another Victoria and another Albert, titles of the lake-sources of the White Nile, come within our borders, and till we finally join hands across the Equator with Natal and Cape Town, to say nothing of the Transvaal and the Orange River on the south, or of Abyssinia or Zanzibar to be swallowed by way of *viaticum* on our journey. And then, with a great empire in each of the four quarters of the world, and with the whole new or fifth quarter to ourselves, we may be territorially content, but less than ever at our ease; for if agitators and alarmists can now find at almost every spot 'British interests' to bewilder and disquiet us, their quest will then be all the wider.

Which, of course, is almost exactly how things turned out over the next twenty years: not only the 'African' part of the analysis, but also Gladstone's peerings into a future when Britain's 'imperial overstretch', to use Paul Kennedy's phrase, could only make her *less* secure. In any case, he insisted in the same essay, Britain did not need colonies. 'The root and pith and substance of the material greatness of our nation lies within the compass of these islands; and is, except in trifling particulars, independent of all and every sort of political dominion beyond them'.[2] That seems unequivocal; a classic statement of the 'Little Englandism' that was a common part of the liberal public discourse in Gladstone's earlier career, and which he was routinely tarred with by his 'new imperialist' critics in later years. Which of course lies at the root of the familiar conundrum surrounding Gladstone: with views and foresight like this, how come it was *he* who was responsible for invading and eventually taking over Egypt; and so – according to most historical accounts – for kicking off the Europe-wide 'new imperialism' that was such an illiberal and arguably ultimately nationally self-destructive feature of the final years both of his life and of the century? Or, to

2 Gladstone, 'Aggression in Egypt and freedom in the east', *Nineteenth Century*, 2 (1877), 149–66.

put it another way: Disraeli was the one who actually lauded 'imperialism', in the 1870s, yet he annexed far less territory – just Cyprus – than did Gladstone, who fought a general election specifically *against* Disraeli's imperialism. Again: how could this be?

Let me kick a couple of canards out of the way first. I don't believe Gladstone was a hypocrite, an imperialist (in his own terms), and just pretending to be an 'anti', perhaps for political reasons. Even Colin Matthew's discovery a few years ago that Gladstone had a substantial financial stake in Egypt – 37 per cent of his investment portfolio was in Egyptian stocks[3] – has not seriously shaken that belief. Today, of course, it would be problematic, which is why there are much stricter conventions regulating the financial interests of government ministers; and even at the time the danger that such investments could compromise a public servant was recognized, which is why members of the colonial and Indian civil services were supposed not to own such interests in the colonies they ruled. So it is vaguely worrying. There can be no doubt that preventing a default on Egyptian bonds was one reason for British intervention; but I'm also prepared to believe that Gladstone thought that that was desirable in *principle*, quite apart from its effect on his own pocket; which for him would have made the national interest perfectly compatible with his personal one. A naïve view, perhaps; but in many ways this was a naïve age. Secondly: I do not think we can blame *God* for Gladstone's invasion of Egypt, as we may be able to in the case of Bush's and Blair's invasion of Iraq (by 'God', of course, I mean the messages these men may have thought they received from God). We know that Gladstone was highly religious; and he once said that he would *answer* to God for his invasion of Egypt (anticipating a similar statement by Tony Blair, that he was responsible only to God for his Iraq policy: a curious doctrine, I thought, for a democrat); but that is not the same as claiming that you were acting on God's direct orders before the event. Neither Gladstone nor Blair was mad enough to claim that.

Then there is the role of chance. I do not want to make too much of this, as I think Gladstone was to blame for at least some of his own bad luck. Yes, General Gordon criminally exceeded his orders when sent to the Sudan simply to evacuate the Egyptian troops there; but Gladstone was fully aware of his failings (chiefly religious fanaticism) when he bowed to what was presented as 'public' pressure to send Gordon there. But it was rather less Gladstone's fault, I think, that Wolseley dawdled so much when sent out to Khartoum to rescue Gordon ('Too Late!', as the famous *Punch* cartoon put it);[4] just as it was not at all Gladstone's fault when the commander of the British troops in South Africa decided off his own bat to attack the Boers of the Transvaal, while Gladstone was already preparing a treaty that would have granted them all they wanted.

---

3 M.R.D. Foot & H.C.G. Matthew (eds), *The Gladstone diaries*, 14 vols (Oxford, 1968–94), x, pp lxxi–lxxii.   4 *Punch*, 14 Feb. 1885.

The resulting defeat at Majuba Hill in 1881, and Gordon's slaying in Khartoum in 1885, were of course the events – outside Ireland – for which Gladstone was most vilified during his second ministry and for long after: 'G.O.M.' was turned around into 'M.O.G.' – 'Murderer of Gordon'. No such excuses, however, can be made in respect of the original invasion of Egypt. That, as it happened, went off terrifically well: as well as the initial capture of Baghdad in 2003; but that is not the point at issue. If Gladstone was not an imperialist, surely his victorious troops should not have been there in the first place?

Then, of course, there is the further excuse that he *liberated* colonies, or tried to, as well as seizing them. The Transvaal is one example. Ireland is another, if you count that as an unequivocal colony. Certainly, many of his opponents objected to Home Rule on imperial grounds – that it would be the first step to the disintegration of the empire as a whole. In 1862–3, a government of which he was a leading member gave up the Ionian Islands (to Greece). Gladstone was similarly involved with a sort of decolonization (devolution) in British North America. And this policy, or aspiration, was not confined (as is sometimes charged against him) to 'white' colonies, of European settlement, alone; in India, for example, Gladstone also embarked (through Lord Ripon) on a policy designed to achieve national self-government there *eventually*. There are several examples while he was prime minister of his turning down new colonies that were offered to him almost on a plate: especially in east and west Africa. So far as his actual acquisitions were concerned, these were undeniably *more than he wanted* to acquire. There is a contrast here with Disraeli, who, however little territory he actually added to the empire, seemed always on the lookout for more: starting, for example, with Abyssinia and Afghanistan. So, Gladstone clearly had an anti-imperial as well as a *query*-imperial side.

Next – in defence of Gladstone's anti- or non-imperialist credentials – there is certainly the consideration that he did not *regard* what he was doing as 'imperialism', for reasons that might seem to us casuistical or even dishonest, but are fully understandable in the context, not perhaps of that time (the 1880s), but of Gladstone's past. The point here is that 'imperialism' is only a *word*, which can be defined any way one wants to, and indeed is defined in some extraordinary ways today (the spread of McDonalds fast food as an instance of American 'imperialism' is one of the more outlandish examples); but which at the time of Gladstone's youth, middle age and early old age (before the 1880s, that is) was almost universally taken to mean one of two things, and two things only: first of all, 'Bonapartism', as exemplified by the two Napoleons, I and III, the latter of whom had been thought to pose a threat to Britain as recently as the 1850s, and to European stability until his fall from power in 1870; and secondly, any sort of international conduct which *resembled* theirs, which was usually taken to be unrestrained aggression, militarism, annexationism and vainglory. These were the characteristics Gladstone most deplored in Disraeli's foreign adventures in the 1870s.[5] They were not, in his view, and I think in fact, features of his own policies. It followed that those policies were not 'imperialistic', by the only definition of that word he could have understood.

They were not, for example, annexationist, strictly speaking. Egypt was never annexed, but remained nominally ruled by its own 'Khedive', with a British *adviser*, only. Of course, this was an almost total fiction; but the effect of it was that Egypt was never, for example, coloured British red on maps. The Sudan was shared between Britain and Egypt; on old maps you will find it coloured in diagonal pink and yellow stripes. Britain took Bechuanaland (now the Republic of Botswana) in 1885, but called it a 'protectorate'; the name intended to indicate not a positive obligation, but a negative one: not that Britain should rule it as a colony, but that she should merely prevent other countries doing so. Other areas of Africa, notably at this time Nigeria and then a little later East Africa and Rhodesia, were given over to capitalist 'chartered companies' to administer, in the belief that this was somehow different from – an alternative to – 'real' colonialism, which meant rule by foreign *governments*. Take all these new acquisitions away from the equation, and it is true that Gladstone's side of it looks lighter: by comparison, for example, with Disraeli's.

But no historian today would allow you to do that. For these days we define 'imperialism' rather more broadly, to embrace 'protectorates', 'spheres of influence' and 'chartered' territories, and indeed much more: like Britain's 'informal' influence through commerce and financial investment; all of which also expanded greatly in these years. But Gladstone could not possibly have recognized that as 'imperialist'. The way he had been brought up, trade and investment were the opposite of, even the antidote to, imperialism. That was in the days when 'free trade' had been the great *internationalist* ideology of the age, the means of bringing all nations and peoples together, rendering the domination of some by others unnecessary and so impossible, and uniting them all – as his old Liberal colleague Richard Cobden had once put it, and as some champions of 'globalization' still hold today – 'in the bonds of eternal peace'.[6] 'Free trade imperialism' – the term Ronald Robinson and Jack Gallagher coined in the 1950s[7] – would have seemed a contradiction in terms. So, we should not blame Gladstone too much for being blind to these kinds of what today we call 'imperialism'; a full seventy years before Robinson and Gallagher, and in view of the fact that most Americans today still seem oblivious to the very similar sort of 'imperialism' that their country has been practising for at least the past fifty years. Imperialism *is* only a word; so their definition is not necessarily any less valid than any other.

5 See, for example, Gladstone's Third Midlothian address, 27 Nov. 1879, printed in *Speeches delivered in Midlothian ... November 1879* (1880).   6 Cobden speech in Manchester, 15 Jan. 1846, quoted in John Bright & Thorold Rogers (eds), *Speeches on public policy by Richard Cobden MP*, 2 vols (London, 1870), ii, 315–16.   7 Ronald Robinson & J.A. Gallagher, 'The imperialism of free trade', *Economic History Review*, 6 (1953), 1–15.

There is one final 'excuse' for Gladstone: which is that he was, in the 1880s, a prisoner of events. Competitive imperialism in the late nineteenth century was inevitable, 'determined', if you like, by great underlying historical forces; you can choose your own from among several possibilities, ranging from the rise of the new German nation, to the 'crisis of capitalism' augured by the so-called 'Great' depression of the 1870s; or even, if you are that way inclined, God's great new plan for bringing the benighted heathen to Him. Looking back on the 1880s and 1890s from the vantage-point of today, the rise of the 'new imperialism' Europe- and also America-wide does appear powerful and inexorable; it is very difficult to imagine those decades turning out very differently in diplomatic terms: but then it is difficult to imagine anything in history turning out differently than it did. Gladstone would certainly *not* have accepted this. There is no sense in that passage quoted above about the dangers of an invasion of Egypt that he believed this to be a solid prediction; more of a *warning*. He thought Disraelian imperialism was an aberration, supported by what he called the 'classes' against the interests of the 'people' (there are echoes of Cobden here, as well as pre-echoes of that great anti-imperial guru of slightly later years, J.A. Hobson). When he came out of retirement to take on Disraelian imperialism in 1880, it was in the full belief that he would be able to put a stop to it immediately, with the help of the 'people', and then retire again. He refused to give in to the pessimistic fatalism that was often associated with and exploited by political conservatism then, as it is today. 'Yes we can' could have been his mantra, if he had thought of it; or, indeed, had been able to express himself as economically as today's political leaders do.

But wait. All this is in the nature of 'excuses' for Gladstone (assuming, of course, that 'imperialism' is something that requires to be excused). That probably needs to be done, not only to make Gladstone more acceptable to our own anti-imperial age (on balance), but also to square some of his actions (especially Egypt) with his professions of anti-imperialism, and with his reputation in later years as the keeper of the ark of the covenant of pure anti-jingo liberalism, in a period when even the Liberal party was becoming increasingly more infected by the imperial virus. Towards the end of the 1890s, the Liberals became sharply – and it was feared even possibly fatally – split over the issue of empire, between 'Liberal Imperialists' (led, albeit lazily, by Rosebery), and what were invariably called the 'Gladstonians'. This, incidentally, is where I first 'met' Gladstone in connection with imperial matters, when I was researching my first book, into 'critics' of empire around the turn of the twentieth century. By that stage, and even before his death in 1898, he was becoming metamorphosed, as most great men and women are, into a useful myth, which was beginning to bear only a partial resemblance to the reality. Anti-imperialism was part of that myth. His anti-imperial champions, if confronted with the invasion of Egypt (as they rarely were), would probably have made the same 'excuses' for it that I have just listed. But these do not do him full justice. For Gladstone's views on imperial matters were far more ambivalent than any full-blown 'anti' could possibly be comfortable with.

For a start, he was certainly not against most forms of overseas intervention *in principle*. When Sir Wilfrid Lawson, a very anti-imperialist Liberal MP, accused him of breaking his principles when he invaded Egypt, he snapped back: 'he seems to think I am a general apostle of non-intervention. I do not, however, see why he should say so; he has quoted nothing that bears out that view'.[8] Nor was he a pacifist, in any sense, even revelling in his army's successes, for example, at the beginning of that Egyptian campaign: asking for church bells to be rung, and guns fired in the London parks.[9] Nor was he opposed to what anyone would regard (even he) as imperialism or colonialism in the formal sense – that is, one country going in and conquering another – in principle. He greatly valued the British Empire of settlement (the 'white' colonies, as they were mis-called), and was immensely proud of the role of its 'prolific British mother' (in his phrase).[10] Indeed, he believed that the British were an inherently imperial people, in this sense. 'It is part of our patrimony', he wrote in 1878; 'born with our birth, dying only with our death; ... interwoven with all our habits ... The dominant passion of England is extended empire'.[11] One wonders whether he could have got that from J.R. Seeley, who was lecturing along these lines at Cambridge University then, though his *Expansion of England* didn't appear until five years later. Sir Charles Dilke is another possible source. Both of these imperial propagandists were also 'dominions' or 'settlement' empire men, not at all keen on the 'dependent' empire of conquest and rule, like India; and saw their empire mainly in terms of the spread of free, democratic, ordered and even self-governing British communities into what were conceived at this time to be the 'waste' regions of the earth (we shall come on to the problems of that in a moment). That may be described as a milder, more liberal form of 'imperialism', perhaps. (It is important to be aware of the distinction. Many writers about British 'imperialism' appear unaware of it.)

But Gladstone was not in principle against the *other* kind of imperialism. This comes out in his attitude to German colonialism in Africa in the mid-1880s, which he actually welcomed, to the great puzzlement of Bismarck, who thought he was provoking Britain by staking claims there; 'if Germany is to become a colonizing power', Gladstone told the House of Commons in 1882, 'all I say is "God speed her!" She becomes our ally and partner in the execution of the great purposes of Providence for the advantage of mankind'.[12] He also took great

8 Foot & Matthew (eds), *Gladstone diaries*, x, p. lxiii.　9 Ibid., x, p. lxxiii.　10 Gladstone, essay on 'Kin beyond the seas' reprinted in *Gleanings of past years* (1879), quoted in Foot & Matthew (eds), *Gladstone diaries*, x, p. xli.　11 Gladstone, 'England's mission', *Nineteenth Century*, 4 (1878), 569–70.　12 Quoted in W.L. Langer, *European alliances and alignments, 1871–1890* (New York, NY, 1931), p. 308.

pride in what Britain had achieved in India (where, incidentally, his son Harry was living and working); 'a most arduous but a most noble duty', was how he described it to his viceroy in 1881.[13]

What he *was*, I think, was a colonial 'nationalist' in principle; but not in an unqualified or absolute sense. That is to say, he was not in favour of giving in to nationalists in every situation; and did not believe that there was a necessary contradiction between nationalism and imperialism in all circumstances. The existing British Empire of settlement was an example, owing its national 'freedoms' – Canadian, Australian, New Zealand, and hopefully Irish in the future – to their guarantee under British protection; which, if it were withdrawn, would be bound to weaken each of these nationalities and so endanger their liberties. 'Nationalists' were not always the best judges of even their own national freedoms. This especially applied in countries where the necessary underlying 'free' institutions and states of mind had not yet had a chance to develop; or perhaps had been repressed for decades, as Gladstone felt was the case under most Muslim governments.[14] Among those institutions and states of mind that Gladstone felt were most vital to the cultivation of 'true' nationality was (as Eugenio Biagini has pointed out)[15] financial probity. Of course, this emphasis appears convenient, even hypocritically so, for the European bondholders (including Gladstone himself) who were so worried about Egypt in the early 1880s. But the old man surely had a point here. Egypt's own 'national' leaders had hugely mismanaged its finances, and as a result hugely compromised its effective national freedom. This has to be borne in mind in connexion with Gladstone's invasion of 1882: that Egypt was not an independent or even a semi-independent country before then, but a *de facto* 'colony' of its European creditors. By restoring its economy to probity, which was his primary aim, and the reason why he chose a scion of the Baring family (Lord Cromer) to run it for him, Gladstone believed he was laying the foundation of a much more stable form of Egyptian nationality in the longer run.

I have been emphasizing one particular phrase, because I think it provides the key to Gladstone's relationship with 'imperialism' and the British Empire. That phrase is 'in principle'. He was not against most forms of imperialism *in principle*. This, I have to say, came as a surprise to me when it first struck me, always having regarded Gladstone (on his own estimation) as a 'principled' man; before I thought for a moment and realized that 'principles' do not necessarily have anything to do with 'morality'. But neither was he *for* imperialism 'in principle'. Indeed, none of Gladstone's policies and decisions in the imperial field seems to me to have been informed by 'principle' at all: unlike, for example,

13 Gladstone to Ripon, 4 Nov. 1881, Foot & Matthew (eds), *Gladstone diaries*, x, p. lxiv.   14 See Gladstone, 1876 & 1877, in ibid., ix, pp xxxiv–xlv.   15 Eugenio Biagini, 'Exporting "western and beneficent institutions": Gladstone and empire' in David Bebbington & Roger Swift (eds), *Gladstone centenary essays* (Liverpool, 2000), pp 202–24.

the famous stand he took over the Bulgarian atrocities in 1876. It is this, I think, that most characterizes his imperial policy. Let me give some examples.

Gladstone believed Britain had done some great work in India, but he still thought it would have been better from Britain's point of view if she had never taken over that country; and he was always hugely sceptical of the increasingly fashionable idea in the 1880s that Britain's work in India was so noble, or India so valuable to Britain, that they needed to extend the empire into other areas (Egypt, for example, and eastern Africa) in order to 'safeguard the routes' there. He also believed that Britain ought to stay in India only as long as the Indians wished. He felt a warm glow about the 'white' dominions, but had no problem contemplating their eventual political separation from Britain, which most Britons expected in the 1860s. On the other hand, he believed that if they were treated fairly and 'freely', they would not *want* to break away; that the Australians, for example, could quite easily cultivate a pride in being both Australian *and* British: which is how things turned out, broadly speaking, in the first half of the twentieth century. One of the things that recommended such colonies to him was that they were cheap and very little trouble to run, as they mainly ran and paid for themselves. Gladstone's main interest *vis-à-vis* Australia while prime minister, in fact, was to try to get her to contribute to her own defence, which would have made 'dominions' imperialism cheaper still.

It would have been nice from a modern liberal point of view (and also from the point of view of what was called the 'Aborigines' Protection' lobby at the time) if, while his attention was on Australia, he had given more thought to the fate of 'native' peoples whom his admired settlers were oppressing in great numbers in the 'waste' places they were colonizing, both there and elsewhere: 'waste' in this context, of course, meaning not 'empty', but merely 'empty of "civilized" people'. Apart from occasionally going through the motions, however – a paper safeguard for natives in the constitution he granted the Transvaal in 1881, for example – he seems not to have been much interested in humanitarian causes, except in the case of white 'civilized' Christians like the Bulgarians. Likewise, he showed no interest in stopping the brutal Arab slave trade in central Africa, placed in the public eye at this time by the explorer Henry Stanley, which could only have been done by means of more imperial intervention and commitment. Of course, slavery might have been a difficult issue for him, in view of his father's slave-owning interests, which he had *seemed* to defend in his maiden speech, way back in the 1830s. But anyway, the point is that he appears to have had few of the humanitarian 'principles' that might have turned him into an 'imperialist', or an 'interventionist'; as happened with other liberals and, much later on, with Tony Blair. For those who would like to push the comparison between these two out further (and lots have tried it: 'Blair' + 'Gladstone' on Google registers 627,000 hits), this probably marks the limit. It is hard to credit this, I realize; but in this regard Blair was (is) holier than Gladstone.

Of course, Gladstone did have principles, but none of them was rooted essentially either in imperialism or its opposite, or, indeed, in any matter intrinsic to the question at all. His main political ideology was, it seems to me, set in the mid-nineteenth century, and moulded by his experience as the great reforming chancellor of that time; it all revolved around free trade, minimal government, gradual reform, financial probity and peace in the world secured by cooperation between peoples (the Concert of Europe); all of which implied a concentration on parochial national concerns only – 'the root and pith and substance of the material greatness of our nation lies within the compass of these islands' – to which everything else in the big wide world should be regarded as strictly ancillary. That sounds narrow, and in many ways unattractively ideological; and it is important to realize that it was not *rigidly* applied to foreign and imperial affairs, as some of his more Radical colleagues might have liked. For Gladstone was not merely ideological, which is easy; he was also wise, which is of course far more difficult; indeed, in my view, he was the wisest prime minister Britain has ever had, rivalled, but not surpassed, by Lord Salisbury, Clement Attlee and – albeit only in flashes – Winston Churchill. It was his wisdom that enabled him to be *flexible*: over Irish nationalism, for example, though he was not a principled nationalist; and over the empire, though he was neither a principled imperialist nor a principled anti-imperialist. Over the first of these two issues he was right, but defeated, tragically; on the question of Egypt he was wrong, as he had (wisely) predicted he would be, but won, disastrously. As a result of that latter 'success', he was probably more responsible for the long, unfortunate and ultimately self-destructive imperialist episode in Britain's history that followed, culminating in the Great War, than any other British statesman, including certainly Disraeli, despite the latter's reputation as much more of an imperialist. Google is wrong here. Punch in 'Disraelian imperialism' and you get 410 hits; 'Gladstonian imperialism' and you get a mere seven. Yet it was Gladstone who was by far the more effective imperialist of the two of them. 'Ironic' hardly seems an adequate word to describe this.

# 'A most arduous but a most noble duty': Gladstone and the British Raj in India, 1868–98[1]

## DAVID OMISSI

### I

How significant was India to Gladstone? The usual answer to this question is 'not very'. As the great Gladstone scholar Richard Shannon has put it, 'The ideal of the beneficent sway of an imperial master race had no attraction for him. India seems hardly to have entered his thoughts'.[2] Indeed, when Gladstone first became prime minister in 1868 he famously announced that his 'mission' was 'to pacify Ireland' – hardly the words of a man preoccupied with India. Gladstone was a prolific writer; and one way of judging India's significance to him is to consider how much he wrote about India, compared with other subjects. Gladstone's diaries are a good place to start. In the index to the diaries, the entry for 'Ireland' runs to sixteen columns, while 'India' and 'Egypt' each get just under three.[3] Gladstone also wrote several articles about Egypt, but none exclusively about India;[4] and his famous 'General Retrospect' of 1896 did not even mention India.[5] India seemed to feature much less than Egypt, let alone Ireland, in Gladstone's concerns. The Gladstone historiography tells a similar story. There are many books and articles about Gladstone and Ireland; there are publications about 'Gladstone and' almost any other conceivable subject (including, of course, Gladstone and Homer); but there are very few works specifically about Gladstone and India.[6]

1 Earlier versions of this essay were presented as papers to the Imperial History Seminar at the University of Leeds and to the Commonwealth History Seminar (in the Colin Matthew Room) at the University of Oxford. I am grateful to the seminar organizers and participants for the opportunity to discuss work in progress. Tony Henderson, Theo Hoppen, Clare Omissi, Simon C. Smith & Andrew S. Thompson provided many helpful comments on drafts of this essay, for which I am very grateful. All remaining errors are entirely my own.  2 R. Shannon, *Gladstone and the Bulgarian agitation, 1876* (London, 1963), p. 8.  3 M.R.D. Foot & H.C.G. Matthew (eds), *The Gladstone diaries*, 14 vols (Oxford, 1968–94), xiv, 672–3, 724–5, 726–34. In references to the diaries, all page numbers in Roman numerals refer to Colin Matthew's introductions; all page numbers in Arabic numerals in references that contain the words 'Gladstone to' or 'entry for' refer to Gladstone's own writings; and all other page numbers refer to Colin Matthew's editorial annotations.  4 For some of his publications from this period, see Foot & Matthew (eds), *Gladstone diaries*, ix, 659–60; xi, 677; xii, 441–2, and xiii, 441–3.  5 Shannon, *Gladstone and the Bulgarian agitation*, p. 111.  6 One of the best is C. Brad Faught, 'An imperial prime minister: W.E. Gladstone and India, 1880–1885', *Journal of the Historical Society*, 6:4 (2006), 555–78.

   This imbalance is perhaps not surprising. The decades from the 1860s to the
1890s have often been seen as the 'golden age' of Britain's Indian empire.
Despite several severe famines (one obvious parallel with Ireland), the period
between the violent upheaval of the Indian mutiny in 1857–8 and the struggles
associated with Indian nationalism, beginning in 1905 with the agitation against
the partition of Bengal, was one of relative political stability. For most of those
years, Indian issues, by comparison with Irish (or even African) ones, were not
particularly salient in British political life. Indeed, by the end of the century,
debates on Indian subjects in the House of Commons were normally guaranteed
to almost empty the chamber.[7]
   This essay will interrogate and challenge the view that India was of only
marginal significance to Gladstone. The fact that British rule over India was a
relatively uncontroversial feature of British political life does not mean that it
was an insignificant one. Consciously or not, British rule in India was part of the
air that Victorian statesmen breathed; and many of Gladstone's contemporaries
simply took for granted India's economic and military significance to Britain. In
1858, as a consequence of the mutiny, political authority over India had been
transferred from the East India Company to the British crown. Thereafter, India
was administered by a governor-general, who answered to a secretary of state for
India[8] – a cabinet appointment made by the prime minister, and accountable,
through parliament, to the British electorate. The government and the defence
of India occasionally became significant electoral issues, as they did for
Gladstone in 1879–80. Furthermore, the autocratic nature of British rule in
India had particular significance for British liberal politicians: it tested liberal
principles of good government, and raised the question of universalism. Which
liberal principles – freedom of the press, equality of all before the law – could,
or should, be applied to India? Gladstone has often been described as an 'anti-
imperialist'.[9] But what did 'anti-imperialism' actually mean in the context of
later Victorian India?[10] How did Gladstone evaluate British rule in India, and
how committed (if at all) was he to its continuation? What sort of relationship
did Gladstone have with British India's leading figures? Gladstone has often
been seen as preoccupied with Ireland; but several scholars have identified
significant interplay between imperial politics in Ireland and in India.[11] What,
exactly, was the relationship between Gladstone's key policies towards Ireland
and his ideas (and those of his opponents) about India?

7 J. Schneer, *London, 1900: the imperial metropolis* (New Haven, CT, 1999), p. 193.   8 Strictly,
secretary of state for India 'in Council': see D. Williams, 'The Council of India and the relationship between the home and supreme governments, 1858–1870', *English Historical Review*, 81:318
(1966), 56–73.   9 C.C. Eldridge, *England's mission: the imperial idea in the age of Gladstone and
Disraeli* (London, 1973), p. 221.   10 J.V. Crangle, 'The decline of anti-imperialism in the age of
Gladstone and Disraeli', *Quarterly Review of Historical Studies*, 13:2 (1973–4), 67–80.   11 For
example, C.A. Bayly, 'Ireland, India and the empire, 1700–1914', *Transactions of the Royal
Historical Society*, 6:10 (2000), 377–97.

II

Gladstone's first premiership began in December 1868. For over five years he led a great reforming government. This government addressed two issues of particular, if indirect, significance to India: the question of Irish land, and the reform of the British Army.

The interplay between Ireland and India has usually been understood in terms of Irish 'influence' in India, and in four main ways. First, Ireland, unlike the self-governing dominions, was represented in the imperial parliament, so Irish MPs had some limited input into Indian policy.[12] Second, there was the influence of people with an Irish background or Irish experience serving in India, notably in the British and Indian armies and the Indian civil service.[13] During Gladstone's first administration, for example, this influence was felt even at the level of viceroy, for Lord Mayo (1822–72), whose appointment Gladstone had confirmed, was a Protestant Irish landowner who had been chief secretary for Ireland in three Conservative ministries, including Disraeli's.[14] Third, there was the influence of Irish 'models' over specific aspects of the administration of British India – most notably the Indian police, the organization and practice of which drew upon the example of the Irish (later Royal Irish) Constabulary.[15] And fourth, Ireland was often treated as a more general point of reference in formulating policy towards India.[16]

This influence, however, sometimes flowed in the other direction. For example, Indian precedent clearly informed Gladstone's first Irish Land Act of 1870. The act marked the end of attempts to precipitate 'a revolution in Irish society by assimilating Irish agriculture to English models',[17] and reflected a growing interest in, and respect for, the ancient and customary laws of 'primitive' agrarian societies. Gladstone intended the act to improve agricultural productivity and to make tenants more secure,[18] using the Ulster tradition of

---

12 E.D. Steele, 'J.S. Mill and the Irish question: reform and the integrity of the empire, 1865–1870', *Historical Journal*, 13:3 (1970), 431. 13 For the latter, see S.B. Cook, 'The Irish Raj: social origins and careers of Irishmen in the Indian Civil Service, 1855–1914', *Journal of Social History*, 20:3 (1987), 507–29. 14 E.D. Steele, 'Ireland and the empire in the 1860s: imperial precedents for Gladstone's first Irish Land Act', *Historical Journal*, 11:1 (1968), 69; R.J. Moore, *Liberalism and Indian politics, 1872–1922* (London, 1966), p. 15. But note R.D. Collison Black, 'Economic policy in Ireland and India in the time of J.S. Mill', *Economic History Review*, 21:2 (1968), 327–8, 330. 15 D. Arnold, *Police power and colonial rule: Madras, 1859–1947* (New Delhi, 1986), pp 25–8; D.M. Anderson & D. Killingray, 'Consent, coercion and colonial control: policing the empire, 1830–1940' in D.M. Anderson & D. Killingray (eds), *Policing the empire: government, authority and control, 1830–1940* (Manchester, 1991), pp 2–4. 16 H. Brasted, 'Indian nationalist development and the influence of Irish Home Rule, 1870–1886', *Modern Asian Studies*, 14:1 (1980), 45. 17 C. Dewey, 'Celtic agrarian legislation and the Celtic revival: historicist implications of Gladstone's Irish and Scottish land acts, 1870–1886', *Past & Present*, 64 (1974), 50. 18 'Secret: case of Irish land law', 9 Dec. 1880, Foot & Matthew (eds), *Gladstone diaries*, ix, 634–5.

tenant right to recognize customary land rights in Ireland more generally.[19] The historicist arguments that Gladstone used to support the act had been inspired by Sir George Campbell's 1869 book *Irish land*, which argued that some forms of Indian tenure could usefully be applied to Ireland.[20] Campbell had significant Indian experience, mainly as a senior administrator and judge, and he wrote extensively on Indian issues.[21] Gladstone read Campbell's pamphlet at least four times between August 1869 and April 1870,[22] noting that 'a vein of truth' ran through its pages.[23] Campbell, in turn, had been influenced by J.S. Mill's 1868 pamphlet *England and Ireland*.[24] Mill also had considerable knowledge of India, being the son of James Mill (the author of the well-known *History of British India*)[25] and having had a long career in the London offices of the East India Company. Mill drew parallels between India and Ireland, arguing that 'those Englishmen who know something of India are ... those who understand Ireland best', and that there were 'many points of resemblance ... between the agricultural economy of Ireland and that of India'.[26] The first Land Act marked the waning of utilitarian influence,[27] a decline in the authority of classical political economy,[28] and a growing acceptance of the validity of custom over contract.[29] Indian knowledge and experience were clearly having an impact on one of Gladstone's core policies towards Ireland.

The second issue relevant to India was the reform of the British Army. Edward Cardwell (1813–86), the Liberal secretary of state for war (and another former chief secretary for Ireland), faced the problem of finding enough men for an expanded British garrison in India (where long-term service was unpopular with British soldiers) on the basis of entirely voluntary enlistment. Cardwell's solution was to reduce the term of service with the colours to six years, and to withdraw British troops from the self-governing dominions.[30] Cardwell then linked the two battalions of each line infantry regiment, with the intention that one battalion would normally serve at 'home' (meaning in either Britain or Ireland) and the other in the empire (normally in India). The battalions could be exchanged, and soldiers rotated between them. The main task of the army at 'home' then became to supply trained drafts to the army in the empire, and to reabsorb those returning from duty overseas.[31] These reforms institutionalized

19 Foot & Matthew (eds), *Gladstone diaries*, vii, p. lvi.  20 Dewey, 'Celtic agrarian legislation', 56–60; Steele, 'Ireland and the empire', 83.  21 G. le G. Norgate, 'Campbell, Sir George (1824–1892)', *ODNB* (Oxford, 2004; online ed. accessed 25 Jan. 2010).  22 Entries for 11 Aug., 9 & 27 Nov. and 1–2 Dec. 1869, and 29 Apr. 1870, Foot & Matthew (eds), *Gladstone diaries*, vii, 114, 166, 181, 184–5, 284; S.B. Cook, *Imperial affinities: nineteenth-century analogies and exchanges between India and Ireland* (New Delhi, 1993), p. 51 n. 34, p. 55 n. 53.  23 Gladstone to C.E. Trevelyan, 13 Aug. 1869, Foot & Matthew (eds), *Gladstone diaries*, vii, 115.  24 Cook, *Imperial affinities*, pp 51, 58. On Mill's pamphlet, see Steele, 'J.S. Mill and the Irish question'.  25 Cook, *Imperial affinities*, p. 52.  26 Quoted in Collison Black, 'Economic policy in Ireland and India', 321.  27 Cook, *Imperial affinities*, pp 68–71.  28 Dewey, 'Celtic agrarian legislation', 31.  29 Cook, *Imperial affinities*, p. 61.  30 Foot & Matthew (eds), *Gladstone diaries*, vii, p. xlix.  31 D.

the relationship between India and the British Army from the 1870s to the 1930s, but at the cost of weakening the home battalions.[32] By the later nineteenth century, one critic could argue that the 'home' battalions had become 'squeezed lemons' and that the 'real' army was now in India.[33]

III

Gladstone announced his retirement in 1874, but was brought back into public life by the Turkish atrocities in Bulgaria in 1876, making an immediate national impact with 'the most famous of all his publications'[34] – his September 1876 pamphlet *Bulgarian horrors and the question of the east*.[35] A number of 'Indian' questions immediately occur. To what extent did Gladstone's reaction to the 'horrors' reflect earlier reactions to the massacres of British women and children during the 1857 mutiny? And how far did Gladstone's anti-Turkish language echo the Islamophobic language of the British press in 1857, in which the Indian mutiny was widely reported, and subsequently understood, as a 'Muslim conspiracy'?[36] Gladstone's reaction may also have owed something to Muslim conspiracy theories about the assassination of Lord Mayo in 1872 by Wahhabi 'fanatics'.[37] Gladstone's long-standing hostility to direct Turkish administration over Christian Slavs in Europe[38] was also significant for India. The Ottoman Empire was British India's 'near abroad', and its stability and survival were widely seen as essential to the defence of India[39] – hence Britain's fairly consistent support for the Ottoman Empire in the nineteenth century. But, to Gladstone, the reunification of the Eastern and Western Christian churches rivalled in importance the integrity of the Ottoman Empire in Europe.

Gladstone's re-engagement with national politics coincided with Disraeli's 'imperialism' of the 1870s. Disraeli outlined his commitment to empire in his 1872 Crystal Palace speech,[40] and gave it practical expression through the British government's purchase of 40 per cent of the shares in the Suez Canal Company

French, *Military identities: the regimental system, the British Army and the British people, c.1870–2000* (Oxford, 2005), pp 14–18.   **32** B. Robson (ed.), *Roberts in India: the military papers of Field Marshal Lord Roberts, 1876–1893* (Stroud, Gloucestershire, 1993), p. 229.   **33** Col. G.F.R. Henderson, quoted in B. Bond, *British military policy between the wars* (Oxford, 1980), p. 100.   **34** Foot & Matthew (eds), *Gladstone diaries*, ix, p. xlviii.   **35** Completed and revised 4–5 Sept. 1876, Foot & Matthew (eds), *Gladstone diaries*, ix, 152. See also *Lessons in massacre* (1877), ibid., p. xlviii.   **36** J.L. Duthie, 'Pressure from within: the "forward" group in the India Office during Gladstone's first ministry', *Journal of Asian History*, 15:1 (1981), 69.   **37** Ibid., 69–70; Bayly, 'Ireland, India and the empire', 388.   **38** W.E. Gladstone, 'Aggression on Egypt and freedom in the east', *Nineteenth Century*, 2 (1877), 163; Foot & Matthew (eds), *Gladstone diaries*, ix, pp xxxiv, xl, xliv–xlvii.   **39** Eldridge, *England's mission*, pp 216–19.   **40** Ibid., pp 172–80; Crangle, 'English nationalisms and British imperialism in the age of Gladstone and Disraeli', *Quarterly Review of Historical Studies*, 21:4 (1981–2), 6–7. See also Disraeli's speech in the House of Commons on 8 Apr. 1878, quoted in Eldridge, *England's mission*, p. 223.

in November 1875.[41] Disraeli's imperialism was more broadly India-orientated,[42] and it included three main elements directly related to India: first, the 1876 Royal Titles Act, which made Queen Victoria Empress of India;[43] second, the 1878–9 Second Afghan War, which was the consequence of Viceroy Lord Lytton's 'forward policy' in defence of India's north-west frontier against Russian expansion;[44] and, third, the 1878 Vernacular Press Act, introduced to curb the resulting Indian public criticism of the war.[45]

Gladstone was implacably opposed to this Tory imperialist 'jingoism' (or 'Beaconsfieldism').[46] During the 'great rhetorical crescendo of 1876–80',[47] Gladstone engaged in a sustained 'public debate of Britain's future responsibilities as a world power'.[48] He articulated a philosophy of imperial governance as applied to India, informed by a deeply moral vision of Britain's enduring imperial responsibilities. What was this vision?

Gladstone, it has been suggested, saw the Royal Titles Act as 'a foolish step backwards ... politically retrogressive and morally shabby'.[49] This verdict seems very plausible. The bill was debated several times in the Commons.[50] On 9 March 1876, speaking before 'an attentive house',[51] Gladstone's response to one of the bill's supporters was acerbic:

> It is true ... that we govern India without the restraints of a law except such law as we make ourselves [and] ... that we have not been able to give to India the benefit and blessings of free institutions. ... I leave it to the right honourable gentleman, if he thinks fit, to boast that he is about to place that fact solemnly upon record. By the assumption of the title of empress, I, for one, will not attempt to turn into glory that which ... I feel to be our weakness and our calamity.[52]

Among other things, Gladstone feared that the bill would 'diminish parliamentary control of India'.[53] Privately, he described the bill as 'of evil omen'.[54]

Gladstone had a notoriously difficult relationship with Queen Victoria, and one which deteriorated over time.[55] His hostility to the Royal Titles Act cannot

41 Eldridge, *England's mission*, pp 209–11. 42 Ibid., p. 226. 43 L.A. Knight, 'The Royal Titles Act and India', *Historical Journal*, 11:3 (1968), 488–507. 44 M. Cowling, 'Lytton, the cabinet and the Russians, August to November 1878', *English Historical Review*, 76:298 (1961), 59–79; Eldridge, *England's mission*, pp 200–4; Faught, 'An imperial prime minister', 565–6. 45 S. Wolpert, *A new history of India* 3rd ed. (Oxford, 1989), p. 254. 46 Foot & Matthew (eds), *Gladstone diaries*, ix, pp xxxiii, li; W.E. Gladstone, 'England's mission', *Nineteenth Century*, 6:560 (1878), passim; Eldridge, *England's mission*, pp 226–7. 47 Foot & Matthew (eds), *Gladstone diaries*, x, p. lii. 48 Ibid., p. xxx. 49 Moore, *Liberalism and Indian politics*, p. 23. 50 Including on 17 Feb., 9 & 23 Mar., and 11 May 1876. 51 Entry for 9 Mar. 1876, Foot & Matthew (eds), *Gladstone diaries*, ix, p. 110. 52 'Royal titles bill: second reading', 9 Mar. 1876, *Hansard* 3:227, 1736–7. See also 20 Mar. 1876. 53 Knight, 'The Royal Titles Act', 494. 54 Entry for 23 Mar. 1876, Foot & Matthew (eds), *Gladstone diaries*, ix, 114. See also Faught, 'An Imperial Prime Minister', 559. 55 J. Chandran, 'Queen Victoria, Gladstone and the viceroyalty

have endeared him to the queen, who personally wished for the formal title of empress (after having used it informally for over a decade), and who was to take the role very seriously.[56] Victoria would retain a 'very long' memory for the opponents of the bill.[57]

Gladstone's underlying assumptions about British rule in India emerged through an acrimonious debate conducted in the pages of the *Nineteenth Century* in 1877 with Edward Dicey (1832–1911), the editor of the *Observer*.[58] Gladstone attacked the then-prevalent idea, advanced by Dicey, that the British occupation of Egypt was imminent, necessary and inevitable.[59] Although Gladstone was highly critical of imperial expansion,[60] and in that sense could be regarded as an 'anti-imperialist',[61] he also made it clear that he wished to maintain, and even valued, British dominion over India. He wrote: 'We are bound to study the maintenance of our power in India ... as a capital demand upon the national honour. ... We have of our own motion wedded the fortunes of that country, and we never can in honour solicit a divorce'.[62] While deploring the Royal Titles Act, Gladstone had no wish to relinquish British rule in India, although he did not believe, as Dicey did, that the retention of India was 'a matter comparable ... with, and next in importance to, our national independence'.[63]

Gladstone had a strong sense of optimism and progress, and he normally tried to act within 'a general context of moral objectives'.[64] These qualities informed his ideas about Britain's imperial role in India. As he put it: 'Our title to be in India depends on a first condition that our being there is profitable to the Indian nations; and on a second condition that we can make them see and understand it to be profitable'.[65] Gladstone, in other words, thought that British rule over Indians was acceptable, and even desirable, provided it was clearly being done for the Indians' own benefit. Notably, he referred to the Indian 'nations' in the plural, rather than 'nation' in the singular – an implicitly anti-nationalist formulation.

Gladstone argued that 'India does not add to, but takes from, our military strength'. In his view, the military greatness of the United Kingdom lay 'within the compass of these islands', and was, 'except in trifling particulars,

of India, 1893–1894', *New Zealand Journal of History*, 3:2 (1969), 175–89. **56** M. Taylor, 'Queen Victoria and India, 1837–61', *Victorian Studies*, 46:2 (2004), 264–6, 271–2; Eldridge, *England's mission*, pp 211–13. **57** Knight, 'The Royal Titles Act', 494 n. 53. **58** E. Dicey, 'The future of Egypt', *Nineteenth Century*, 2 (1877); Eldridge, *England's mission*, pp 219–21; Shannon, *Gladstone and the Bulgarian agitation*, p. 215. **59** Gladstone, 'Aggression on Egypt'. Gladstone probably began the article, at the editor James Knowles' 'instance' in July: entry for 21 July 1877, Foot & Matthew (eds), *Gladstone diaries*, ix, 237. **60** Foot & Matthew (eds), *Gladstone diaries*, ix, p. xliii. **61** Ibid., p. lxxii, and n. 3. **62** Gladstone, 'Aggression on Egypt', 153. **63** Ibid. For Dicey's reply, see 'Mr Gladstone and our empire', *Nineteenth Century*, 2 (1877). **64** Foot & Matthew (eds), *Gladstone diaries*, vii, p. xxxvi. **65** Gladstone, 'Aggression on Egypt', 154.

independent of all and every sort of political dominion beyond them'.[66] Gladstone presumably had in mind British industry and the Royal Navy; but many of his contemporaries (like many historians), would have questioned his dismissal of India's military significance. India was in fact a major military resource for Britain throughout this period, until, and arguably well beyond, the Great War.[67] Gladstone's denial of the military value of India to Britain was, however, a significant underpinning to his philosophy of imperial governance. It underlined the idea that British rule in India had a moral and progressive purpose: it was not just a selfish matter of strategic expediency or economic advantage. 'We have no interest in India', Gladstone wrote, 'except the wellbeing of India itself'.[68]

This debate with Dicey was not the only occasion on which Gladstone underlined the importance of Britain's morally driven imperial mission in India.[69] As early as 1872, Gladstone had told the viceroy, Lord Northbrook, that his desire for India's future was simply that 'we may labour steadily to promote the political training of our fellow-subjects', and 'that when we go, if we are to go, we may leave a clear bill of accounts behind us'.[70] This vision, with its recognition of the possible end of the British Raj after a long period of political tutelage, 'would have startled many of his contemporaries', although Gladstone 'made no moves to encourage its realization'.[71]

Gladstone expressed similar views in a letter to Lord Ripon (then viceroy of India) in November 1881:

> To the actual ... strength of the empire, India adds nothing. She immensely adds to the responsibility of government; and ... by our army arrangements we (at home) have made her the means of fastening upon us large military expenditure which might well have been avoided. But none of this is to the purpose. We have undertaken a most arduous but a most noble duty. We are pledged to India, I may say to mankind, for its performance, and we have no choice but to apply ourselves to the accomplishment of the work [and to] the redemption of the pledge, with every faculty we possess.[72]

---

66 Ibid., 153; see also Foot & Matthew (eds), *Gladstone diaries*, ix, p. xliii.   67 See, for example, S. Akita, 'The Second Anglo-Boer War and India', *Journal of Osaka University of Foreign Studies*, 8 (1993), 117–35.   68 Gladstone, 'Aggression on Egypt', 153.   69 See also 'England's mission', especially 578–81. The article was begun on 9 Aug. and finished on 22 Aug. 1878: Foot & Matthew (eds), *Gladstone diaries*, ix, 337, 339.   70 Gladstone to Northbrook, 15 Oct. 1872, Foot & Matthew (eds), *Gladstone diaries*, vii, p. xlviii.   71 Ibid., p. xlviii; see also Faught, 'An imperial prime minister', 574–6.   72 Gladstone to Ripon, 24. Nov. 1881, Foot & Matthew (eds), *Gladstone diaries*, x, 166. The expression 'a most arduous but a most noble duty' echoes the phrase 'the most arduous and perhaps the noblest trust, that ever was undertaken by a nation' employed by Gladstone in a speech at Glasgow on 5 Dec. 1879 and quoted in Eldridge, *England's mission*, p. 239.

These words are simply not those of an anti-imperialist who gave hardly any thought to India.

The Indian vernacular press was another issue that occupied Gladstone in the later 1870s. The Indian press of the mid-nineteenth century has been (accurately) described as 'a small world of journalism'.[73] In 1873, the largest circulation of any one Indian vernacular paper was only about 3,000, and the total readership of the so-called 'native papers' was around 100,000,[74] at a time when India's population was nearly 250 million.[75] But concerns were growing about the political impact of vernacular newspapers. There was a danger, Lytton thought, of such papers being read out in bazaars,[76] with the aim of creating 'agitation'; so in 1878 he introduced the Vernacular Press Act to muzzle criticisms of the British administration, and in particular of its conduct of the Second Afghan War.[77] The act allowed British officials to demand bonds from printers and publishers, and to confiscate the bond, press machinery and all copies of a paper if 'objectionable' matter were published. The act has been described as 'a flagrant violation of democratic principle and of constitutional practice [and of] the principles of British rule in India'.[78] Again there was an interplay between Irish and Indian politics – the act had been inspired by Irish precedents, in this case the Peace Preservation (Ireland) Act of 1870.[79]

Gladstone denounced the Indian Press Act in the Commons as 'painful',[80] in print as 'deplorable and senseless',[81] and in private as 'monstrous'.[82] As well as attacking the act, Gladstone 'defended the Indian press from charges of disloyalty'.[83] This was not just a question of upholding the principle of free speech: Gladstone had some personal contact with the world of Indian journalism. For example, he had discussed politics with the educated Bengali Keshav Chandra Sen during the latter's visit to England in the later 1860s.[84] Sen had edited the English-language *Indian Mirror* since 1865, and his friends included J.S. Mill and the Oxford indologist Max Müller.


IV


Gladstone sought re-election in 1879–80, treating the election as a sort of 'referendum on imperialism', and campaigning principally on foreign and imperial issues, of which the expensive 'forward' policy and resulting war in Afghanistan

73 U. Das Gupta, 'The Indian press, 1870–1880: a small world of journalism', *Modern Asian Studies*, 11:2 (1977), 213–35. 74 Ibid., 229–31. 75 B.R. Tomlinson, *The economy of modern India, 1860–1970* (Cambridge, 1993), p. 4. 76 Das Gupta, 'The Indian press', 221. 77 Faught, 'An imperial prime minister', 562. 78 S. Gopal, *British policy in India, 1858–1905* (Cambridge, 1965), pp 118–19. 79 Cook, *Imperial affinities*, p. 33; Brasted, 'Indian nationalist development', 45. 80 On 23 July 1878. 81 Gladstone, 'England's mission', 580. 82 Gladstone to Ripon, 24 Nov. 1881, Foot & Matthew (eds), *Gladstone diaries*, x, 166. 83 Ibid., ix, 332 n. 11. 84 Das Gupta, 'The Indian press', 224–5.

was one of the most significant.[85] Before massed audiences during his
Midlothian campaign, Gladstone denounced the 'vainglorious imperialism' that
had shaken the foundations of the Indian Empire, had 'broken Afghanistan to
pieces', and had 'driven mothers and children forth from their homes to perish
in the snow'.[86] He urged the electorate to remember that 'the sanctity of life in
the hill villages of Afghanistan ... is as inviolable in the eye of Almighty God as
can be your own'.[87]

How did the soldier at the heart of the matter view the prospect of Gladstone
becoming prime minister? Writing from Kabul in February 1880, Frederick
Roberts (1832–1914), the British commander in Afghanistan, was privately
optimistic about the outcome of the election:

> I am glad to hear ... that the [Conservative] ministry are likely to
> remain in office. It would certainly be a calamity if the Liberals got
> into power now. They tell me that Mr Gladstone has done for himself
> in Scotland, and now has no chance of being returned for Mid
> Lothian.[88]

In fact, Gladstone's Midlothian campaign was a major factor in the Conservative
defeat in the election of March 1880,[89] and Gladstone became prime minister for
the second time in April.[90]

Relations between Lord Roberts and Gladstone's second administration seem
to have been fairly typical of the 'generally poor' relationship between the
Liberal party and the army in this period.[91] In April, Lytton noted that Roberts
had become 'specially obnoxious' to a 'powerful section' of the Liberal party, and
feared that he would be made a 'victim of party feeling'.[92] On 27 July, a British
and Indian force was heavily defeated at Maiwand in Afghanistan.[93] In August,
Roberts swiftly marched his forces from Kabul to Kandahar to retrieve the situation, which he did, in what became irreverently known as the 'race for the
peerage'.[94] When rewards for the campaign were published in the summer of
1881, however, Roberts received 'only' a baronetcy and £12,500. These rewards,

85 Foot & Matthew (eds), *Gladstone diaries*, ix, p. lxvii. Gladstone's preparations for the
Midlothian campaign including reading a recent article by Henry Creswicke Rawlinson
(1810–95) in the *Nineteenth Century* about the Afghan War: entry for 10 Nov. 1879, ibid., 457.
From 1868 to 1895 Rawlinson was a military member of the Council of India. See also Faught,
'An imperial prime minister', 559–60.  86 Eldridge, *England's mission*, pp 228–9. See also R.
Quinault, 'Afghanistan and Gladstone's moral foreign policy', *History Today*, 52:12 (2002), 32.
87 Quinault, 'Afghanistan', 28.  88 Roberts to O.T. Burne, India Office, Kabul, 1 Feb. 1880,
Robson, *Roberts in India*, p. 157.  89 Eldridge, *England's mission*, p. 231; Robson, *Roberts in
India*, p. 435.  90 Entry for 23 Apr. 1880, Foot & Matthew (eds), *Gladstone diaries*, ix, 506–7.
91 Ibid., vii, p. li.  92 Viceroy to Cranbrook, secretary of state for India, Pinjore, 16 Apr. 1880,
Robson, *Roberts in India*, p. 186.  93 T.A. Heathcote, *The Indian Army: the garrison of British
imperial India, 1822–1922* (Newton Abbot, Devon, 1974), pp 175–80, 193–5; Robson, *Roberts in
India*, p. 114.  94 Robson, *Roberts in India*, p. 115.

he felt, 'contrasted meagrely' with those given to his rival Sir Garnet Wolseley (1833–1913) for the 1873–4 Ashanti campaign.[95]

One of Gladstone's strengths as the keystone in the liberal arch was his ability to formulate principles of foreign and imperial policy that other leading liberals found difficult.[96] Imperial policy was one of the chief areas in which Gladstone 'intended to restore right conduct and right principles after the disasters of Beaconsfieldism'.[97] Gladstone, indeed, had been 'willing to fit India into his Midlothian programme'; and, in a manifesto to the electors of Britain and Ireland, the Indian Association (a forerunner of the Indian National Congress), had come out 'against the return of the Conservative government'.[98]

Although the viceroy of India (unlike the secretary of state) was not normally a 'political' appointment, one of Gladstone's first acts as prime minister was to find a suitable candidate to replace Lytton, who had resigned. In the context of the Afghan War, Gladstone said that he attached more importance to the viceroyalty than to all except one or two cabinet posts at home.[99] Lord Kimberley, then George Goschen, both turned the viceroyalty down, however,[1] before Lord Ripon accepted, leaving for India in May 1880.[2] Ripon – the antithesis of the arch-Conservative Lytton – has been described as 'Gladstone's political reflection in India',[3] and as 'the apostle of Gladstonian Liberalism'[4] through whose influence 'Gladstonian Liberalism became a permanent element in the political scene of British India'.[5]

Ripon wished to find bold solutions to India's political problems.[6] Like Gladstone, he regarded the Vernacular Press Act as 'detestable and a disgrace';[7] and, acting on 'virtually a specific mandate from Gladstone',[8] who considered the Press Act a 'really urgent case',[9] immediately sought its repeal. Although he encountered some opposition, the act was eventually repealed in early 1882.[10] Gladstone told Ripon that he was 'delighted at your success about that disgraceful Press Act', and described its repeal as 'one of the last steps in the great undoing process which the last government bequeathed to us'.[11]

Unsurprisingly, Indian editors rejoiced at the repeal of the act, and Indian

95 Ibid., p. 230; see also Roberts to Mountstuart Grant Duff, 25 Dec. 1882, and Roberts to Childers, 26 Dec. 1882 in ibid., pp 273–5. 96 Foot & Matthew (eds), *Gladstone diaries*, x, p. liii. 97 Ibid., p. lxii. 98 Brasted, 'Indian nationalist development', 56. 99 Gladstone to Kimberley, 24 Apr. 1880, Foot & Matthew (eds), *Gladstone diaries*, ix, 508. 1 Gladstone to Kimberley, 25 Apr. 1880, ibid., 509; T.J. Spinner, *George Joachim Goschen: the transformation of a Victorian liberal* (Cambridge, 1973), p. 65. 2 Cabinet, 3 May 1880, Foot & Matthew (eds), *Gladstone diaries*, ix, 513. 3 Wolpert, *A new history of India*, p. 256. 4 Moore, *Liberalism and Indian politics*, p. 27. See also Faught, 'An imperial prime minister', 567. On Lytton's Tory views, see Cowling, 'Lytton, the cabinet and the Russians', 70 and n. 4. 5 Gopal, *British policy in India*, p. 129. 6 Foot & Matthew (eds), *Gladstone diaries*, x, p. xlviii. 7 Moore, *Liberalism and Indian politics*, p. 30. 8 Gopal, *British policy in India*, p. 144. 9 Gladstone to Hartington, 16 June 1880, Foot & Matthew (eds), *Gladstone diaries*, ix, 542. 10 Moore, *Liberalism and Indian politics*, pp 30–1. 11 Gladstone to Ripon, 13 Mar. 1882, Foot & Matthew (eds), *Gladstone diaries*, x, 221. See also Faught, 'An imperial prime minister', 565.

papers were full of praise for the decision. The response of the Calcutta weekly *Ananda Bazar Patriká* was typical. On 9 January 1882, the paper reported that Lord Ripon was 'becoming increasingly popular with [the] natives of this country. His public acts and speeches have exceedingly gratified them'.[12] The positive reaction of the Bengali press was particularly striking, given that the press in that province had been 'almost uniformly hostile' to the Royal Titles Act.[13] A group of Indian editors presented Ripon with an address of thanks in March. He replied that 'a free press, wisely conducted, must always be of great assistance to the government', and that the limited extent to which representative institutions existed in India made 'the provision of an unfettered press especially important'.[14]

In the 1879–80 Midlothian campaign, Gladstone had attacked the Tories for saddling India with 'the costs of an imperialism wholly ours'.[15] Once in office, one of his aims was to secure complete withdrawal from Afghanistan.[16] He achieved this by May 1881. He also wanted to share out the cost of the war, as he did not want the Indian taxpayer to bear the whole burden.[17] Gladstone's government accordingly offered a subsidy of £5 million from the United Kingdom to the government of India to help pay for the war.[18]

How did Gladstone regard India's economic relationship with Britain more generally? He thought that imperial expansion was economically damaging,[19] certainly to the United Kingdom, and probably to India as well. Most educated, nationally minded Indians would have agreed with him. Like most British liberals, however, Gladstone had a deep commitment to orthodox political economy, including a belief (although held to a much lesser extent in the context of Irish land legislation) in the beneficially corrective forces of the free market and free trade.[20] He was therefore hostile to protectionism.[21] The main nationalist critique of British rule in India was embodied in the famous 'drain theory', which blamed some aspects of British rule for Indian poverty and famines.[22] Drain theorists often saw free trade, and particularly free trade in manufactured cloth, as detrimental to the economic interests of many Indians, particularly those engaged in handicrafts; but the Gladstone administration abolished Indian

12 Bengali, 700 weekly, Report on native newspapers, Bengal, 1882, British Library, India Office records, L/R/5/8, p. 16.   13 Knight, 'The Royal Titles Act', 506.   14 Gopal, *British policy in India*, pp 144–5. See also *Bhárat Mihir* (Mymensing, Bengali, 671 weekly), 14 Mar. 1882, Report on native papers, Bengal, 1882, British Library, India Office records, L/R/5/8, p. 101.   15 Moore, *Liberalism and Indian politics*, p. 68.   16 Foot & Matthew (eds), *Gladstone diaries*, ix, pp lxxi–lxxii; Gladstone to Rosebery, July 1880, ibid., 554; and Gladstone to Ripon, 10 Sept. 1880, ibid., 579–80.   17 Gladstone to Hartington, 8 & 12 May and 9 June 1880, Foot & Matthew (eds), *Gladstone diaries*, ix, 517–18, 522, 536–7; and entries for 12 Mar., 21 June, 6 Sept., 4 & 5 Oct. 1880, ibid., ix, 491, 517–18, 522, 544, 576, 590.   18 Gladstone to Hartington, 8 Feb. 1881, and entry for 5 Mar. 1881, ibid., x, 17–18, 27.   19 Ibid., p. xxxvi.   20 Ibid., vii, p. xxxix and ix, p. xxvi; and entries for 15 & 16 Dec. 1879, ibid., ix, 467–8.   21 Ibid., x, p. xxxvii.   22 Schneer, *London, 1900*, pp 192–3, 197–8.

LABOUR AND REST.

Ex-Head Gardener (*retired from business*). "WELL, WILLIAM, YER DON'T SEEM TO BE MAKIN' MUCH PROGRESS—*DO* YER!"
New Head Gardener. "WHY NO, BENJAMIN; YOU LEFT THE PLACE IN SUCH A PRECIOUS MESS!!"

11.1 Head gardener Gladstone clearing the 'precious mess' left by 'Beaconsfieldism' (*Punch*, 19 June 1880).

duties on the import of manufactured cotton, Britain's chief export to India, in 1882.[23]

The following year, the administration faced a controversy over the Indian judiciary. In February 1883, the new law member of the viceroy's council, Sir Courtenay Ilbert (1841–1924), had 'introduced a bill abolishing the principle of jurisdiction on the basis of race', and extending to country areas the right of Indian magistrates to preside over cases involving British defendants.[24] The 'Ilbert Bill' was immediately, deeply, and bitterly unpopular with all classes of the European community in India.[25] Faced with such opposition, Ripon soon accepted that the introduction of the bill had been 'an error in tactics' – a view

23 Moore, *Liberalism and Indian politics*, p. 70.  24 Gopal, *British policy in India*, pp 148–9.
25 See, for example, Roberts to Viceroy, 8 Mar. 1883, Robson, *Roberts in India*, pp 275–6; Moore, *Liberalism and Indian politics*, pp 37–8; and Faught, 'An imperial prime minister', 568–9.

in which Gladstone cautiously concurred.[26] However, Ripon felt that the bill had now become a 'test question', and that it could not be withdrawn without abandoning 'principles of equal justice'.[27] Gladstone's 'interest in the question' was 'great',[28] his feelings were 'strongly with Ripon',[29] and he gave Ripon his full support.[30] In the event, Ripon proved willing to compromise; and a much watered-down and 'almost unrecognizable' version of the bill was eventually passed.[31] This partial climb-down was a major victory for British opinion in India over the government of India and the Liberal government in Britain, and it became an important stimulus to the development of Indian nationalist opinion and organization.[32]

V

In June 1885, the Conservatives under Lord Salisbury briefly replaced the Liberals in government. The outgoing Commander-in-Chief in India, Sir Donald Stewart (1824–1900), hastened his retirement to give Roberts the opportunity to succeed him. He wrote to Roberts:

> Put all your irons into the fire *without delay* if you want to succeed me. I may have to go home sooner than I expected, and I am all the more willing to do so as you may have a better chance of succeeding me under the present [Conservative] government than if Gladstone comes in again, as he is likely to do in November. Don't ask any questions but write home at once as I may resign before the election comes off. Keep this entirely to yourself and lose no time in looking after your interests in this matter.[33]

Both Salisbury and Randolph Churchill (1849–95), the new secretary of state for India, were in favour of Roberts,[34] and in July 1885 he was duly appointed Commander-in-Chief in India, a post he would hold until 1893.

Under the Conservatives, with the Ulster peer Lord Dufferin as viceroy, the government of India pursued a more aggressive foreign policy. In response to

26 Gladstone to Ripon, 17 Apr. 1883, Foot & Matthew (eds), *Gladstone diaries*, x, 433. 27 Moore, *Liberalism and Indian politics*, p. 39. 28 Gladstone to Ripon, 1 June 1883, Foot & Matthew (eds), *Gladstone diaries*, x, 456. 29 Gladstone to Kimberley, 22 May 1883, ibid., 451. 30 Moore, *Liberalism and Indian politics*, p. 39. Gladstone was being kept aware of European opinion through the letters of his third son Harry, then working in Calcutta: Faught, 'An imperial prime minister', 571–3. 31 Gopal, *British policy in India*, p. 152; Faught, 'An imperial prime minister', 570. 32 M. Cumpston, 'Some early Indian nationalists and their allies in the British parliament, 1851–1906', *English Historical Review*, 76:299 (1961), 291. 33 Stewart to Roberts, 17 July 1885, Robson, *Roberts in India*, p. 325. 34 Robson, *Roberts in India*, p. 233; R. Foster, *Lord Randolph Churchill: a political life* (Oxford, 1981), p. 184.

King Theebaw's signing of a commercial treaty with France in January 1883, and because of growing disorder in Burma, British and Indian forces invaded Upper Burma in November 1885.[35] The capture of Mandalay was announced on 1 December. Randolph Churchill celebrated the New Year as usual at FitzGibbon's house in Howth, just outside Dublin. At the stroke of midnight, he raised his glass and proclaimed that Burma was now being formally annexed to the Queen's Dominions as a 'New Year's gift' to Empress Victoria.[36] Burma became a full province of British India (not, it should be noted, a princely state under British paramountcy) on 1 March.[37]

Contemporaries as well as historians have found it ironic that the Liberal government that assumed office in 1880 on a platform of curtailing imperial responsibilities should have added so much to them in South Africa, Egypt and the Pacific.[38] While Gladstone's change of direction over Egypt is very well known,[39] it is also worth noting that Gladstone came to support the annexation of Upper Burma. Gladstone's speeches in the House of Commons in early 1886 reveal the troubled 'moral conscience of an anti-imperialist' cautiously reasoning in favour of annexation.[40] The process of annexation turned out to be far from straightforward.[41] The initial military success in Burma was followed by prolonged guerrilla resistance,[42] and it took over 30,000 British and Indian troops five years to conduct a campaign of 'pacification'.[43]

VI

In mid-December 1885, just as Burma was being absorbed into British India, Gladstone's conversion to the cause of Irish Home Rule became public knowledge.[44] Several historians have noted the close interplay between Ireland and India over the Home Rule issue.[45] Tories and Liberal Unionists alike drew parallels with India in order to undermine the case for Home Rule.[46] Home Rule for Ireland, they argued, would be the first 'domino' in the collapse of the British Empire.[47] Lord Salisbury, a former secretary of state for India, was a leading

35 Foster, *Randolph Churchill*, p. 211; A. Herman, *Gandhi and Churchill: the epic rivalry that destroyed an empire and forged our age* (London, 2008), p. 43.   36 Herman, *Gandhi and Churchill*, p. 43.   37 Thant Myint-U, *The making of modern Burma* (Cambridge, 2001), pp 191–7. 38 Entry for 24 July 1880, Foot & Matthew (eds), *Gladstone diaries*, ix, 562; ibid., x, p. lxi n. 2. 39 For an excellent discussion of the historiography, see A.G. Hopkins, 'The Victorians and Africa: a reconsideration of the occupation of Egypt, 1882', *Journal of African History*, 27:2 (1986), 363–91.   40 Moore, *Liberalism and Indian politics*, p. 48.   41 Herman, *Gandhi and Churchill*, p. 44.   42 Robson, *Roberts in India*, p. 327.   43 Foster, *Randolph Churchill*, pp 209–10.   44 Entry for 30 Jan. 1886, Foot & Matthew (eds), *Gladstone diaries*, xi, 485. 45 Including Moore, *Liberalism and Indian politics*, pp 51–2, and Bayly, 'Ireland, India and the empire', 392–3.   46 Foot & Matthew (eds), *Gladstone diaries*, ix, p. xxxv.   47 Brasted, 'Indian nationalist development', 43.

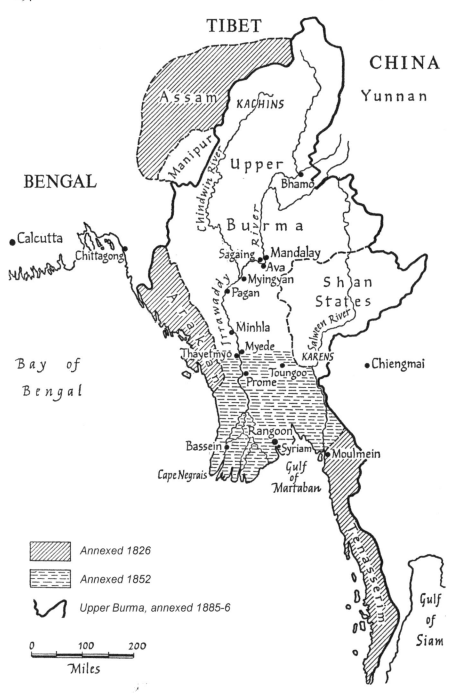

**11.2** British annexations in Burma, 1826–86.

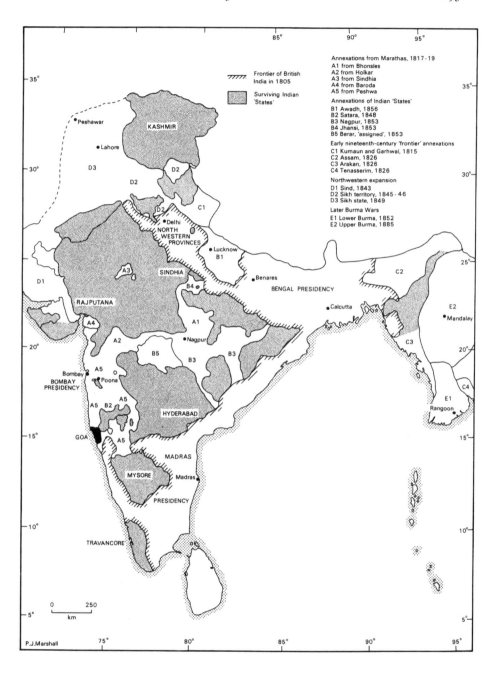

**11.3** British expansion in India, 1805–86. Upper Burma is marked 'E2' (after A.N. Porter (ed.), *Atlas of British overseas expansion* (London, 1991), p. 90).

advocate of this idea.[48] In an 1883 article, ominously entitled 'Disintegration',[49] he argued that granting Home Rule for Ireland would be 'an avowal ... that all claims to protect or govern anyone beyond our own narrow island were at an end'.[50] Home Rule for Ireland would mean Home Rule for India, and 'the final disintegration of the empire'.[51] Indeed, Gladstone accepted the annexation of Burma partly because he was aware that his opponents might try to exploit the India–Ireland connection to upset his plans for Irish Home Rule.[52]

The supporters of Home Rule also drew parallels with India. It became 'an integral part of Irish parliamentary policy' to intervene in imperial issues, and Irish Home Rulers often spoke out in the Commons on behalf of India.[53] The most prominent of them was Frank Hugh O'Donnell (1846–1916), who advocated a policy of 'Home Rule all round', and who in 1875 had helped set up a short-lived 'Constitutional Society of India'.[54] O'Donnell believed that the Irish MPs were the 'natural representatives and spokesmen of the unrepresented nationalities of the empire'.[55] On 15 March 1884, he said in the Commons that

> English tyranny in Ireland was only part of that general system of the exploitation of suffering humanity which made the British Empire a veritable slave empire. ... Parliamentary agitation would not be very effective until the Irish people, crushed down under their present tyranny, effected a coalition with the oppressed natives of India and other British dependencies, and all regarded England as the common enemy.[56]

Nationally minded Indians, too, made the connection with Irish Home Rule.[57] Although their wider ideas about civic institutions and political liberty were drawn from British, French and Italian liberal and revolutionary traditions, Ireland was the day-to-day example of actual nationalist practice that supplied

---

48 M. Bentley, *Lord Salisbury's world: Conservative environments in late-Victorian Britain* (Cambridge, 2001), p. 235. 49 Presumably as a conscious echo of Disraeli's 24 June 1872 Crystal Palace speech, in which he said that 'there has been no effort so continuous, so subtle, supported by so much energy, and carried on with so much ability and acumen, as the attempts of Liberalism to effect the disintegration of the empire of England': Foot & Matthew (eds), *Gladstone diaries*, vii, p. l. 50 Anon. [Lord Salisbury], 'Distintegration', *Quarterly Review*, 312:156 (1883), 594; Brasted, 'Indian nationalist development', 43. See also Bentley, *Lord Salisbury's world*, p. 235. 51 [Salisbury], 'Disintegration', 595. See also Dicey, 'The future of Egypt', 5. 52 Moore, *Liberalism and Indian politics*, p. 48. 53 Brasted, 'Indian nationalist development', 46; Cumpston, 'Some early Indian nationalists', 281–6. 54 Brasted, 'Indian nationalist development', 50. See also Cook, 'The Irish Raj', 519. 55 M. Cumpston, 'The discussion of imperial problems in the British parliament, 1880–85', *Transactions of the Royal Historical Society*, 13 (1962), 37; Cumpston, 'Some early Indian nationalists', 282; Schneer, *London, 1900*, p. 187. See also Crangle, 'The decline of anti-imperialism', 78 n. 63. 56 Quoted in Cumpston, 'Imperial problems', 39, and Cumpston, 'Some early Indian nationalists', 297 n. 1. 57 Schneer, *London, 1900*, pp 194, 200–1.

the principal external frame of reference for the early Indian nationalist movement. These ideas were disseminated mainly through the Indian vernacular press, which, by the 1880s, was full of Irish–Indian parallels. Ireland, however, could serve both as a good example and as a horrible warning. This dichotomy was particularly evident around questions of agitation and political violence. In some parts of India (but not others) the activities of the Land League were applauded, and in more radical (if not moderate) nationalist circles there was open admiration of Parnell.[58] The main Indian nationalist organization, the Indian National Congress, was founded in 1885, two years after the Ilbert Bill controversy and partly because of it.[59] In some imperial circles, this step was read as evidence that India was about to go the same way as Ireland, except on a much bigger scale.[60] In fact, very few Indian nationalists demanded Home Rule, still less outright independence; most of them merely wanted better representation in government for educated Indians. In 1889, to pursue this goal, the British Committee of the Indian National Congress was founded as a vehicle for lobbying within Westminster.[61] The following year, the Committee's English-language newspaper, *India*, was established as a voice for congress in British politics. This lobbying strategy seemed to bear some fruit when (in 1892) the Parsi politician Dadhabhai Naoroji (1825–1917) was elected to the House of Commons as the Liberal member for Central Finsbury, to become the first Indian MP (albeit with a wafer-thin majority of three).[62] Significantly, perhaps, Naoroji was known (echoing Gladstone) as the 'Grand Old Man' of Indian politics. Naoroji, a good friend of Michael Davitt (1846–1906), was also well known in Irish political circles, and had several times tried, 'through Davitt's offices', to secure an Irish constituency.[63] After the 1892 election, many in congress hoped that some of their programme might be realized, and that they might obtain what they called 'justice and fair play for India'.[64] By 1895, these hopes had not been realized: Ireland remained the dominant imperial issue.[65] Naoroji then lost his precarious seat in the 1895 election.[66] Gladstone, preoccupied with Ireland, mentioned Naoroji only once in his diaries.[67]

Gladstone's final illness and death were, however, closely followed in the pages of *India*. On 20 May 1898, his death was the lead story on a black-bordered front page. 'In the profound and universal sorrow which his death has caused',

58 Brasted, 'Indian nationalist development', 37–42, 51–63. 59 Faught, 'An imperial prime minister', 570–1. 60 Brasted, 'Indian nationalist development', 44–5. 61 Cumpston, 'Some early Indian nationalists', 294–6; Schneer, *London, 1900*, pp 188–91, 195; N. Owen, *The British left and India: metropolitan anti-imperialism, 1885–1947* (Oxford, 2007), pp 22–48. 62 Moore, *Liberalism and Indian politics*, p. 66; *India*, 15 July 1892. 63 Brasted, 'Indian nationalist development', 49; Cumpston, 'Imperial problems', 38; Cumpston, 'Some early Indian nationalists', 285. 64 *India*, 26 Aug. 1892. 65 Faught, 'An imperial prime minister', 575. Gladstone's Irish priorities were made clear in Gladstone to Wedderburn, 8 June 1893, Foot & Matthew (eds), *Gladstone diaries*, xiii, 248. 66 Schneer, *London, 1900*, p. 191. 67 Entry for 9 Aug. 1893, Foot & Matthew (eds), *Gladstone diaries*, xiii, 276.

remarked the paper, 'the people of India will sincerely share'. To Indians, his name was 'a synonym for justice, wisdom and high resolve'.[68] The particular way in which *India* chose to remember him was through his speech in the House of Commons in March 1880, in which he urged that the UK should bear a substantial share of the cost of the Second Afghan War, rather than leaving the Indian taxpayer to foot the entire bill. His gesture was contrasted with the refusal of Salisbury's Conservative government to contribute anything towards the cost of recent wars on India's north-west frontier. Gladstone's very long obituary in *The Times*, on the other hand, mentioned India only once, in passing, in a piece dominated by Ireland.[69]

VII

One of Gladstone's most significant Indian legacies was the thriving late-Victorian Indian vernacular press,[70] which often provided a 'loyalist', but highly critical, perspective on British policy,[71] and which contrasted itself favourably with the heavily censored press of imperial Russia. The first Gladstone administration left an important military legacy in the form of the Cardwell system; and the second in the abandonment for a generation of the 'forward' policy on India's north-west frontier. Gladstone also left an Indian legacy at the level of personal connection. John Morley – 'the disciple of Mill, the friend and biographer of Gladstone', as one leading Indian nationalist described him[72] – was to become the reforming secretary of state for India (1905–10) in Asquith's Liberal government. Morley had been chief secretary for Ireland in two Gladstone governments (1886 and 1892–5),[73] and brought his Irish experience to bear on Indian problems, not least through his hostility to coercion. Although Morley did not believe that India was ready for self-government, the 1909 Morley–Minto reforms, which aimed at making the bureaucracy more responsive to elected Indian politicians, could be seen as the fulfilment in India of Gladstonian liberalism. In some respects, Gladstone's attitude to India was inconsistent: the implacable opponent of Tory expansionism in Afghanistan became the cautious defender of the annexation of Burma; and the campaigner who denounced 'imperialism' as an unacceptable economic cost came to support the abolition of Indian tariffs on British cotton goods. In other respects, however, Gladstone's attitude to India was consistent, particularly in its emphasis on

68 *India*, 20 May 1898; there was also a full-page obituary on 27 May.  69 *The Times*, 19 May 1898, also reproduced in I. Brunskill & A. Sanders (eds), *Great Victorian lives: an era in obituaries* (London, 2007), pp 445–86.  70 Schneer, *London, 1900*, p. 195.  71 C. Kaul, *Reporting the Raj: the British press and India* (Manchester, 2003), p. 101.  72 B. Porter, *The lion's share: a short history of British imperialism, 1850–2004*, 4th ed. (London, 2004), p. 212.  73 Cook, *Imperial affinities*, p. 28 n. 39.

Britain's moral duty towards the good governance of India. Through his hostility to Disraeli's Tory jingoism, and to the 'oriental' pomp associated with the Royal Titles Act, Gladstone articulated a more idealistic vision of imperial governance in India informed by moral and progressive purposes – a vision which many nationally minded, educated Indians could, and did, share. In that sense at least, neither Gladstone nor congress were 'anti-imperialist'. India had an uneven significance for Gladstone, and his concern with India waxed and waned – as one would expect from a senior politician and party leader rather than from a minister with particular responsibility for India, or from a backbencher consistently committed to Indian issues. When Gladstone died, it is notable that Indian nationalists chose to remember in particular what he had said in 1880, rather than anything before or after. India had indeed been most salient for Gladstone during the decade from 1876 to 1886 – from the Royal Titles Act to the annexation of Upper Burma. From 1886, Ireland was to become *the* major imperial issue in British politics, overshadowing India and all other imperial questions. But Ireland could eclipse India only because Ireland had become aligned with India. British dominion over India was part of the context in which Gladstone, his contemporaries and their immediate successors had to engage with the relationship between Britain and Ireland. India remained important to Gladstone, precisely because Ireland was important to Gladstone; and the interplay between Ireland and India ensured that India's significance to Gladstone was long-standing, even if he often felt India's influence only indirectly.

# A statue of Gladstone for Dublin

## PAULA MURPHY

Shortly after the death of William Gladstone in May 1898, a writer for *The Spectator* mused on the various ways in which the statesman might be commemorated and – approaching the end of a century that was recognized for its statuemania – identified that sculpture would certainly feature. 'There will be a statue, of course, probably many statues, and they will most of them be good, for Mr Gladstone's face and form were of the kind which lend themselves to sculpture'.[1] It transpired that there would certainly be three statues, one of which was proposed for Dublin.

Gladstone was much portrayed in his lifetime and after his death. The many portraits include several busts and statues in bronze and marble by English sculptors John Adams-Acton, Thomas Woolner, Edward Onslow Ford and Thomas Brock. London-based, Irish-born sculptor Albert Bruce Joy (1842–1924) also portrayed the statesman in both bust and statue format. Gladstone sat for Bruce Joy in the sculptor's studio and in Downing Street.[2] The resulting statue, erected in 1882 in Bow Road, London, received favourable criticism and was thought to be 'meritorious as sculpture and as portraiture'.[3]

In the immediate aftermath of the death of the politician, the Gladstone National Memorial Fund was established and the trustees of the fund proposed three monuments, one each for London, Edinburgh and Dublin. English sculptor Hamo Thornycroft's London monument was unveiled on the Strand in 1905. Scottish sculptor James Pittendrigh MacGillivray's monument, designed in 1902, originally intended for Coates Crescent in Edinburgh, where it is now located, was unveiled instead in St Andrew's Square in 1917.[4] The proposal, in 1898, to erect a memorial to Gladstone in Dublin proved more problematic.

This was not the first time that a statue of Gladstone was proposed for Dublin. In the mid-1880s there had been a proposal to convey such an honour on the politician, but the project was postponed.[5] A new proposal to commemorate Gladstone in the Irish capital was proffered in a letter, dated 15 July 1898, from the duke of Westminster to the lord mayor of Dublin, then Daniel Tallon.

---

1 Quoted in the *Irish Times*, 1 June 1898.  2 Bruce Joy in interview in *New York Times*, 9 July 1911.  3 *Magazine of Art*, 1881/2, Appendix, Art Notes, xxix.  4 John Gifford, Colin McWilliam & David Walker et al., *Edinburgh*, Buildings of Scotland (London, 1984), p. 371. 5 *Freeman's Journal*, 5 Aug. 1898.

The duke was writing in his capacity as chairman of the general committee of the Gladstone National Memorial Fund. On 8 August 1898, the letter was read at a meeting of Dublin City Council, where it met with vehement opposition. The council passed a motion stating 'that no statue should be erected in Dublin in honour of any Englishman until at least the Irish people have raised a fitting monument to the memory of Charles Stewart Parnell'.[6] Many newspaper articles drew attention to the inappropriate nature of the proposed commemoration, querying whether it should be tolerated 'that such a man should have one of the prominent public places in the capital of Ireland for a statue' and describing the suggestion as 'a daring insult to the memory of Parnell'.[7] This is not without irony, as Parnell had supported the earlier proposal to commemorate Gladstone in Dublin with a statue, stating that the man had already done enough for Ireland 'to deserve a monument at our hands'.[8] Not everyone was opposed to the monument in 1898. Some saw its rejection as 'an act of the blackest ingratitude' and wondered whether Limerick or Cork might have been more receptive to the proposal.[9] The issue was widely analyzed in the Irish and British press at the time, revealing evidence of politics at play, with the statue serving as the perfect vehicle for feuding between Dillonites and Parnellites.

However, the decision of the City Council in 1898 did not rule out the possibility of a Gladstone commemoration being erected at a later date, and in 1910, with the understanding that the government had given its approval,[10] the monument committee proceeded with the commission and a formal contract to carry out the work was signed by Irish sculptor John Hughes (1865–1941) on 24 December. The sum agreed for the work was £6,000 and the proposed location for the monument was the People's Garden in Dublin's Phoenix Park. The year in which the contract was signed is not insignificant, as a statue of Parnell for Dublin, the work of Irish-American sculptor Augustus Saint-Gaudens (1848–1907), was completed in 1907 and the monument of which it formed part was to be erected in O'Connell Street in 1911. The choice of Hughes for the Gladstone commemoration will likely have been influenced by his completion of the Queen Victoria Monument, which was unveiled in the grounds of Leinster House in 1908.

The committee that was formed to oversee the putting in place of the Gladstone memorial in Dublin was presided over by Lord Crewe, with Lord Pentland as Hon. Secretary. Hughes submitted a sketch model for the monument to the committee long before the signing of the contract. In a letter

---

6 *Minutes of Dublin City Council*, meeting held 8 Aug. 1898, motion no. 287. Dublin City Library and Archive.  7 *Irish Daily Independent*, 8 Aug. 1898.  8 *Freeman's Journal*, 5 Aug. 1898.  9 *Irish Times*, 15 Aug. 1898.  10 Letter, Lord Pentland to Robin L. Hunter, 23 Dec. 1910 in Alan Denson, *John Hughes, sculptor, 1865–1941: a documentary biography* (Kendal, 1969). Many of Hughes's letters on the Gladstone memorial and on other topics are published in Denson's documentary biography.

12.1 The statue of Gladstone in the grounds of St Deiniol's Library, Hawarden (image courtesy of St Deiniol's Library, Hawarden).

to Lord Pentland, he indicated his 'endeavour to represent Gladstone, at the fateful moment, when full of fiery energy, he fought his great battle for Ireland'.[11] In 1886, during his student years in London, Hughes had the opportunity to see Gladstone at close quarters and was hugely impressed by his physiognomy, but most especially by his 'splendid, fearless eyes.'[12] Hughes was also keen to make reference in the monument to Gladstone's classical scholarship and to his 'marvellous grasp of figures'.[13] Perhaps most importantly, the sculptor chose to include in his design a specific reference to Ireland in the figure of Erin, as he had done on the Victoria monument. The completed monument, therefore, comprises a standing portrait of Gladstone, accompanied by allegorical representations of Erin, Classical Learning, Finance and Eloquence. Erin takes pride of place, positioned to the front of the monument, somewhat awkwardly posed, looking upwards towards the politician in, as the sculptor said, 'hopeful expectancy', awaiting 'the victorious issue of the battle which [Gladstone] began. Then shall the music of her long-silent harp be heard once more in the glens and valleys of Ireland'.[14] Hughes' comments, in conjunction with the prominent positioning of the harp on the Gladstone monument, give a strong

11 Letter, Hughes to Lord Pentland, 22 May 1910 in Denson, *John Hughes*, p. 257.    12 Letter, Hughes to Henry Gladstone, 14 July 1925 in Denson, *John Hughes*, p. 363.    13 Letter, Hughes to Lord Pentland, 22 May 1910 in Denson, *John Hughes*, p. 257.    14 Letter, Hughes to Rt Hon. Mr Justice Boyd, spring 1908 in Denson, *John Hughes*, p. 213.

indication of his continuing concern for his homeland, in spite of the fact that he was at that stage living outside the country.

The sculptural work for the monument was carried out in Paris, where, in 1911, Hughes hired a studio in the Rue Vercingétorix specifically for the Gladstone work, as his studio in the Avenue du Maine was not sufficiently large for the purpose.[15] Hughes proceeded with the modelling of the figures and organized for the stone pedestal to be made in England by the Kirkpatrick Brothers of Manchester.[16] The portrait of Gladstone and the four allegorical figures were ready for casting in bronze in July 1914. It had always been intended that the casting would be carried out in Paris. However, as most of the foundry workmen were mobilized during the war and the French government requisitioned large stocks of the available copper, rendering the price of metal exorbitant, there was a long delay before the casting could be contemplated. After the war, this situation did not resolve itself with any speed, and ultimately, in 1919, an agreement was made with a foundry in Brussels, the Compagnie des Bronzes, to cast Hughes' models.

The casting of the five bronze figures was completed in November 1920, by which time Hughes had already indicated his awareness of what he described as the 'unsettled state in Ireland'.[17] In spite of this, in 1924, there was 'general agreement in Dublin' that the statue could be erected. There was, however, to be a slight change in the location of the monument. While still proposed for the Phoenix Park, it was no longer to be sited in the public space that was the People's Garden, but rather in the private space that formed the grounds of the Viceregal Lodge.[18] This was to afford the monument protection from those who had declared war on imperial statues across the country and who had already targeted several monuments in Dublin. Hughes, who had never given up hope that the Gladstone memorial would be erected in Dublin, was invited to select a site in the grounds of the lodge and to oversee the erection of the monument there. In June 1924, he travelled to Dublin from Florence, where he was living at the time, but shortly after he had selected an appropriate site, the government once more postponed the decision to accept the work.

By this time, Gladstone's sons had become involved in the discussions and were of the belief that 'it was a grave error of judgment to press the statue on Ireland'.[19] Other locations began to be suggested, including Oxford and Hawarden, Caernarfon and Cardiff. Hawarden, in Flintshire, Wales, where Gladstone had lived, was finally decided upon and the monument was offered to the Trustees of St Deiniol's Library. This was a fitting location, as the building

15 Letter, Hughes to W.T.S. Hewett, 4 Oct. 1916 in Denson, *John Hughes*, p. 274.  16 Letters between Hughes and Kirkpatrick Bros dating to 1912 in Denson, *John Hughes*, pp 267–8.  17 Letter, Hughes to H. Shand, 14 Oct. 1918 in Denson, *John Hughes*, p. 280.  18 Letter, Lord Crewe to Timothy Healy, 7 May 1924 in Denson, *John Hughes*, p. 316.  19 Letter, Herbert Gladstone to Henry Gladstone, 3 July 1924 in Denson, *John Hughes*, p. 329.

of the library was also the result of the Gladstone National Memorial Fund. Once the decision was made, the putting in place of the monument proceeded swiftly, with the bronze statues making the journey from Brussels and the stone pedestal from the Portland quarry in the south of England. Erected without much ceremony in April 1925, an unnamed trustee is recorded as having said that 'if at some future date, the political situation in Ireland makes it possible to erect the statue in Dublin, it should be released and presented to Ireland as originally intended'.[20] But the president of the Dublin Memorial Committee, Lord Crewe, was of the opinion 'that the stone base will be well covered with green moss before the Irish government ask for this memorial'.[21] Herbert Gladstone was firm in his belief that the Irish would want to remember his father: 'Sooner or later Ireland will put up a statue. When that time comes they will probably prefer to put up a statue of their own and make it a real Irish tribute'.[22] This did not prove to be the case.

Although aware that his work ended up in Hawarden, Hughes was not present for its installation. He was nonetheless pleased with the photographs that were sent to him showing the monument in situ in the grounds of St Deiniol's and with the kind words of Henry Gladstone, who was complimentary about his work and thought the monument a success.

20 Letter, Hon. Revd C.F. Lyttelton to H. Shand, 2 Dec. 1924 in Denson, *John Hughes*, p. 348. 21 Letter, Lord Crewe to H. Shand, 27 August 1924 in Denson, *John Hughes*, p. 338. 22 Letter, Herbert Gladstone to Henry Gladstone, 3 July 1924 in Denson, *John Hughes*, p. 329.

# Index